BOOM

TO BACKLASH

DK BARTLEY
GLOBAL DEI EXPERT

BOOM
TO BACKLASH

GEORGE FLOYD'S LEGACY ON DEI AS A BUSINESS IMPERATIVE

WILEY

Library of Congress Cataloging-in-Publication Data is Available:

ISBN: 9781394351459 (cloth)
ISBN: 9781394351466 (ePub)
ISBN: 9781394351473 (ePDF)

COVER DESIGN: PAUL MCCARTHY
COVER ART: © GETTY IMAGES | COLORS HUNTER - CHASSEUR DE COULEURS
SKY10099915_040325

To my mom and dad, who taught me the value of perseverance and authenticity, and why it's important to build a more inclusive world where everyone can contribute their full potential.

Contents

Introduction: Beyond Black and White

IF YOU BELIEVE Diversity, Equity, and Inclusion (DEI) is just about "checking boxes" or hiring less qualified people to meet racial quotas, you've been lied to.[1] In fact, quite the opposite is true. Practicing DEI is about recognizing that businesses all over the world are *currently* hiring less qualified people because unconscious biases are built into the way we operate at every level. By identifying and correcting these biases, we can cast a wider net and find the most exceptional talent for every role. It has nothing to do with handing out jobs to people who don't deserve them. It is about finding potential superstars who are overlooked by the recruiting, hiring, management, and promotion practices that are currently in place.

When organizations truly embrace inclusion, they create a culture where every individual, regardless of background, has the chance to contribute, be heard, and succeed. This shift toward true equity fosters an environment where innovation thrives, creativity flourishes, and businesses are positioned to outperform their competitors. As research from Deloitte reveals, companies with inclusive cultures are six times more likely to innovate and twice as likely to exceed their financial goals.[2] The research shows that inclusive cultures are more innovative and drive better business outcomes. But understanding the

1

real-world application of these principles requires more than just data—it requires lived experience.

In 2013, Microsoft faced a critical crossroads in the tablet market. Apple's iPad dominated with a commanding 43.6 percent market share, setting records with 52.5 million devices sold. Microsoft's new product, the Surface RT, struggled to gain traction, failing to even break into the top five manufacturers.[3] The Surface was a key part of the company's strategy, but it failed to resonate with consumers, leading to a staggering $900 million write-down on unsold inventory.[4]

At the time, I was working at Dentsu, one of the largest networks of marketing and advertising agencies in the world, and my team was chosen to step in and help Microsoft navigate this turbulent moment. The solution we proposed wasn't groundbreaking in its complexity—it was about shifting perspectives. Rather than relying on traditional hiring pipelines, we sought out professionals who could connect with communities Microsoft had overlooked. We found people who understood the nuances of local cultures and needs. Over the next several months, we helped build diverse teams across Houston, Atlanta, Seattle, Detroit, and New York—people who weren't just familiar with these communities but could engage with them authentically. This shift in approach didn't just create more meaningful connections; it generated $66 million in new revenue for Microsoft in a single year. This wasn't an accident; it was the result of recognizing that diverse talent brings more than just different perspectives—it brings the ability to solve problems in new and innovative ways.

This focus on diversity as a driver of business performance isn't just anecdotal. A groundbreaking study published in *Nature* found that papers authored by diverse teams received 10.63 percent more citations than those from homogeneous groups, demonstrating their higher impact and influence in the scientific community.[5]

The stakes for getting this right have never been higher. In the aftermath of George Floyd's murder in 2020, corporate America made unprecedented commitments to diversity, equity, and inclusion. Major corporations pledged billions toward racial equity initiatives, with the financial sector alone committing over $50 billion.[6]

But, by 2023, a concerning trend had emerged. Major companies rolled back their DEI initiatives, with some completely dismantling all their diversity-focused programs.[7] Job postings with "DEI" in the title dropped by 23 percent,[8] and many organizations began quietly distancing themselves from their earlier commitments.

Yet the most successful companies aren't abandoning DEI, they're evolving their approach. They're focusing on integrating diversity and inclusion into their core business strategies. They are moving beyond demographic targets to create truly inclusive cultures that drive innovation and growth.[9]

In today's global economy, the ability to identify, develop, and retain the best possible talent isn't just a business advantage—it's a necessity. The World Economic Forum's latest Global Talent Competitiveness Index reveals that countries excelling at attracting and developing diverse talent experience up to 50 percent higher innovation output and stronger economic growth.[10] This is not about lowering standards or meeting quotas. It's about building systems that discover and nurture exceptional talent from all walks of life.

As organizations begin to see the importance of these principles, the shift is already happening. Forward-thinking companies are moving beyond simple demographic goals to create inclusive cultures that directly link DEI strategies to business outcomes.[11] These data-driven approaches show measurable results from implementing DEI best practices, such as up to 30 percent higher market share in key demographics and 45 percent improved employee retention rates.

This book is the culmination of everything I've learned from these experiences and from the world of business. Whether you're a CEO looking to transform your company, a manager building a diverse team, or a professional navigating your own career, this book will give you the tools to turn inclusion into a competitive advantage. I've witnessed DEI evolve from being a buzzword to one of the most powerful drivers of innovation and growth. The companies that thrive in the future will be those that understand the link between excellence and inclusion—not those that treat diversity as a checkbox exercise or believe that excellence and diversity are mutually exclusive.

As Business Insider's comprehensive analysis shows, companies that maintained or strengthened their DEI initiatives during the 2023–2024 downturn are now seeing tangible benefits: higher employee engagement, increased innovation, and stronger financial performance.[12] In the past five years, DEI has become one of the most contentious political battlegrounds, but also one of the biggest hidden drivers of success among the world's leading companies. The field is shifting, and those who stay on the cutting edge will reap the rewards, while those who fall behind will struggle to compete in an evolving marketplace.

Which will you be?

1

Breaking the Silence

ON MAY 25, 2020, George Floyd woke up to a typical Minneapolis spring morning.[1] A thin layer of clouds hung in the sky and the air was hot and heavy with moisture.[2] Floyd pulled himself out of bed. At 46 years old, he was working to rebuild his life after moving from his hometown of Houston, Texas, to Minnesota for a fresh start.[3] Known as "Big Floyd" to his friends and family, he cut an imposing figure at 6′4″ but was thought of by those who knew him as a "gentle giant." In fact, his high school football coach later recalled, "If you said something to him, his head would drop … he just wasn't going to ball up and act like he wanted to fight you."[4]

That morning, Floyd likely thought about his daughters back in Houston.[5] He may have said a prayer. Floyd was known in his community as a man of faith who had worked extensively with a Christian ministry called Resurrection Houston to mentor young men. "The things that he would say to young men always referenced that God trumps street culture," recalled Ronnie Lillard, who performed with Floyd under the name Reconcile. "I think he wanted to see young men put guns down and have Jesus instead of the streets."[6] Perhaps he spent some time worrying that morning about making ends meet. The COVID-19 pandemic had thrown millions out of work, including Floyd, after the restaurant where he worked as a bouncer was forced to close.[7]

5

George Perry Floyd Jr. was born in Fayetteville, North Carolina, and raised in Houston's Third Ward, where his mother moved the family seeking better opportunities.[8] Growing up in the Cuney Homes housing project, known locally as "The Bricks," Floyd found refuge in sports and music. His childhood friend Herbert Mouton remembered him as someone who could always lighten the mood after a tough loss: "He never wanted us to feel bad for too long," Mouton recalled. The housing project's challenges were real. Residents created a self-deprecating song: "I don't want to grow up, I'm a Cuney Homes kid. They got so many rats and roaches I can play with."[9]

He was the first of his siblings to go to college, attending South Florida State College on a basketball scholarship before transferring to Texas A&M University–Kingsville.[10] His college basketball coach, George Walker, remembered specifically seeking Floyd out: "I was looking for a power forward, and he fit the bill. He was athletic, and I liked the way he handled the ball."[11] Though he didn't graduate, his family remembered how proud he was to be the first to make it to college. As a young boy in second grade, he had written an essay expressing his dream of becoming a Supreme Court Justice. "When I grow up, I want to be a Supreme Court judge," young Floyd wrote. "When people say, 'Your Honor, he did rob the bank,' I will say, 'Be seated.' And if he doesn't, I will tell the guard to take him out."[12]

Life hadn't been easy for Floyd. He struggled with addiction at times and had run-ins with the law, including a 2007 armed robbery conviction that resulted in a five-year prison sentence.[13] But after his release, he was committed to turning his life around. He participated in Christian outreach programs in Houston's Third Ward, using his experience to mentor younger men and steer them away from violence. In one video message, he pleaded: "Our young generation is clearly lost, man … Come on home, man. One day, it's gonna be you and God. You're goin' up or you're goin' down, you know what I'm sayin'? That's gonna be it."[14]

In Minneapolis, Floyd worked as a security guard at the Salvation Army's Harbor Light Center homeless shelter and later at Conga Latin Bistro, where he was known as a friendly face who would walk cowork-ers to their cars after late shifts.[15] His employer at Conga Latin Bistro, Jovanni Thunstrom, remembered Floyd's warm personality: "Always cheerful ... He would dance badly to make people laugh. I tried to teach him how to dance because he loved Latin music, but I couldn't because he was too tall for me. He always called me 'Bossman.' I said, 'Floyd, don't call me Bossman. I'm your friend.'"[16] When COVID-19 hit and restaurants closed, Floyd, like millions of Americans, found himself out of work.[17]

On that fateful Memorial Day evening, Floyd walked into Cup Foods, a corner store he'd visited many times before. Like everyone else during those strange pandemic days, he wore a face mask.[18] The store's owner, Mike Abumayyaleh, would later tell NBC News that Floyd was a regular customer with whom they had "never had an issue." The teenage clerk who served Floyd that day was new to the job. When Floyd used what appeared to be a counterfeit $20 bill, the clerk initially intercepted it and returned it to Floyd, who then left the store. When Floyd returned about 10 minutes later and used another $20 bill, the clerk suspected both bills were counterfeit. Following store protocol, he informed his supervisor and called the police.[19]

At 8:08 PM, Officers Thomas Lane and J. Alexander Kueng arrived at Cup Foods.[20] Lane, who had been on the force for only four days, drew his gun and ordered Floyd to show his hands.[21] Floyd was cooperative but visibly distressed. "I'm sorry, I'm sorry," Floyd said. "I didn't do nothing ... What did I do though? What did we do, Mr. Officer?" He begged the officers not to shoot him, telling them he had been shot before. When officers tried to put him in the squad car, he told them he was claustrophobic and had recently recovered from COVID-19.[22]

Officers Derek Chauvin and Tou Thao arrived later. What happened next would be captured on multiple cameras and viewed by millions around the world. Darnella Frazier, a 17-year-old bystander who had been walking with her 9-year-old cousin to the store, recorded the incident on her phone. "Although this wasn't the first time I've seen a Black man get killed at the hands of police," she would later write, "this is the first time I witnessed it happen in front of me. Right in front of my eyes, a few feet away."[23] For 9 minutes and 29 seconds, Chauvin kept his knee on Floyd's neck.[24] Even after Floyd became unresponsive, even after bystanders begged the officers to check his pulse, Chauvin didn't move. A Cup Foods employee called the owner crying, telling him, "'Mike, Mike. What should I do? The guy can't breathe. They're killing him.' 'Call the police on the police,'" Abumayyaleh recalled telling the employee. "And make sure it's recorded."[25] When the ambulance finally arrived, Floyd had no pulse. He was pronounced dead at 9:25 PM at the Hennepin County Medical Center.[26]

George Floyd couldn't have known that his death would become a turning point in American history.[27] He couldn't have known that his last words, "I can't breathe," would echo in protests from Seoul to Sydney, and London to Lagos.[28] He couldn't have known that his name would become a rallying cry for racial justice that would transform institutions around the globe.

Ripples in the Corporate World

The first call came minutes after George Floyd was pronounced dead. I let it go to voicemail, hoping to take a moment to process what I'd just witnessed on my screen. Then another call came. And another. The sound pierced through the quiet of my kitchen, where I sat with my takeout growing cold. The shrill beeping shook me out of my numbness.

I knew what these calls meant. As a DEI expert practitioner, I'd received similar calls before. Every time we received a tragic reminder of America's unresolved racial trauma my phone would ring. But something felt different this time. The calls weren't just from my usual network of DEI colleagues. They came from CEOs, board members, and HR directors I hadn't heard from in years.

One company offered me a million-dollar base salary (plus very competitive long-term incentives) on the spot to become their Chief Diversity Officer. I turned it down. It was obvious they didn't want real change; they wanted a poster child, someone they could point to and say, "look, we're doing something. See? We hired a top expert. We care!" But as my phone continued to light up with calls from corporate leaders across the country, I realized we were witnessing something unprecedented.

The response began locally. On May 26, hundreds gathered in Minneapolis at the site of Floyd's death. By May 27, protesters took to the city streets in growing numbers. Within a week, demonstrations had spread to almost every major US city, and most minor ones too, marking one of the largest protest movements in American history.[29] The unprecedented scale of documentation made this movement different from any before. Live streams of more than 400 protests were viewed over 1.4 billion times, creating what analysts called a "perfect storm" of visibility: there was simply no way to look away or deny what was happening.[30]

As people across the country protested police violence, law enforcement officers often responded, ironically, with escalating force. Medical experts documented the devastating impact of the "less lethal" weapons used to break up crowds during these rallies. Rubber bullets penetrated skin, broke bones, ruptured eyeballs, and even caused traumatic brain injuries. Despite manufacturer guidelines specifying that these weapons should only be aimed at the lower body, videos showed officers frequently targeting protesters' heads and upper bodies.[31] These efforts only spurred the protesters on, as citizens grew more justified in their anger. The very tactics meant to silence the demonstrations instead amplified them, broadcasting police aggression to millions of viewers worldwide.

Those still sheltering in place took to the internet to express their outrage and support. According to Pew Research Center, the phrase "Black Lives Matter" appeared on Twitter an average of 2 million times a day in the weeks following Floyd's death, with the hashtag being used nearly 47.8 million times between May 26 and June 7, 2020, marking the highest volume of daily tweets using the hashtag since the platform began tracking it.[32]

On June 2, 28 million Instagram users participated in Black Out Tuesday, a movement that originated within the music industry but quickly spread across social media platforms. Major music labels including Atlantic Records, Capitol Music Group, Warner Records, and Sony Music joined the protest by pausing all business operations for the day.[33] Instead of posting traditional content, millions of users uploaded simple black squares to their Instagram feeds. Though well-intentioned, Black Out Tuesday revealed the complexity of digital activism—many critics pointed out that the black squares were drowning out information and resources being shared by organizers on the ground.

Within weeks, the calls for justice had crossed oceans. More than 70 countries held solidarity protests and demonstrations.[34] In London, thousands of protesters flooded Trafalgar Square, kneeling in solidarity for a minute's silence before chanting "no justice, no peace." Signs bearing Floyd's last words, "I can't breathe," were raised alongside the names of Black Britons who had died in police custody. The demonstrations spread across the UK, with protests erupting in Manchester, Cardiff, Leicester, and Sheffield.[35]

In Paris, a crowd of 20,000 people gathered outside their US Embassy, defying a police ban on large gatherings during the COVID-19 pandemic. The protests quickly evolved to encompass France's own struggles with police violence, with demonstrators carrying signs that read "Justice for Adama" alongside "Justice for Floyd."[36] In Sydney, Australia, tens of thousands marched through the heart of the city after winning a last-minute court appeal to authorize the demonstration. What began as a protest against American police brutality transformed into a powerful statement about Indigenous deaths in Australian police custody.[37]

These weren't just expressions of solidarity with American protesters—people in other countries saw their own struggles reflected in Floyd's death. In France, demonstrators drew explicit parallels to the killing of Adama Traoré, a young Black man who died in French police custody in 2016 after telling officers, "I can't breathe." Traoré's sister, Assa, became a leading voice in the French protests, telling crowds, "What's happening in the United States is happening in France."[38]

Australia's Indigenous community, which has long faced systemic discrimination and police violence, found kinship with the Black Lives Matter movement. In the 12 days following Floyd's death, more than 25,000 Australians donated over $1.5 million to Indigenous rights campaigns, marking an unprecedented surge in support for Aboriginal justice initiatives.[39] From Brazil to South Korea, local activists connected Floyd's murder to their own battles against state violence and systemic racism, transforming an American tragedy into a global rallying cry for justice.[40]

Artists around the world created powerful murals honoring Floyd's memory, from the streets of São Paulo to the walls of Paris to public spaces in Lithuania. These weren't just artistic expressions, they became powerful catalysts for change. Local artists transformed city walls into memorials that sparked conversations about justice and equality in their own communities.[41]

The corporate world, caught in this storm of global outrage, faced unprecedented pressure to respond. It wasn't enough to issue vague statements about "standing against racism" or making nominal donations to civil rights organizations. Employees were demanding real action. Customers were scrutinizing company practices. Activists were calling out corporate hypocrisy. The very tools companies had used to build their brands—social media, corporate communications, carefully crafted public images—became channels for holding them accountable.

Consider what happened to CrossFit. When founder and CEO Greg Glassman responded to the protests with a flippant tweet comparing Floyd's murder to the pandemic ("Floyd-19"), the response was swift and devastating. Within days, more than 1,000 affiliated gyms abandoned the CrossFit name, and major sponsor Reebok immediately announced they would end their partnership when their contract expired at the end of the year.[42]

This wasn't just another news cycle that companies could wait out. The combination of undeniable evidence, a captive audience, and the amplifying power of social media had created something new: a moment of sustained moral clarity that demanded more than performative activism. Companies that had successfully avoided meaningful conversations about race for decades now faced a choice: transform or be transformed.

The initial corporate response revealed just how unprepared most companies were for this moment. For years, Black deaths at the hands of police had gone unremarked in corporate America. Now, companies that had previously remained silent found themselves scrambling to respond.[43] Startups suddenly grappled with diversity strategies, while major corporations faced pressure from both employees and customers to take meaningful action.[44]

Universities and colleges across the nation were forced to confront their own institutional biases. Analysis of 356 statements issued by higher education institutions showed a dramatic shift in how they addressed racism, moving from "color-blind" messaging to explicitly acknowledging systemic racism.[45]

The financial response was unprecedented. Major banks, histori-cally hesitant to wade into social issues, pledged billions toward racial equity initiatives. According to the Harvard Law School Forum on Corporate Governance, corporations announced more than $50 bil-lion in commitments to racial justice causes.[46] PepsiCo committed $400 million over five years specifically to increase Black representa-tion in management and support Black-owned businesses.[47]

But the most significant changes weren't just about money, they were about how companies fundamentally operated. PNC Bank, for example, developed an $88 billion community benefits plan focused on economic empowerment in low- and moderate-income areas and communities of color.[48] Netflix went beyond statements about sup-porting Black lives; they moved $100 million of their cash holdings to Black-owned banks, fundamentally changing how they thought about even their routine business operations.[49]

Companies began sharing unprecedented levels of transparency about their workforce demographics. Google and Microsoft not only published detailed diversity reports but set specific, measurable goals for improvement.[50]

Banks began leveraging their multicultural employee networks in new ways. M&T Bank, for instance, established 100 new multicultural banking centers, staffed by bilingual employees, and designed specifi-cally to serve diverse communities.[51]

Most significantly, companies began tying executive compensation to diversity goals. Starbucks announced that executive compensa-tion would be directly linked to meeting diversity targets, aiming for 40 percent BIPOC representation in retail and manufacturing roles by 2025.[52] DEI wasn't a separate initiative anymore: it became a board-level priority, with executives being held personally accountable for progress.[53]

The transformation that began in American boardrooms soon rip-pled across the globe. Companies began scaling up their DEI initia-tives internationally, adapting their approaches to different cultural contexts while maintaining core commitments to equity and inclusion.[54]

Major global corporations began transforming their approach to diversity and inclusion. Sony Music Group made history by appointing

Tiffany R. Warren as its first-ever Executive Vice President and Chief Diversity and Inclusion Officer. Warren, known for founding ADCOLOR, the premier organization celebrating diversity in creative industries, brought decades of experience in building inclusive corporate cultures. Her appointment signaled a fundamental shift in how Japanese corporations approached leadership and representation.[55]

The transformation manifested differently across cultures and industries, but the conversation reached the highest levels of global business leadership. At the World Economic Forum in Davos, diversity and inclusion became central themes in discussions about the future of work. Leaders examined how these issues intersected with technological change, economic recovery, and the growing skills gap in the global workforce. The Forum highlighted how companies that embraced diversity were better positioned to address future challenges, from climate change to digital transformation.[56]

Global shipping giant A.P. Møller-Maersk demonstrated how multinational corporations could implement practical changes. They conducted comprehensive leadership training programs that embedded diversity and inclusion principles for over 1,100 first-time leaders, creating a ripple effect throughout their global operations. This training went beyond traditional diversity workshops, focusing on practical skills for building and leading inclusive teams in a complex, multicultural environment.[57]

These changes weren't just about doing the right thing; they reflected a growing understanding that diversity drives innovation and performance in an increasingly interconnected world. Companies began recognizing that their ability to compete and grow depended on building organizations that could harness diverse perspectives and serve diverse markets effectively.

Why Now?

To understand why this moment catalyzed such unprecedented change, we need to first confront an uncomfortable truth: state-sanctioned violence against minorities had become disturbingly routine in America. Statistics showed a consistent and troubling pattern of fatal police shootings, with the numbers increasing year over year.[58]

Seven years earlier, in 2013, George Zimmerman was acquitted in the shooting of Trayvon Martin. Public outcry in response to this, and other white-on-Black shootings, led to the creation of a new hashtag: #BlackLivesMatter.[59]

Eric Garner's plea of "I can't breathe" became a rallying cry in 2014, when an NYPD officer held him in an illegal chokehold. The New York City medical examiner's office officially ruled his death a homicide, citing "compression of neck (chokehold), compression of chest and prone positioning during physical restraint by police" as the cause of death.[60]

That same year, Michael Brown, an unarmed Black teenager, was shot and killed by police officer Darren Wilson in Ferguson, Missouri. His death sparked weeks of protests that revealed the depths of Black grief and anger. Brown's body was left lying in the street for four hours after his death, an image that would become emblematic of the dehumanization of Black lives by law enforcement.[61]

Then there was 12-year-old Tamir Rice, shot by Cleveland police while playing with a toy gun in a park near his home. Officer Timothy Loehmann shot Rice within seconds of arriving at the scene. Security footage showed he fired less than two seconds after exiting his patrol car. The boy died the next day at MetroHealth Medical Center.[62]

In April 2015, Freddie Gray died from spinal injuries sustained while shackled in the back of a Baltimore police van. Gray had made eye contact with police and ran, leading to his arrest. During his transport, he suffered a severe spinal cord injury that would prove fatal. Despite clear evidence of "rough rides," a practice where handcuffed suspects are thrown around in the back of police vans by erratic driving, all criminal charges against the officers were eventually dropped, though the city reached a $6.4 million civil settlement with Gray's family.[63]

Just months before Floyd's death, Breonna Taylor, a 26-year-old emergency room technician, had been shot dead in her Louisville apartment during a botched no-knock raid. Police had burst in at 12:40 AM while Taylor was asleep in bed with her boyfriend, Kenneth Walker. When Walker fired a warning shot, believing intruders were breaking in, officers responded with 32 bullets. Six struck Taylor, who was pronounced dead at the scene.[64]

That same spring, Ahmaud Arbery, a 25-year-old Black man, was chased down and shot while jogging through a Georgia neighborhood. The men responsible, Gregory McMichael, his son, Travis, and their neighbor, William Bryan, weren't even arrested at first. Local authorities initially accepted their claim of attempting a citizen's arrest, citing Georgia's Civil War–era law. It took 74 days, public outcry, and cell phone footage showing Arbery being hunted down for charges to finally be filed.[65]

Each death sparked outrage. Each led to protests. Each prompted calls for change. But none transformed corporate America's approach to racial equity.

George Floyd's murder would prove different. According to McKinsey's analysis of Fortune 1000 companies, the corporate response was unprecedented in both scale and scope. Companies didn't just issue statements; they made specific, measurable commitments backed by billions in funding.[66]

Why was this event such a turning point? The answer lies in the convergence of four distinct but related forces that turned what could have been just another tragedy into a moment of irreversible change.

The first force was the undeniable visual evidence. For 9 minutes and 29 seconds, people around the world watched the slow, agonizing murder of a fellow citizen.[67] It wasn't a split-second decision that could be explained away. It wasn't a chaotic situation open to interpretation. It was methodical, deliberate, and captured from multiple angles by bystanders who recognized the gravity of what they were witnessing.

Thanks to the courage of 17-year-old Darnella Frazier, who filmed the entire ordeal while walking her 9-year-old cousin to the store, we saw a clear and complete picture of what happened. Her act of bearing witness, which would later earn her a special citation from the Pulitzer Prize board "for courageously recording the murder of George Floyd," became a pivotal moment in American history. The Pulitzer board specifically praised her for "highlighting the crucial role of citizens in journalists' quest for truth and justice," recognizing how her split-second decision to record transformed a local tragedy into a catalyst for global change.[68]

The video, swiftly posted on Facebook, showed in excruciating detail what so many had tried to ignore for so long. While the initial

Minneapolis police statement clinically claimed, "Man Dies After Medical Incident During Police Interaction," deliberately obscuring the officers' actions, the public saw the unvarnished truth. The 200-word police statement not only failed to mention the knee on Floyd's neck but actively worked to minimize police involvement, stating only that officers "noted he appeared to be suffering medical distress" and "called for an ambulance." Meanwhile, bystander videos showed Officer Derek Chauvin keeping his knee on Floyd's neck even after he lost consciousness, and even as onlookers begged him to stop.[69]

Multiple bystanders recorded different angles of the incident. Expert witnesses, including veteran police officers, would later testify that Floyd did not resist arrest and was completely unarmed. Police use-of-force expert Sgt. Jody Stiger would testify that the force used was "excessive" from the moment Floyd was put on the ground, noting that the proper response would have been to put Floyd in a "side recovery position" to help him breathe. Instead, Chauvin maintained his position even after Floyd had stopped moving.[70] When he cried out for his mother, the sound pierced through the hearts of parents everywhere.

Everyone I spoke to who had children, especially white parents from different parts of the country and even internationally, said the same thing: "That would never happen to my child." For the first time, they were understanding "this race thing" a bit better. They realized their children might be stopped by police, might even do something wrong, but they wouldn't be killed for it. The situation was impossible to misinterpret. No amount of public relations spin could change what we all witnessed.

The second force that made George Floyd a turning point was a growing anxiety among Americans trapped in one of the most challenging periods of modern history. The spring of 2020 was a crucible. A deadly worldwide pandemic created by the COVID-19 virus, and the extreme uncertainty around the proliferation of the disease, left the population feeling scared and vulnerable. On top of that, a litany of harsh economic and social effects accrued as well.

According to the Bureau of Labor Statistics, the unemployment rate had increased by an unprecedented 10.3 percentage points to 14.7 percent, marking both the highest rate and the largest over-the-month increase since the BLS began collecting data in 1948. In a single month, the unemployment rate jumped higher than it had during the entire two years of the Great Recession.[71]

April alone saw the loss of more than 20.5 million jobs, nearly triple the job losses of the entire 2008 Great Recession. The carnage was widespread but uneven. Leisure and hospitality lost 7.7 million jobs, nearly half its entire workforce. Professional and business services shed 2.1 million positions. Retail trade lost 2.1 million jobs. Even healthcare, typically resistant to economic downturns, lost 1.4 million jobs as non-emergency procedures were canceled nationwide.[72]

The impact was devastatingly divided across racial lines: while white unemployment peaked at 12.4 percent, Black Americans faced a record 16.8 percent job loss. Hispanic workers were hit even harder, with their unemployment rate soaring to 18.9 percent. These numbers represented the largest disparity in unemployment rates between Black and white Americans in the past five decades.[73]

The disparities didn't end with job loss. According to the Centers for Disease Control data, Black and Hispanic Americans were being hospitalized for COVID-19 at rates 2.8 and 3.0 times higher than their white counterparts, respectively. The death rates revealed an equally stark divide: Black Americans were dying at 1.9 times the rate of white Americans, while Pacific Islanders faced mortality rates 2.4 times higher than white populations. Indigenous Americans were being hospitalized at 3.7 times the rate of white Americans, and Latino communities were experiencing infection rates up to three times higher in many regions.[74] These deep-seated injustices were present long before the pandemic, but in 2020, the disparities became clearer than ever, providing a bleak backdrop for the growing anxiety and stress sweeping the nation.

The third force that made George Floyd different was the forced isolation of those working and schooling from home during the COVID-19 pandemic. Under these conditions, Americans found themselves consuming media at unprecedented rates. Nielsen's data showed that people spent 70 percent more time on the internet and consumed 95 percent more news than usual. The patterns were striking: streaming content consumption surged by 61 percent, with local news viewing increasing 23 percent. Social media engagement skyrocketed, with platforms reporting record-breaking usage levels. Facebook reported a 50 percent increase in messaging, while Twitter saw its daily active users jump by 24 percent.[75] We had more empty hours than ever before, and we were spending most of them consuming media, witnessing our collective pain mirrored back at us through our screens.

The fourth force was the most surprising: corporate vulnerability. For the first time in modern history, companies found themselves unable to control their own narratives. As the BBC reported, this marked a dramatic shift from previous instances of racial injustice, where corporate America had largely remained silent. Nike took a strong stance with the message, "For once, Don't Do It," a play on their famous slogan, urging people not to turn their backs on racism. Ben & Jerry's went further, issuing a detailed statement titled "We Must Dismantle White Supremacy" that called for specific police reforms, including the passage of HR 40, legislation that would create a commission to study reparations. Even traditionally conservative brands felt compelled to speak out. NASCAR banned Confederate flags at its events, while Walmart committed $100 million to create a center on racial equity.[76]

In an age where social platforms amplify voices instantly, the very nature of social media left corporations with little choice but to issue statements—and to do so quickly. No longer could companies stay uninvolved in racial issues. If you were at a company where others like Netflix were speaking out and your company remained silent, employees wanted to know why. Even if your business couldn't take direct action due to its nature, you needed to explain your position to your employees. Silence was no longer an option. But, amid a growing "cancel culture," that could potentially devastate companies who took a stand their customers did not like, responding in just the right way became its own challenge.

These four forces—undeniable evidence, a growing unease and anxiety, a captive audience, and corporate vulnerability—created perfect conditions for change.

The Current Challenge

The story, however, gets more complicated. As the changes resulting from Floyd's murder began to show results, they also sparked intense public debate. By 2024, the pushback had reached the highest levels of business and politics. Billionaire Elon Musk sparked controversy when he tweeted that "DEI is just another word for racism," drawing immediate criticism from other business leaders. Mark Cuban publicly challenged Musk's statement, arguing that business leaders should focus on finding the best talent regardless of background. Their exchange highlighted the growing divide in corporate America over DEI initiatives, with Cuban emphasizing that diverse hiring pools increase competition and raise standards.[77]

The political sphere amplified these tensions. Then-former President Trump intensified the rhetoric during a major policy speech, claiming that "Every institution in America is under attack from this Marxist concept of equity." He called for the complete dismantling of equity initiatives in federal agencies, framing DEI programs as a direct threat to American meritocracy. His speech specifically targeted federal contractor requirements and diversity training programs, calling for their immediate elimination.[78]

The rhetoric quickly transformed into action. On his first day back in office, Trump issued a series of executive orders abolishing DEI positions across the federal government, placing hundreds of employees on immediate leave. Through the newly created Department of Government Efficiency, led by Elon Musk, the administration moved to slash what it claimed was over $120 billion in annual DEI spending. The White House also required tens of thousands of federal contractors to certify they did not operate any "unlawful forms of DEI," while establishing a tip line for workers to report attempts to disguise such programs through "coded or imprecise language."[79]

The impact of this backlash became increasingly visible in corporate America. Major companies began rolling back their DEI initiatives, with each announcement creating a domino effect across industries. Walmart's retreat proved particularly significant given its position as America's largest private employer. The retail giant's carefully worded statement to Newsweek reflected the delicate balance companies tried to strike: "We've been on a journey and know we need to constantly evolve our approach." This announcement followed similar moves by Toyota, which had begun reviewing all its DEI policies, and several major financial institutions that had previously been industry leaders in diversity initiatives.[80]

The retreat manifested in concrete ways across industries. Job postings with "DEI" in the title declined significantly, while companies that had previously trumpeted their diversity achievements began speaking about these efforts in more muted terms. Corporate diversity officers, once highly sought after, reported finding their roles and resources diminished. Some companies began rebranding their diversity initiatives under different names, while others quietly merged their DEI departments with general human resources functions.[81]

The pressure on companies to abandon their DEI commitments sometimes came from unexpected sources and could escalate rapidly. The case of Jack Daniel's parent company, Brown-Forman, proved particularly illustrative. When faced with threats of an "anti-woke" boycott on social media, the spirits giant quickly announced plans to pull back on their DEI initiatives. The company's rapid reversal came despite their previous commitments to diversifying their workforce and supplier base. This demonstrated how vulnerable these programs could be to coordinated pressure campaigns, even at well-established companies with long histories of community engagement.[82]

With the conservative, "anti-DEI" political force on the apparent ascendancy under President Trump's second term, it may seem that, at least superficially, the dramatic changes that began five years ago in response to the murder of George Floyd are on their way out. However, in my experience working with organizations across sectors, I've observed that the most successful companies aren't retreating from DEI, they're evolving their approach. Rather than abandoning their commitments entirely, they're finding ways to integrate DEI principles into their core business practices. They understand that this isn't about politics or public relations. It's about competing in a global economy where innovation and growth depend on our ability to identify, develop, and retain the best possible talent. It's about building organizations that can spot opportunities others miss and solve problems others can't crack.

Through decades of working with organizations worldwide, I've come to understand that excellence and inclusion strengthen each other. Whether companies call it DEI-AB (adding Accessibility and Belonging); Merit, Excellence, and Intelligence (MEI); or use another framework entirely, I've consistently seen that formalizing the way organizations bring different perspectives together tends to make them stronger and more innovative.

In the chapters that follow, I'll share what I've learned about how we reached this point, which approaches I've seen work effectively, and how some organizations have turned diversity into a competitive advantage. Drawing from my extensive experience in this field, we'll examine the evolution of corporate DEI practices, including the impact of significant changes I've witnessed since George Floyd's murder. Finally, I'll explain why, in my analysis, some companies are thriving while others struggle to accept and adapt to this new reality and offer practical solutions.

As someone who has dedicated their career to this work, I believe the key question facing organizations isn't whether to embrace inclusive practices, but whether they'll lead or follow in this transformation.

2

The Long Road to Change

THE HISTORY OF corporate America's relationship with diversity didn't begin in 2020. To understand the seismic changes that followed George Floyd's death, we must first be aware of the long and complex journey that preceded it. This evolution unfolded across three distinct eras, each building upon the lessons and limitations of the previous phase while responding to broader societal changes. The story that emerges is not one of steady progress, but rather of successive attempts to address increasingly complex challenges, each era revealing new dimensions of the work required for true equity.

The first era, spanning roughly from the 1960s through the late 1970s, might be called "The Foundation Years." This period marked the fundamental shift from legally sanctioned discrimination to the establishment of basic civil rights protections in the workplace. Companies moved from being able to openly discriminate to facing new legal requirements for equal treatment, spurred by landmark legislation and social upheaval. The compliance-focused approaches of this era would later prove insufficient, but they created the basic framework that future efforts would build upon—establishing the principle that workplace discrimination was not just morally wrong but legally prohibited.

The second phase, "The Standardization Era" of the 1980s and 1990s, emerged from the recognition that mere compliance wasn't enough. Organizations began developing standardized hiring practices, formal policies, and structured programs aimed at increasing representation. This period was characterized by the rise of diversity training programs, employee resource groups, and the first attempts to connect diversity to business performance. While these systematic approaches often fell short of creating true inclusion, they helped organizations recognize that achieving equity required comprehensive, organizationwide changes rather than isolated initiatives.

The third phase, "The Measurement Period" of the early 2000s through the late 2010s, arose from the realization that good intentions and formal programs weren't sufficient without accountability. Companies began implementing sophisticated tracking systems, analyzing detailed workforce demographics, and measuring the impact of their diversity initiatives. This era saw the rise of unconscious bias training, the impact of the #MeToo movement, and growing pressure from investors for transparency around diversity metrics. The data-driven approaches developed during this period would prove crucial in 2020, providing companies with the tools to assess their starting points and measure their progress toward new commitments.

Each of these eras brought its own innovations and challenges, revealing both the progress made and the persistent barriers to true equity in corporate America. As Portocarrero and Carter note, this evolution wasn't always straightforward[1]—early diversity professionals often lacked guidance and evidence-based insights, leading them to develop initiatives without the necessary expertise to evaluate their effectiveness. Yet each phase laid essential groundwork for what would follow, creating the infrastructure, practices, and measurement tools that companies would draw upon as they responded to the racial reckoning of 2020.

The limitations of each era helped shape the next. The shortcomings of pure compliance drove the move toward systematic approaches; the superficial nature of many standardized programs led to demands for measurement and accountability; and the stark data revealed during the measurement era helped create the conditions for rapid change in 2020. When George Floyd's death forced corporate America to confront racial inequity with new urgency, companies didn't start from scratch—they built upon decades of evolving practices, learning from both the successes and failures of previous approaches.

To understand the transformative impact of George Floyd's death on corporate diversity efforts, we must first examine these earlier phases in detail. Their legacy lives on in today's DEI initiatives, which combine the legal foundation of the first era, the systematic approaches of the second, and the data-driven accountability of the third. Let's explore each phase in turn, beginning with the foundational period that emerged from the civil rights movement.

The Foundation Years: Civil Rights to Corporate Change

The modern corporate diversity movement emerged from the crucible of the Civil Rights Movement, at a time when America was grappling with profound social transformation. Prior to the 1960s, workplace discrimination was not only legal but commonplace—employers could openly refuse to hire Black applicants, mandate that pregnant women resign, and maintain completely segregated workforces.[2]

The first governmental crack in this system came with President Kennedy's Executive Order 10925 in 1961, which required federal contractors to take "affirmative action" in employment. The term itself had emerged from labor relations—first used in the Wagner Act of 1935 regarding unfair labor practices, and later applied to racial discrimination in 1945 when New York passed the first state antidiscrimination law using the term.[3] When drafting Kennedy's order, Hobart Taylor Jr., a young African American lawyer from Detroit, chose the phrase "affirmative action" for its alliterative quality, unknowingly crafting terminology that would define decades of social policy.[4]

The Equal Pay Act of 1963 marked another early step, prohibiting wage discrimination based on gender. The Act required equal pay for equal work, covering all forms of compensation including salary, overtime, bonuses, stock options, profit sharing, and benefits. Studies leading to the Act's passage had found stark disparities—women were earning $8–$20 less per week than men for the same office work (equivalent to $4,260–$10,760 per year in today's dollars). Female college graduates were earning substantially less than their male counterparts, a pattern that would persist for decades.[5]

As these initial policy changes were taking shape, American cities erupted in racial violence that forced corporate America to confront inequality in unprecedented ways. The pattern began with multiple urban uprisings across the country in 1964: a three-day riot in Rochester leaving four dead; unrest in New York City's Harlem and Bedford-Stuyvesant neighborhoods involving 4,000 people; a three-day disturbance in Philadelphia following a Black couple's arrest; and protests in Chicago after a Black woman was attacked by a store owner.[6]

The Watts Rebellion of 1965 in Los Angeles marked a turning point. What began as a routine traffic stop escalated into six days of unrest, resulting in 34 deaths, over 1,000 injuries, and $40 million in damages. The uprising revealed deep divisions in perception—while 75 percent of white Los Angeles County residents said the riots "hurt the Negro's cause," only 24 percent of local Black residents agreed. To the Black community, these events represented not mindless violence but a revolt against systemic inequality. A survey found that 56 percent of local Black residents said the unrest had a purpose or goal, and 58 percent expected it to have favorable effects.[7]

Two years later, the Detroit riots proved even more devastating, with 43 deaths, 342 injuries, and nearly 1,400 buildings burned. The unrest emerged from a powder keg of conditions: about 60,000 low-income residents crammed into the Virginia Park neighborhood's 460 acres, a police force with only about 50 African American officers, and widespread accusations of racial profiling and police brutality. The city's economic situation had grown increasingly dire—the east side of Detroit alone had lost over 70,000 jobs in the decade following World War II, and from 1950 to 1960, Detroit lost almost 20 percent of its population as white residents fled to the suburbs.[8]

In the aftermath of the unrest in Detroit and Newark, New Jersey, President Johnson appointed the National Advisory Commission on Civil Disorders, known as the Kerner Commission. The commission identified more than 150 riots or major disorders between 1965 and 1968. Their report's conclusion was stark: "Our nation is moving toward two societies, one Black, one white—separate and unequal." The commission placed responsibility on racial segregation and discrimination in housing, education, employment, and law enforcement.[9]

These upheavals catalyzed both government and corporate action. Some companies, like Xerox, didn't wait for government mandates. When race riots erupted in Rochester, New York, where Xerox was headquartered, the company's leadership took aggressive action. As Joseph Wilson, Xerox's CEO at the time, noted: "We are among those who are compelled to accept the indictment of the National Advisory Commission on Civil Disorders . . . We, like all other Americans, share the responsibility for a color-divided nation; and in all honesty, we need not look beyond our own doorstep to find out why."[10]

Xerox's response was comprehensive and groundbreaking. Company chairman Joseph Wilson and President Peter McColough wrote a letter to all managers in 1968, explicitly condemning discrimination and committing to intensive minority recruitment. They made line managers directly responsible for success and backed this commitment with concrete actions—funding a minority-owned manufacturing plant and sponsoring television programs about Black history and culture.[11]

In 1970, this commitment was tested when a group of Black employees at Xerox gathered after hours in Webster, New York, frustrated by watching their talents go unrecognized while less qualified colleagues advanced. This group became BABE (Bay Area Black Employees), the first Xerox caucus group. Their methodical approach—documenting patterns, tracking promotion rates, comparing performance reviews, and gathering detailed data about project assignments and mentorship opportunities—led to significant changes. By 1970, they had convinced regional management to give Black employees a major role in recruiting and hiring. A system was developed where a Black Xerox employee was present whenever white managers interviewed a Black candidate.[12]

The results were transformative. Between 1964 and 1974, the percentage of minority employees at Xerox grew from 3 percent to

14.6 percent. More importantly, this growth wasn't just in entry-level positions; the percentage of minorities in official and managerial positions increased from 1 percent to 6.9 percent.[13]

The Civil Rights Act of 1964 also marked a watershed moment, with Title VII prohibiting workplace discrimination based on race, color, religion, sex, and national origin. Yet the law itself provided little implementation guidance, leaving personnel managers, rather than civil rights leaders or legal scholars, to largely determine what compliance looked like in practice.[14] Many executives and managers were concerned that the Act might require quotas that would take jobs away from white employees, a specific manifestation of the broader fear that extending rights to African Americans would necessitate taking them away from whites.[15]

The creation of the Equal Employment Opportunity Commission (EEOC) in 1965 added enforcement power to these new requirements. The commission pioneered innovative approaches to data collection and investigation, requiring employers to submit detailed workforce statistics that could reveal discrimination patterns. Although the Act created the EEOC, in its final form it excluded any stated quotas or enforcement powers. The EEOC was to respond to citizen complaints, not defend the public interest in eliminating patterns of discrimination. By 1972, when Congress expanded its authority through the Equal Employment Opportunity Act, the EEOC had developed sophisticated methods for identifying systemic discrimination.[16]

President Johnson moved to strengthen these initiatives through Executive Order 11246 on September 24, 1965. This order created the Labor Department's Office of Federal Contract Compliance (OFCC, later the OFCCP), giving it specific responsibilities for enforcing anti-discrimination laws among federal contractors. The creation of the OFCC took affirmative action out of the White House and placed it in the Department of Labor with a staff designated for enforcement. Initially focused on racial minorities, the order was amended in 1967 to include discrimination against women.[17]

Several major corporations emerged as early leaders in diversity efforts. IBM's initiatives during this period were pioneering—the company had included Black and female employees since its founding in 1911, but in the 1960s and 1970s it significantly expanded its equal opportunity efforts. IBM wrote its first formal Equal Opportunity Policy in 1953, a decade before the Civil Rights Act, and continued to lead through innovations in recruitment, training, and advancement programs.[18] Similarly, Avon recognized that their predominantly white sales force struggled to reach Black consumers and launched targeted recruitment programs for Black representatives. This initiative proved highly successful—the new representatives significantly outperformed their counterparts in Black communities, demonstrating the business value of diversity.[19]

The Supreme Court's decision in *Griggs v. Duke Power Co.* (1971) established the legal precedent for "disparate impact" lawsuits. The case challenged a power company's requirement that employees pass an intelligence test and obtain a high-school diploma to transfer out of its lowest-paying department. Prior to the Civil Rights Act, Duke openly discriminated, allowing Black employees to work only in the Labor Department, where the highest-paying jobs paid less than the lowest-paying jobs in the other four "operating" departments reserved for whites.[20]

The Court's unanimous decision fundamentally changed how discrimination would be evaluated in the workplace. Chief Justice Warren Burger, a conservative nominated by President Nixon, wrote that Title VII "proscribes not only overt discrimination but also practices that are fair in form, but discriminatory in operation." The ruling established that employment tests must be "related to job performance," effectively prohibiting the use of arbitrary requirements that could discriminate against minority groups. Importantly, the Court held that even if an employer doesn't intend to discriminate, employment practices that disproportionately exclude minority groups are illegal unless they relate to job performance.[21]

The Philadelphia Plan of 1967 represented another development in corporate diversity efforts. The program emerged from a half century of discriminatory practices by construction unions that had successfully relegated skilled African Americans to the less skilled "trowel" trades. Such workers could find employment in private home construction in segregated neighborhoods, but the more lucrative large-scale projects were controlled by the unions, whose membership tended to be passed down from white father to son or uncle to nephew.[22]

Initially declared illegal in 1968, the Plan was successfully revived by the Nixon administration. George Shultz, Nixon's labor secretary, and Arthur Fletcher, his assistant secretary, redesigned the program to require Philadelphia government contractors in six construction trades to set goals and timetables for hiring minority workers or risk losing valuable contracts. While no specific quotas were set, giving businesses autonomy in determining how to meet the goals, the plan faced significant opposition. Labor unions saw it as threatening their gains in collective bargaining since the 1930s, while the US Chamber of Commerce and National Association of Manufacturers objected to the requirements.[23]

The Plan became a political wedge issue for the Nixon administration, which saw an opportunity to divide two reliably Democratic constituencies: African Americans and organized labor. Despite this political calculation, the Plan succeeded in integrating the skilled construction unions in Philadelphia and several other cities. However, as construction unions lost control over the hiring process during the 1970s, its long-term impact on integrating the skilled workforce at jobsites diminished.[24]

By the late 1970s, the federal government's approach to enforcement evolved in response to emerging challenges. The establishment of the Office of Federal Contract Compliance Programs (OFCCP) required federal contractors to develop written affirmative action plans with specific goals and timetables. The OFCCP's mandate expanded through the Rehabilitation Act of 1973 and the Vietnam Era Veterans' Readjustment Act of 1974, extending protections to individuals with disabilities and veterans.[25]

Yet progress remained uneven across corporate America. Many companies focused on developing elaborate documentation systems rather than addressing root causes of inequality. As Dobbin and Kalev note in their comprehensive study of corporate diversity programs, firms often created complex bureaucratic procedures that gave the appearance of fairness without fundamentally changing how decisions were made.[26]

The federal government's evolving stance created new pressures and opportunities. In 1978, under Executive Order 12086, President Jimmy Carter consolidated all equal opportunity contract compliance enforcement powers into the Department of Labor. This reorganization streamlined oversight but also highlighted the growing complexity of diversity requirements.[27]

Research during this period revealed persistent gaps between policy and practice. A comprehensive review of workplace dynamics found that referral networks tended to be highly segregated by race, with workers more likely to refer candidates of their own racial background. In companies where management was predominantly white, referral programs effectively created a pipeline of mostly white candidates.[28]

By the end of the 1970s, growing evidence suggested that purely compliance-based approaches had reached their limits. While companies had become adept at documenting their diversity efforts, many struggled to achieve meaningful integration at higher levels of management. A study by the Economic Policy Institute found that racial wage gaps expanded during this period, despite increased attention to workplace equality.[29]

This period nonetheless established precedents that would shape corporate diversity efforts for decades to come. Companies learned to gather and analyze demographic data, create formal policies and procedures, and connect diversity initiatives to business objectives. While many of these early efforts focused more on compliance than transformation, they created infrastructure and expectations that would support more substantive changes in later years. Most importantly, they demonstrated that meaningful progress on workplace equality required sustained commitment and systematic approaches, not just good intentions.

These insights would become increasingly important as corporate America entered the 1980s and began shifting from basic compliance toward more systematic approaches to diversity management.

The Standardization Era: Making Diversity Systematic

As corporate America entered the 1980s and 1990s, the approach to diversity began shifting from mere compliance toward systematic integration into business practices. Companies started recognizing that success in an increasingly diverse marketplace required more than just meeting legal requirements—it demanded fundamental changes in how organizations operated.[30]

This shift manifested in the rise of standardized hiring practices. Companies adopted uniform applications and interviews, ostensibly to ensure fair treatment for all candidates. The introduction of fax machines and overnight mail revolutionized recruitment processes, allowing companies to cast wider nets for talent. Job seekers began to trust recruiters more, and in-person networking events like job fairs became popular venues for direct engagement between candidates and employers.[31]

A series of Supreme Court decisions in this era provided guidance on the permissible scope of corporate diversity efforts. In *United Steelworkers v. Weber* (1979), the Court upheld voluntary affirmative action plans in private companies, finding that Title VII's prohibition on racial discrimination did not condemn all private, voluntary, race-conscious affirmative action plans. The case involved a plan that reserved 50 percent of openings in a craft-training program for Black employees until the percentage of Black craftworkers matched the local labor force.[32]

Chief Justice Brennan, writing for the majority, emphasized that Congress's primary concern in enacting Title VII was with "the plight of the Negro in our economy," and the prohibition against racial discrimination was primarily addressed to "opening opportunities for Negroes in occupations which have been traditionally closed to them." The Court found the plan acceptable because it didn't "unnecessarily trammel the interests of white employees" and was a temporary measure to eliminate racial imbalance.[33]

This precedent was extended to gender in *Johnson v. Transportation Agency* (1987), where the Court upheld a voluntary affirmative action plan that considered gender as one factor in promotions. The case involved a female employee, Diane Joyce, who was promoted over a male employee despite scoring slightly lower on initial interviews. The Court emphasized that such plans were permissible when they sought to eliminate manifest imbalances in traditionally segregated job categories. In this case, none of the 238 Skilled Craft Worker positions had ever been held by a woman.[34]

A landmark development was the Department of Labor's Glass Ceiling Initiative in 1989. Through pilot studies of nine Fortune 500 companies, the initiative documented systemic barriers preventing qualified minorities and women from reaching senior management positions.

The study revealed several deeply concerning patterns about corporate diversity practices. First, while companies typically monitored equal access and opportunity at lower organizational levels, they almost never considered it a corporate responsibility for senior management positions. The investigation also found that appraisal and compensation systems determining salary, bonuses, and perquisites were not monitored for potential bias. Record-keeping was another major issue, with a general lack of adequate documentation tracking advancement opportunities. Perhaps most troublingly, the study found that development practices and credential-building experiences, which were crucial for career advancement, were often not as available to minorities and women as they were to white male employees.[35]

This initiative led to the creation of the Glass Ceiling Commission through the Civil Rights Act of 1991. The Commission's findings revealed stark disparities: among Fortune 1000–sized companies studied, women represented 37.2 percent of all employees but only 6.6 percent of executive-level managers. The numbers were even lower for minorities at just 2.6 percent of executive positions.[36]

The Los Angeles riots of 1992, following the Rodney King verdict, became a pivotal moment forcing corporate America to confront racial inequities. The scope of destruction was unprecedented in modern American history. Fifty-two people lost their lives during the unrest, while another 2,499 were injured. Law enforcement recorded over 16,000 riot-related crimes during the period. The economic toll was equally staggering, with property damage exceeding $446 million across 1,120 buildings. The impact on the business community was particularly severe, as nearly 94 percent of the damaged buildings were commercial enterprises, predominantly retail stores.[37]

The riots' economic impact forced many companies to reassess their diversity programs and community engagement. In response, Mayor Tom Bradley formed Rebuild LA (RLA), choosing Peter

Ueberroth to chair the organization. RLA's strategy evolved through two distinct phases. From 1992 to 1994, the organization took an initial "top-down" approach, focusing on stimulating private investments through what they termed a "three-legged stool" of business, government, and community cooperation. This approach showed early promise, generating $500 million in corporate commitments before being stalled by the 1994 Northridge earthquake. From 1994 to 1997, RLA shifted to a "bottom-up" approach, concentrating on developing businesses that would serve residents' needs while simultaneously strengthening existing businesses through collaborative projects.[38]

The Texaco discrimination lawsuit and settlement in 1996 marked another important moment for corporate diversity efforts. The case began when six highly qualified African American employees filed a class action complaint alleging systematic discrimination in promotions and compensation.

The investigation into Texaco's practices revealed stark disparities in leadership representation and systematic barriers to advancement. Among Texaco's top 498 executives, only four were Black, a statistic that spoke volumes about the company's promotion practices. Investigators uncovered the existence of a "secret" high-potential list used for promotions that included no African Americans whatsoever. The company's affirmative action plans were found to be poorly implemented, with little meaningful effort to increase minority representation in higher-level jobs.[39]

The situation at Texaco took an even more dramatic turn when secret recordings of executive meetings came to light. These tapes captured senior leaders making openly racist remarks and mocking Black employees. In one particularly egregious instance, executives were recorded referring to Black employees as "black jelly beans stuck to the bottom of the bag." The recordings also revealed executives plotting to destroy documents relevant to the discrimination case. Their derision of diversity celebrations like Kwanzaa demonstrated a culture of deep-seated racism at the highest levels of the organization.[40]

The settlement that eventually emerged from this case was unprecedented in both scope and scale. At its core was a massive cash payment of $115 million to be distributed among 1,500 class members, making it the largest settlement of its kind at that time. Beyond this immediate compensation, Texaco committed to substantial ongoing investments in equity. This included $26.1 million in pay raises over five years for Black employees and an additional $35 million allocated specifically for sensitivity and diversity training programs. The settlement also mandated the creation of an independent Equality and Tolerance Task Force to oversee the company's diversity efforts moving forward. The economic impact extended beyond the direct beneficiaries. The settlement was estimated to have created or sustained 4,608 jobs, demonstrating how addressing discrimination could have positive ripple effects throughout the economy.[41]

The Americans with Disabilities Act (1990) marked another expansion of corporate diversity considerations. The Act's Title I established comprehensive protections, specifically prohibiting discrimination on the basis of disability across the full spectrum of employment aspects. This included everything from initial job application procedures through hiring and advancement decisions, extending to employee compensation, job training, and all other terms and conditions of employment.

To comply with the new law, companies had to undertake significant organizational changes. This began with a thorough review of all personnel policies, manuals, and handbooks to identify and eliminate potentially discriminatory language. Organizations also needed to revise their job descriptions to clearly state essential functions, ensuring that qualification criteria were truly job-related rather than arbitrarily exclusive. The law prohibited pre-employment medical examinations, fundamentally changing how companies assessed job candidates. Perhaps most significantly, businesses were required to develop comprehensive policies for reasonable accommodations, creating systematic processes for adapting workplace conditions to support employees with disabilities.[42]

Some organizations began recognizing these systemic barriers and taking more comprehensive approaches. Employee Resource Groups (ERGs) evolved significantly during this period, transforming from their origins as race-based employee groups in the 1960s into sophisticated business resources. Xerox pioneered this movement with the first

ERG, the National Black Employee Caucus, in 1970, followed by the Black Women's Leadership Caucus in 1980. By the 1990s, ERGs had expanded to include various dimensions of diversity and were increasingly aligned with business objectives.[43]

The most forward-thinking companies started tying diversity goals to business performance. IBM's approach under CEO Lou Gerstner became a landmark example of this integration. Rather than treating diversity as a philanthropic effort, IBM made it a core business strategy. The company established diversity task forces and made executives accountable for developing minority talent. During meetings of the senior team, executives were expected to be able to discuss any high-potential manager at any moment, with explicit effort made to ensure minorities and women were discussed alongside white males. This practice, known as the "five-minute drill," became a powerful tool for accountability.[44]

The results at IBM were remarkable. The company saw a dramatic 370 percent increase in female executives, while the number of ethnic minority executives rose by 233 percent. Perhaps most striking was the 733 percent gain in LGBTQ+ executive representation. These demographic shifts corresponded with significant business growth, particularly in the company's Market Development organization, which expanded its revenue from $10 million in 1998 to hundreds of millions by 2003 through focused efforts on women-owned and minority-owned businesses.[45]

Yet progress remained uneven across corporate America. Research from the 1990s showed that standardized hiring practices had not eliminated racial discrimination. A meta-analysis of field experiments through 2015 found that white applicants received 36 percent more callbacks than equally qualified African Americans and 24 percent more callbacks than Latinos.[46]

By the end of the 1990s, the business case for diversity was becoming clearer, but so were the challenges of creating genuine change. Despite apparent progress in corporate policies and practices, workplace segregation remained stubbornly persistent. Research showed that between 1990 and 2000, there was little change in overall workplace segregation patterns, suggesting that surface-level changes in hiring practices were insufficient to address deeper structural issues.[47]

The Measurement Period: From Tracking to Understanding

As corporate America entered the new millennium, a fundamental shift occurred in how companies approached diversity: they began adopting more sophisticated measurement and analysis tools. Companies increasingly recognized that "if it doesn't get measured, it doesn't get done."[48] This shift manifested in multiple ways, with companies analyzing detailed workforce metrics and examining patterns in hiring, retention, advancement, and compensation. McKinsey's research revealed stark disparities in early career advancement. Women were 20 percent less likely than men to get promoted from entry-level positions to first-level management, with this gap widening throughout the career pipeline.[49]

A landmark study of Fortune 500 companies revealed the power of detailed metrics to uncover hidden patterns. Among 244 Fortune 500 companies studied, 139 of 171 companies (81 percent) showed significant gaps between minority and white representation at leadership levels. Perhaps most striking, 38 companies had four or fewer minority executives in their entire leadership team. These disparities persisted even in companies that appeared diverse at lower levels.[50]

The rise of sophisticated measurement coincided with growing evidence that diversity initiatives could meaningfully impact business performance. Research examining market reactions to diversity efforts during different presidential administrations found that DEI initiatives supporting specific social groups yielded varying financial returns depending on the broader political climate. During the Obama administration, companies implementing LGBTQ-focused DEI initiatives saw their stocks decrease by 0.34 percent, while those focusing on veterans saw increases of 0.65 percent. These patterns notably reversed during the Trump administration.[51]

Technology played a role in this evolution. HR systems progressed from basic personnel tracking to sophisticated analytics platforms capable of analyzing multiple dimensions of the employee life cycle. Modern systems could track not just basic demographics but also promotion velocities, pay differentials, and retention patterns across different demographic groups. This technological advancement enabled companies to identify specific points where diverse talent got stuck or pushed out of the pipeline.[52]

The rise of detailed metrics also revealed uncomfortable truths about existing diversity initiatives. A comprehensive review of diversity training programs found that mandatory diversity training often produced negative results, with some companies seeing up to a 10 percent decline in Black women in management positions after implementing required training. The study found that US businesses spent between $200 million and $300 million annually on diversity training, but many programs were more symbolic than substantive. When attendance was voluntary, diversity training showed positive results, but forcing participation often created resistance and backlash.[53]

Pay equity emerged as a particular focus during this period, with some companies developing sophisticated analysis methodologies. Google implemented a rigorous annual pay analysis system where compensation recommendations (including base salary, bonus, and equity) were made "blind" to gender, with analysts not having access to employees' gender data. Managers had limited discretion to adjust suggested amounts and needed to provide legitimate rationale for any changes.[54]

Salesforce's pay equity journey became a notable case study in this period. The initiative began when two executives, Cindy Robbins and Leyla Seka, presented the idea to CEO Marc Benioff. Though initially skeptical, Benioff became convinced after seeing preliminary data. The company undertook an analysis of 16,000 employees' salaries, making adjustments for both men and women. Importantly, they discovered that achieving pay equity required ongoing monitoring rather than just one-time fixes.[55]

Companies also expanded their measurement focus beyond internal workforce metrics, developing sophisticated approaches to measuring diversity throughout their value chains. Leading organizations implemented comprehensive supplier diversity measurement systems that tracked not just spending with diverse suppliers but also the economic impact of these relationships on local communities. They measured metrics such as job creation, wealth generation in underserved communities, and the growth trajectory of minority-owned businesses within their supplier networks.[56]

Technology played an increasingly central role in enabling more sophisticated measurement approaches. New HR analytics platforms emerged that could integrate data from multiple sources to provide real-time insights into diversity metrics. These systems could automatically flag potential inequities in hiring, promotion, and compensation decisions before they became systemic issues. Machine learning algorithms began to be employed to identify patterns in employee data that might indicate subtle forms of bias or exclusion. However, organizations had to carefully monitor these systems to ensure the algorithms themselves didn't perpetuate existing biases.[57]

Legal and regulatory requirements increasingly shaped measurement practices during this period. The Dodd-Frank Act's requirements for workforce disclosure, state-level pay equity laws, and the EEOC's reporting requirements all drove companies to develop more rigorous measurement systems. California's SB 973, for example, required companies to submit annual pay data reports broken down by gender, race, and ethnicity across job categories and pay bands. This regulatory pressure led many organizations to implement more sophisticated pay equity analysis tools and regular audit processes.[58]

Several companies emerged as leaders in measurement innovation during this period. Intel, for example, developed a comprehensive "warmth score" that measured not just representation but also inclusion and belonging across different demographic groups. Microsoft implemented a "Diversity Dashboard" that provided real-time metrics on hiring, promotion, and retention patterns, making this data available to all managers to inform their decision-making. Bank of America created a supplier diversity economic impact report that measured both direct spending with diverse suppliers and the broader economic ripple effects in local communities.[59]

Public accountability increased significantly during this period, driven largely by investor pressure. By 2020, major institutional investors began demanding greater transparency around diversity metrics. The New York City Comptroller, overseeing $206 billion in retirement assets, sent letters to 67 companies in the S&P 100 demanding release of EEO-1 workforce demographic data. This pressure produced results. At cybersecurity company Fortinet's annual meeting, 70 percent of shareholders voted to back a resolution to report on workforce diversity, a record high for similar resolutions. However, only 32 companies in the Russell 1000 initially made this information public.[60]

Despite increased measurement and monitoring, research revealed persistent gaps between data collection and meaningful change. A study by the Economic Policy Institute found that racial wage gaps expanded during this period.[61]

Organizations gradually recognized that measurement alone couldn't create inclusion. According to research from Notre Dame University, the most successful companies moved beyond pure representation metrics to focus on creating environments where everyone could thrive.[62] The most effective organizations developed what researchers termed "meaningful impact metrics," which went beyond simple headcount to assess actual influence and participation. For instance, rather than just tracking the number of women in leadership positions, companies began measuring their participation in key decisions, their influence on corporate strategy, and their success in mentoring the next generation of leaders.[63]

The evolution of measurement also revealed the importance of connecting diversity metrics to business outcomes. Companies discovered that diverse teams offered varied approaches to problem-solving and drove business innovation. Studies of S&P 500 companies found that firms with greater diversity demonstrated more resilience during economic crises. During the 2008 financial crisis, inclusive companies listed on that index saw a 14 percent increase in their share prices, while the index overall had a 35 percent decline.[64] This data helped make the business case for diversity more concrete and measurable.

The impact of the #MeToo movement in late 2017 further accelerated the focus on measurement and accountability. Research showed that firms with all-male boards experienced negative market reactions as the movement gained momentum, while those with three or more women directors saw positive returns. This finding suggested that investors viewed board gender diversity as a signal of corporate culture and risk management capability.[65]

In the wake of #MeToo, companies began tracking not just incidents of harassment but also measuring the effectiveness of their response mechanisms. A CAHRS White Paper found that 35 percent of firms noted an increase in harassment reports after #MeToo, though this didn't necessarily correlate to increased substantiation rates. Of firms experiencing an increase, 82 percent reported a minimal increase, while 18 percent highlighted a significant increase, with reports doubling at more than one firm.[66]

These insights would shape the next phase of corporate diversity efforts—a phase supercharged by the immediate and dramatic response to the death of George Floyd. This pushed organizations to think more holistically about equity and inclusion while maintaining rigorous measurement practices. Companies began developing more sophisticated metrics for assessing racial equity, including examining promotion velocity differences between demographic groups, measuring pay equity across intersectional categories, and tracking the effectiveness of inclusion initiatives through employee sentiment analysis and retention patterns.

3

The Corporate Awakening

THE MURDER OF George Floyd didn't just spark unprecedented protests—it ushered in a fourth distinct phase in corporate America's approach to diversity, equity, and inclusion. While the Foundation Years (1960s–1970s) established basic legal protections, the Standardization Era (1980s–1990s) created systematic approaches, and the Measurement Period (2000s–2010s) brought data-driven accountability, this new Post-Floyd Era would fundamentally transform how companies thought about inclusion.

What distinguished this fourth phase wasn't just its unprecedented scale—though the financial commitments would dwarf any previous corporate diversity initiative. The real revolution came in how companies began approaching equity and inclusion. Rather than treating diversity as a separate initiative managed by a dedicated department, organizations started integrating inclusive practices into every aspect of their operations.

This shift manifested differently across industries but followed a consistent pattern. Target didn't just hire more diverse employees—they reimagined how their stores served urban communities. Microsoft didn't just increase representation—they fundamentally changed how they developed AI systems. WarnerMedia transformed not just who told stories, but how stories were developed, funded, and distributed. JPMorgan Chase didn't simply hire more minority bankers—they revolutionized their approach to community banking. Google didn't just set hiring goals—they rebuilt their entire approach to product development.

The scale of this transformation was staggering. Between May 2020 and October 2022, Fortune 1000 companies pledged approximately $340 billion to driving racial equity, with $141 billion of those commitments coming between May 2021 and October 2022 alone.[1]

The distribution of these commitments revealed both the scope of corporate America's response and its limitations. Financial institutions led the way, with 16 finance companies accounting for 93 percent of total commitment values. Retail companies contributed 4.5 percent of commitments, food and restaurant businesses 1.3 percent, with all other sectors contributing less than 1 percent each. This distribution raised questions about sector-specific barriers to change, particularly given that sectors employing the highest percentages of Black workers often made the smallest commitments.[2]

The deployment of these commitments revealed evolving corporate priorities. While early pledges in 2020 focused heavily on housing and small business initiatives (accounting for 78 percent of commitments), by 2021–2022 only 20 percent of financial commitments targeted these areas. Companies shifted toward broader-based initiatives, though tracking specific impacts became more challenging as many organizations pooled funds into collective initiatives or grant-making foundations. Notably, while overall commitment levels remained high, only 10 percent of new commitments focused on external community initiatives, with just 2 percent directed toward internal organizational changes.[3]

The effectiveness of these commitments varied significantly. By October 2022, 60 percent of Fortune 1000 companies had not made any public statements supporting racial justice. Among those that did make commitments, the healthcare industry—which employs the largest share of Black workers at 21 percent—pledged just 0.2 percent of total corporate commitments between May 2021 and October 2022.[4]

Perhaps the most visible changes came in corporate leadership. Board diversity underwent dramatic transformation in the wake of Floyd's murder. The percentage of Russell 3000 companies with no racial/ethnic diversity on their boards plummeted from 38 percent in 2020 to just 10 percent in 2022. Even more significantly, the percentage of companies with two or more racially/ethnically diverse directors nearly doubled, rising from 29 percent in 2020 to 55 percent in 2022.[5]

By 2022, all S&P 500 companies included at least one racially/ethnically diverse director—a historic first. The progress accelerated beyond simple representation: 36 percent of S&P 500 companies now have three racially/ethnically diverse directors, while 31 percent have four. However, progress remained uneven—Hispanic/Latin American directors occupied only 5 percent of S&P 500 board seats despite comprising 18.5 percent of the US population.[6]

Institutional investors emerged as powerful drivers of this transformation. The market response to corporate diversity initiatives proved telling—companies that engaged in purely passive discussions about racial issues saw their stock values decline by 2.1 percent on average. However, shareholders rewarded firms that took concrete action, particularly those that appointed Black board members without expanding board size—suggesting markets valued substantive change over symbolic gestures.[7]

The corporate response extended far beyond America's borders, forcing multinational companies to navigate different cultural contexts and histories. Major global brands took unprecedented public stances—Nike reversed its iconic "Just Do It" slogan in an online video, declaring "For once, Don't Do It" and directly addressing racism. In a remarkable show of solidarity transcending business competition, rival Adidas retweeted Nike's message, adding "Together is how we make change."[8]

While the initial flood of commitments and public statements was unprecedented, the real story of this era would emerge in how companies translated these pledges into fundamental changes in how they operated. The following stories of five companies—Target, Microsoft, WarnerMedia, JPMorgan Chase, and Google—illustrate different aspects of this transformation, revealing both the challenges and opportunities organizations encountered as they moved from diversity as a program to inclusion as a competitive advantage.

Target: When Local Tragedy Drives Global Change

In February 2020, just months before Minneapolis would become the epicenter of a national reckoning on race, Target's marketing team was celebrating the success of their "Black Beyond Measure" campaign. The displays, featuring Black women with natural hair and celebrating Black excellence, seemed to represent everything the company stood for. The campaign wasn't just another corporate diversity initiative—it had been created by Target's African American Business Council, a 1,000-member strong employee resource group established five years earlier.[9]

For Target, whose red-and-white bullseye had been a fixture of Minnesota retail since its first store opened in Roseville in 1962, this felt like a natural evolution. The company had long viewed diversity and inclusion as business imperatives, with a formal strategy dating back more than 15 years. Every business unit leader tracked and reported on diversity goals, and the company had built what appeared to be a comprehensive approach to inclusive retail.[10]

But in just three months, the murder of George Floyd less than three miles from Target's corporate headquarters would shatter any complacency about the company's progress on racial equity. As protests erupted across Minneapolis, several Target stores were damaged, including the Lake Street location near where Floyd was killed. The store, which sat across from the Minneapolis Third Police Precinct, became a focal point of demonstrations—and a symbol of deeper tensions the company had failed to recognize.[11]

The Lake Street store's history embodied these tensions. It had been what one security engineer described as Target's "experimental site for loss prevention and surveillance policies geared toward poor people." While Target denied this characterization, the store had come to represent something larger about the relationship between corporate America and urban communities—a relationship that was about to be fundamentally tested.[12]

For Target CEO Brian Cornell, watching his hometown become the epicenter of a national uprising on race forced a profound realization: the company's previous efforts at diversity and inclusion, however well intentioned, had barely scratched the surface. "I know this trial cannot erase the pain that comes from years of inequalities and inequities," Cornell would later write to employees after Derek Chauvin's conviction. "What I want to offer today is my promise that we as a company will continue to use our values and actions to advance empathy and understanding and to confront individual bias and systemic racism."[13]

What followed would be more than just another corporate diversity initiative. It would force Target to fundamentally rethink everything from store layouts to supplier relationships, ultimately leading to a transformation that would survive even as the company faced intense backlash from those who thought it had gone too far. But in those early days of June 2020, as Target executives gathered to craft their response to Floyd's murder, they had no way of knowing just how deeply this crisis would transform their company.

Target's initial response came quickly. Within two weeks of Floyd's death, the company pledged $10 million to social justice organizations and committed to providing 10,000 hours of pro bono consulting services for business owners of color in the Twin Cities. More significantly, they established a Racial Equity Action and Change committee, known as REACH, composed of senior leaders tasked with reimagining the company's approach to racial equity.[14]

But for Kiera Fernandez, Target's chief diversity and inclusion officer, these immediate responses weren't enough. "We have an opportunity here in the Twin Cities to demonstrate to the rest of this country this is how you bridge community," she explained. "This is what it looks like to stand for diversity and equity and inclusion and have this representative workforce and partners and companies and CEOs and leaders that say, 'We stand for the value of inclusion.'"[15]

The company began by looking inward. In September 2020, Target released its Workforce Diversity Report and announced plans to increase Black representation across the company by 20 percent over three years. But the more profound transformation began when

Target's leadership started examining how their stores served—or failed to serve—urban communities.[16]

The Lake Street store in Minneapolis became a laboratory for change. Rather than simply rebuilding what had been damaged during the protests, Target conducted extensive listening sessions with local leaders and residents via Zoom, asking what they wanted in a neighborhood store. The answers revealed how far the company's standard approach had strayed from community needs. The pharmacy needed to be more accessible for elderly customers. The grocery section lacked the spices and foods locals cooked with. Even the store's entrance felt unwelcoming.[17]

"By being based in Minneapolis—by being based in the eye of the storm of George Floyd—they had a huge responsibility to produce a pretty elaborate plan," explained Anthony Thompson, a professor at NYU's Center on Race, Inequality, and the Law. The reimagined Lake Street store would become a model for a new kind of urban retail, one that reflected rather than ignored its community.[18]

This store-level transformation was matched by broader structural changes. In May 2022, Target announced a commitment to spend $2 billion with Black-owned businesses by the end of 2025. The company launched Forward Founders, an accelerator program designed to help Black entrepreneurs navigate the retail industry. By 2023, Target had increased its investments with Black-owned brands, companies, and suppliers by more than 50 percent compared to 2020 and more than doubled its Black-owned brand product offerings.[19]

Microsoft: Recognizing Biases in Facial Recognition

On a crisp fall day in 2015, Joy Buolamwini sat at her desk in MIT's Media Lab—nicknamed the "Future Factory"—absorbed in what should have been a lighthearted project. As a first-year graduate student in a class called "Science Fabrication," she was pursuing an enchanting vision: creating a modern-day magic mirror inspired by the shape-shifting stories of Anansi the spider, a trickster figure from her Ghanaian heritage. The assignment seemed perfectly aligned with the Media Lab's reputation as a cocoon for dreamers, a place where the messiness of the real world could be temporarily forgotten in pursuit of technological wonder.

Her project, which she called the Aspire Mirror, used half-silvered glass placed over a laptop screen to create an illusion of transformation. When she projected an image of Serena Williams, her favorite athlete, and saw the tennis star's features align with her own, it felt like pure magic. "It was spellbinding," Buolamwini would later recall.[20]

But as she worked to enhance the illusion by adding face-tracking capabilities, the dream began to crack. The system, built on widely used artificial intelligence software, simply couldn't detect her face. Puzzled, Buolamwini tried an experiment. She drew two horizontal lines for eyes, an L for a nose, and a wide U for a smile on her palm—essentially a child's drawing of a face. The software detected it instantly. Even more telling, when she held up a white costume mask she had bought for Halloween, the system had no trouble tracking it. The implications were staggering: the AI could recognize a cartoon face drawn on a hand or a plastic mask, but not the real face of a young Black woman.[21]

"Coding in whiteface was the last thing I expected to do when I came to MIT," Buolamwini would later write. The experience transformed her from an optimistic technologist into what she called an "accidental advocate." This personal encounter with what she termed the "coded gaze"—a technological bias as pervasive as the "male gaze" in art or the "white gaze" in literature—drove her to look deeper.[22]

What began as one student's troubling experience evolved into a rigorous scientific investigation. By 2018, Buolamwini and fellow researcher Timnit Gebru had assembled a groundbreaking study. They created a dataset of more than 1,270 faces, carefully coded on the Fitzpatrick scale of skin tones, and tested major companies' AI systems against it. The results were shocking: commercial facial recognition systems from major tech companies, including Microsoft, IBM, and Amazon, showed significant racial and gender biases. The results were stark: while these systems could identify light-skinned male faces with near-perfect accuracy, they failed dramatically when analyzing images of darker-skinned women.[23]

For Microsoft, the numbers were particularly damning. While their system achieved perfect accuracy when identifying light-skinned males, it had an error rate of 21 percent for darker-skinned females.[24]

The irony was sharp. Microsoft, a company that proudly proclaimed its mission to "empower every person and every organization on the planet to achieve more," had built AI systems that effectively discriminated against a significant portion of humanity.[25]

The research sent shockwaves through the tech industry. IBM responded by releasing a new "Diversity in Faces" dataset containing 1 million images meant to sample a more diverse group of faces. However, this effort backfired when it was revealed that IBM had scraped these photos from Flickr without permission from either photographers or subjects.[26]

Microsoft's initial response was more measured. In a statement, the company acknowledged the research's importance and said it had "taken steps to improve the accuracy of its facial-recognition technology." Microsoft emphasized it was "investing in improving its training datasets" and believed "the fairness of AI technologies is a critical issue for the industry and one that Microsoft takes very seriously."[27]

Then came 2020, and the murder of George Floyd changed everything. The impact reverberated through Microsoft's halls, virtual and physical, forcing a deeper confrontation with racial inequity than any technical analysis had achieved. For Darrell Booker, a Microsoft employee with 25 years in the technology industry, the aftermath of Floyd's death marked the first time in his career he couldn't focus on his job. "I felt like a zombie at work," he would later recall. "I was 100% distracted."[28]

When a company vice president scheduled an all-hands meeting to discuss racism, Booker initially didn't trust himself to speak. But something had fundamentally shifted. He found himself being the first to speak up, telling his colleagues that while he wasn't upset with Microsoft's initial response, he believed the company could do more to reach out to Black communities. Within hours, that conversation had sparked a new program, which would soon become part of Microsoft's comprehensive Racial Equity Initiative.

The company's response to Floyd's murder went far beyond public statements of support for racial justice. In June 2020, Microsoft made a decisive move: it would not sell facial recognition technology to police departments until there were national laws, grounded in human rights, governing its use.[29] This wasn't just another corporate policy change—it represented a fundamental shift in how Microsoft approached the ethics of AI development.

The transformation accelerated rapidly. By 2021, Microsoft had established a comprehensive Responsible AI Standard, introducing new safeguards and requirements for AI development. The company created a "sensitive uses process" that required review and oversight of high-impact AI applications. This wasn't just bureaucracy—it led to real decisions to decline business opportunities when the company wasn't confident it could deploy AI systems ethically.[30]

Perhaps the most dramatic evidence of Microsoft's evolving approach came in 2022, when the company made an unprecedented decision: rather than continuing to try to fix the biases in their facial analysis AI, they would retire entire capabilities. Features that claimed to infer emotional states, gender, age, and facial features would be completely discontinued. It was a stark admission that some AI applications weren't just biased—they were fundamentally problematic. "These efforts raised important questions about privacy," the company acknowledged, along with concerns about "the lack of consensus on a definition of 'emotions,' and the inability to generalize the linkage between facial expression and emotional state across use cases, regions, and demographics."[31]

WarnerMedia: A Cultural Transformation

For decades, Hollywood faced criticism for its lack of diversity both on screen and behind the camera. Study after study revealed a troubling pattern: minorities made up nearly 40 percent of the US population but were dramatically underrepresented in lead roles, directing, and writing positions across film and television.[32]

Within the entertainment industry, WarnerMedia stood as a microcosm of these systemic issues. By 2019, the company's CEO John Stankey acknowledged they had "more work to do at every level," even while claiming diversity and inclusion were "important to our employees, our creative partners, our customers, and to our success."[33]

But it was the murder of George Floyd that catalyzed a deeper transformation. "In 2020 there was a lot of pressure for organizations to hire these roles, but not a real understanding of what the jobs were," recalled Jeanell English, who would later become executive vice president of impact and inclusion at the Academy of Motion Picture Arts and Sciences. "You're bringing me in to really challenge, question, rebuild, dismantle the systems that your organization has been built on. And that is fundamentally uncomfortable if you're not ready to receive and respond to that level of critique."[34]

WarnerMedia's response went far beyond typical corporate statements. The company created what would become one of the entertainment industry's most comprehensive diversity initiatives. They developed "The Red Book," a first-of-its-kind catalog of diverse suppliers working in entertainment production and began sharing it with other studios to increase diversity across the entire industry.[35]

Under the leadership of Karen Horne, who became Senior Vice President of Equity and Inclusion Programs, WarnerMedia launched ambitious pipeline programs targeting every sector of their vast enterprise—from animation to games, news to sports. "I've always wanted to work in this field," Horne would later explain. "Also, I've never had a plan B." Her approach went beyond mere funding, focusing on mentorship and providing invaluable access to top creatives across WarnerMedia's many divisions.[36]

The company's commitment to transparency set new standards for the industry. In 2021, they released detailed data about diversity across their workforce and content creation, revealing both progress and persistent challenges. While their global workforce was reaching gender parity with 54 percent men and 46 percent women, management-level positions remained less diverse, with whites comprising 72 percent of senior executives. However, recent hiring and promotion data showed movement toward change, with only 58 percent of new senior management hires being white.[37]

By 2022, WarnerMedia had built an unprecedented equity and inclusion division with more than 50 diverse leaders—an unheard-of number in an industry that typically recruited only a handful of full-time employees for such work. Through six strategic pillars—content, programs, workforce, international, corporate social responsibility, and marketing and communications—the division worked to drive systemic change throughout the organization.[38]

The company's initial diversity report laid bare uncomfortable truths that many in Hollywood preferred to ignore. A McKinsey analysis revealed that the entertainment industry was leaving $10 billion in annual revenues on the table simply by neglecting diverse audiences. Black-led projects were consistently underfunded and undervalued, despite often earning higher relative returns. Films with Black leads were distributed in 30 percent fewer international markets, based on the persistent myth that they wouldn't "travel well"—yet when they did reach global audiences, they earned nearly the same box-office sales as films with white leads.[39]

"Marketing teams need to be on board to select a film," explained one Black executive in the McKinsey report, "but if they don't feel comfortable with the story, it limits the number of buys." The same executive added pointedly: "When executives feel like they can't personally relate to your content, they don't bid."[40]

Growing up as a young biracial kid in New Jersey with a single mom, Karen Horne brought personal understanding to her role at WarnerMedia. "It's always been very important to me that voices who haven't been given a seat at the table have this opportunity," she explained. Her work wasn't just ignited by George Floyd's murder, but "really accelerated by it," as she noted. "It accelerated what our efforts at WarnerMedia were going to be and provided us an opportunity to really address systemic racism in our industry."[41]

The progress was evident in specific divisions. By 2021, Cartoon Network had fundamentally reimagined its approach to character development, with 54 percent of animated protagonists in development being female. Warner Bros. Animation followed suit with 52 percent of lead characters in development being female.[42]

Yet challenges persisted. As showrunner Brigitte Muñoz-Liebowitz experienced with her Latinx coming-of-age show, *Gordita Chronicles*, which was canceled despite strong performance: "We got great reviews, we had great ratings. It's hard to not come to a conclusion that there was some kind of bias." The incident highlighted how deeply entrenched resistance to change remained, even as evidence mounted that diverse content could deliver both critically and commercially.[43]

JPMorgan Chase: From Redlining to Reinvention

In January 2017, on a cold winter morning in Manhattan, JPMorgan Chase executives gathered to address an uncomfortable reality: the nation's largest bank was about to settle yet another racial discrimination lawsuit. The charges were damning—the bank's independent mortgage brokers had systematically charged at least 53,000 Black and Latino borrowers higher fees and interest rates than white borrowers with the same credit profiles. "Chase's pattern of discrimination has been intentional and willful, and has been implemented with reckless disregard of the rights of African American and Hispanic borrowers," the Justice Department's complaint stated bluntly.[44]

The $55 million settlement was just the latest in a series of similar cases. In 2013, the bank had paid $13 billion to settle Justice Department charges over predatory mortgage practices that disproportionately affected minority borrowers.[45] Even as the bank worked to put these lawsuits behind it, its actions seemed to perpetuate patterns of exclusion. A troubling analysis by S&P Global Market Intelligence found that JPMorgan was closing branches in majority-Black neighborhoods at a far higher rate than in other areas—and perhaps most tellingly, wealthy majority-Black areas were just as likely to lack a branch as low-income areas.[46]

For JPMorgan Chase, the largest bank in America with over $3.5 trillion in assets, these issues weren't just moral failings—they represented a profound strategic blind spot.[47]

But it would take the shocking murder of George Floyd in May 2020 to catalyze a fundamental rethinking of the bank's approach to racial equity. CEO Jamie Dimon's response was swift and emotional. "We are watching, listening, and want every single one of you to know we are committed to fighting against racism and discrimination wherever and however it exists," he wrote in a memo to employees. The death of Floyd, he acknowledged, "coupled with the COVID crisis, highlights the inequities Black and other diverse communities have and continue to face every day and it strengthens our resolve to do more as individuals, as a firm, and in our communities."[48]

For America's largest bank, this would not be just another corporate statement of solidarity. Instead, it would mark the beginning of what Dimon called a "wake-up call"—one that would lead to the most ambitious corporate commitment to racial equity in American banking history, and ultimately transform how the nation's largest bank thought about the relationship between inclusion and growth.

The scale of JPMorgan's response matched the gravity of the moment. In October 2020, the bank announced a $30 billion commitment over five years to help close the racial wealth gap. This wasn't just the largest such commitment by any US corporation in the wake of Floyd's killing—it was structured to fundamentally reshape how the bank did business in underserved communities.[49]

"Systemic racism is a tragic part of America's history," Dimon declared as he announced the initiative. "We can do more and do better to break down systems that have propagated racism and widespread economic inequality, especially for Black and Latinx people. It's long past time that society addresses racial inequities in a more tangible, meaningful way."[50]

The commitment was notable not just for its size, but for its comprehensive scope. The bank assembled a task force of community advocates, fair housing experts, and financial inclusion specialists to identify areas where reform was most urgently needed. The resulting plan included $8 billion in mortgages to help an additional 40,000 Black and Latino households purchase homes, $14 billion to finance 100,000 affordable rental units, $2 billion in small business loans, and $2 billion in philanthropic capital.[51]

But perhaps most significantly, the bank committed to opening new branches in underserved communities—a direct reversal of its previous pattern of branch closures in minority neighborhoods. One of the first of these new locations opened in Anacostia, a historically Black neighborhood in Washington, DC where the poverty rate was 46 percent, about two-and-a-half times the city average. The branch wasn't just a banking center—it was designed as a community hub, with space for financial education workshops and small business mentoring.[52]

"We view this as an important opportunity to say, 'Let's grow this region, but let's grow it in an inclusive way. Let's grow it in a way that truly creates opportunity for more people,'" explained Peter Scher, JPMorgan Chase chairman of the Mid-Atlantic region.[53]

The bank's commitment went beyond just opening branches. It revamped its lending practices, creating new programs specifically designed to increase access to credit in majority-minority communities. One of the most significant changes was the creation of a special purpose credit program—the first of its kind nationally—specifically designed to expand credit access for small businesses in majority Black and Latino communities.[54]

For many observers, these changes seemed almost too good to be true, given the bank's troubled history with racial equity. The real test would come not in the immediate aftermath of Floyd's murder, but in the years that followed, as public attention inevitably began to fade and corporate America's commitment to racial justice faced growing pushback.

By the end of 2022, the numbers told a compelling story. JPMorgan had deployed nearly $29 billion of its $30 billion commitment, financing the preservation of nearly 170,000 affordable housing rental units and helping thousands of Black and Latino families purchase homes. The bank expanded its $5,000 Chase Homebuyer Grant program to include over 11,000 majority Black, Hispanic, and Latino communities, providing about 2,700 grants totaling $13.5 million. The commitment to small business wasn't just rhetoric either—when Jamie Dimon visited Houston, he met Sherice and Steve Garner, owners of Southern Q barbecue, who had previously been running their business from a personal bank account. JPMorgan helped them secure a small business loan to purchase their business location.[55]

Google: When Employee Activism Drives Corporate Change

On a warm August morning in 2017, Google's Mountain View campus was buzzing with tension. A 10-page internal memo titled "Google's Ideological Echo Chamber" had just gone viral, first internally and then across Silicon Valley. Written by software engineer James Damore, the document argued that biological differences between men and women might explain the gender gap in tech and criticized Google's diversity initiatives as discriminatory.[56]

For many of Google's employees, particularly women and underrepresented minorities, the memo's viral spread felt like a betrayal. Here was proof that beneath Google's progressive exterior—its pride in being consistently ranked as one of the best places to work, its famous "don't be evil" motto—lurked the same biases that had long plagued the tech industry. Even more troubling was how many employees seemed to agree with Damore's arguments. One engineer reportedly wrote that the memo had caused "irreparable harm . . . to 1000s of Googlers."[57]

The company's response was swift. CEO Sundar Pichai cut short his vacation to address the crisis, and Damore was fired for violating the company's code of conduct.[58] In his response, Pichai wrote to employees: "To suggest a group of our colleagues have traits that make them less biologically suited to that work is offensive and not OK . . . Our co-workers shouldn't have to worry that each time they open their mouths to speak in a meeting, they have to prove that they are not like the memo states, being 'agreeable' rather than 'assertive,' showing a 'lower stress tolerance,' or being 'neurotic.'"[59]

Despite Pichai's strong stance, the memo's impact couldn't be undone with a single personnel decision. It sparked what would become years of internal activism and debate over Google's approach to diversity, equity, and inclusion.[60] The company's published diversity metrics revealed the scale of the challenge: as of 2019, women made up only 31.6 percent of Google's global workforce, and in the United States, just 3.3 percent of employees were Black+, and 5.7 percent were Latinx+.[61]

Then came 2020, and George Floyd's murder changed everything. For a company that prided itself on having data-driven answers to every problem, Floyd's death—and the national reckoning that followed—posed a different kind of challenge. In a watershed moment, Sundar Pichai addressed the company directly, acknowledging the systemic nature of the problem: "Listening to the personal accounts of members of our Black Leadership Advisory Group and our Black+ Googlers has only reinforced for me the reality our Black communities face: one where systemic racism permeates every aspect of life, from interactions with law enforcement, to access to housing and capital, to health care, education, and the workplace."[62]

The company's initial response came in June 2020, when Pichai announced a series of concrete commitments, including an ambitious goal to improve leadership representation of underrepresented groups by 30 percent by 2025.[63] To achieve this, Google committed $175 million in financing and funding to support Black business owners, startup founders, job seekers, and developers, alongside YouTube's separate $100 million fund to amplify Black creators and artists.[64]

Under the leadership of Chief Diversity Officer Melonie Parker, the company began to see tangible results. In the first two years of Parker's role, Google increased the annual percentage of Black hires within the United States from 5.5 percent in 2019 to 9.4 percent in 2021, while Latino US hires rose from 6.6 percent to 9.0 percent. By 2021, Google achieved its largest percentage of new Black and Latino hires in the United States. Additionally, women came to account for 32.6 percent of Google's global leadership, an increase of 5.9 percent since 2019.[65]

The transformation began with a fundamental reimagining of Google's hiring practices. The company launched a comprehensive initiative to address unconscious bias, developing workshops and training programs that were rigorously tested for effectiveness. In an experiment during new hire orientation, Google found that employees who participated in bias training "showed statistically significant increases in awareness and understanding of unconscious bias, and motivation to overcome it." Even more notably, follow-up surveys revealed that workshop participants were "significantly more likely to perceive Google's culture as fair, objective, and as valuing diversity, than those in the control group."[66]

To ensure lasting change, Google created a dedicated Retention and Progression team focused on addressing systemic barriers. As Rachel Spivey, Head of the Stay and Thrive Team at Google, explains: "We try to make sure that retention and progression rates are at parity across race and gender lines." Initially a small initiative that "no one wanted," the team grew dramatically following Google's 2020 equity commitments, eventually quadrupling in size.[67]

The company also revolutionized its approach to accountability through transparent reporting. Since publishing its first Diversity Annual Report in 2014, Google has consistently expanded its data collection and reporting methods. By 2019, the company was tracking not only basic demographic information but also intersectional data combining race and gender, as well as voluntary self-identification data for LGBTQ+ status, disability status, military experience, and gender identity.[68] This commitment to transparency yielded measurable results: by 2022, Google achieved "its best hiring year yet for women globally (37.5 percent of hires) and Black+ and Latinx+ hires in the U.S."[69]

Chief Diversity Officer Melonie Parker attributes this progress to a data-driven, systematic approach: "Everything I've done and the work I've led has been completely powered and informed by data," she explains. "We use data to understand where we have gaps to parity, and we're then able to set goals and rally the company in ensuring we make progress in those areas." Importantly, Google doesn't keep this methodology to itself; the company open sources its diversity data using BigQuery so other leaders can use it to inform their own strategies.[70]

Beyond just focusing on hiring and retention metrics, Google recognized that true transformation required addressing workplace culture at a deeper level. The company expanded its Employee Resource Groups (ERGs), which by 2019 had grown to include more than 25,000 active members across 16 groups. These ERGs became powerful forces for change within the company. For example, the Black Googler Network spans 30 chapters and launched initiatives like the #YouTubeBlack Brand Summit, while the Women@Google network grew to over 15,000 members across multiple countries, running programs like the #IAmRemarkable empowerment workshops that have reached 25,000 women both inside and outside Google.[71]

The company also took concrete steps to make its workspaces more inclusive. In one notable example, Google reformed its security practices after recognizing potential bias in its "tailgater" monitoring system, where employees were expected to watch for unauthorized visitors. After extensive research and listening to Black Googlers' experiences, the Global Security and Resilience team developed new security procedures that maintained safety without relying on employee badge-checking, which had been identified as susceptible to bias.[72]

Google's transformation extended beyond its own walls to impact its products and services. The company established a systematic approach to product inclusion, implementing guidelines that prompt product managers, researchers, and UX designers to question whether their products are inclusive of diverse users. As explained by Senior Vice President Hiroshi Lockheimer, who leads teams responsible for Android, Chrome, Google Play, and Photos: "Our products have to meet billions of different needs, and we can't succeed without inclusive products designed for all users, no matter who they are or where they come from." This approach led to concrete improvements, such as developing the Pixel camera technology to take better pictures of all skin tones and shades.[73]

By 2022, the impact of these comprehensive changes was becoming clear. Employee sentiment data showed that 87 percent of Googlers reported feeling comfortable being themselves at work (up 3 percent year over year), and 91 percent said their work groups valued diverse perspectives (up 2 percent). More significantly, for the first time ever, Black+ attrition in the United States became comparable to Google-wide attrition levels.[74]

Despite these gains, Google's leadership acknowledges that significant work remains. As Melonie Parker reflects, "If you see talent as an asset, what do you think your talent needs to ensure your company is not only successful, but profitable? Not just experiences or competencies, but what conditions do people need to bring their best selves to your company every day?" Her approach emphasizes that "leaders should re-recruit their talent every day, remind people of why they're there. We do that by investing in their career development and really examining the culture of the company to make sure it's fair and supportive for everyone."[75]

The company's commitment continues to evolve in response to new challenges. Parker emphasizes that one of the biggest challenges in a global workforce is "ensuring our strategy is truly global to the point where our workforce worldwide sees themselves reflected in our DEI strategy." She approaches this through a learning mindset: "I'm always reading, researching, studying, and talking to people to learn more."[76]

Looking toward the future, Google has expanded its focus to include long-term investments in education and community development. The company has implemented programs like Computer Science Summer Institute (CSSI), a three-week introduction to computer science for graduating high school seniors, with 92 percent of the most recent cohort identifying as Black+, Latinx+, or women. The company also conducts outreach at 13 historically Black colleges and universities (HBCUs) and 30 Hispanic-serving institutions (HSIs), while programs like Tech Exchange provide immersive learning opportunities on Google's campus.[77]

However, as Parker notes, "Even incremental progress in hiring, progression, and retention is hard-won. Only a holistic approach to these issues will produce meaningful, sustainable change. We must continue our work to expand the talent pool externally, and improve our culture internally, if we want to create equitable outcomes and inclusion for everyone."[78] This recognition that sustainable change requires both systematic measurement and cultural transformation has become central to Google's approach to diversity, equity, and inclusion, setting a new standard for how large technology companies can respond to calls for racial and gender equity. Additionally, the benefits of their focus on racial equity have directly advanced Google's DEI ecosystem related to gender, the pride community, neurodiversity, abilities, accessibility, veterans, generational, well-being, lifestyle, and host of other affinity stakeholders at Google.

The company's journey from the Damore memo crisis to its current state of exceeding all its publicly stated racial equity goals is a testament to what can happen when DEI is planned, implemented, and executed correctly. It proves that moments of crisis, when met with sustained commitment and systematic action, can catalyze meaningful transformation. As Parker puts it, "We're taking an enterprise-wide approach in our five-year racial equity goals, looking at our milestones on a continual basis and reporting it out annually to allow for transparency internally and externally. This way, our partners, users, creators and workforce are not only aware of the progress we're making, but also are able to participate."[79]

From American Crisis to Global Transformation

The stories of Target, Microsoft, WarnerMedia, JPMorgan Chase, and Google reveal a remarkable pattern in how American corporations transformed in the wake of George Floyd's murder. Each company had considered itself a leader in diversity and inclusion before that fateful day in Minneapolis. Each had programs, initiatives, and metrics they could point to with pride. Yet for each, Floyd's murder sparked a revelation that their previous efforts had barely scratched the surface of what real inclusion required.

What followed wasn't just another round of corporate diversity programs. These companies undertook fundamental examinations of their business models, confronting uncomfortable truths about how their standard practices perpetuated exclusion. Microsoft discovered how its AI systems encoded bias. WarnerMedia realized its traditional approaches to storytelling marginalized diverse voices. JPMorgan Chase recognized how its lending practices reinforced racial wealth gaps. Target saw how even its store layouts could make communities feel unwelcome. Google found that its product development processes weren't accounting for diverse user experiences.

The transformations that followed went far deeper than new hiring goals or sensitivity training. Microsoft rebuilt its approach to AI development from the ground up. WarnerMedia revolutionized how it developed and distributed content. JPMorgan Chase reimagined community banking. Target transformed everything from store designs to supplier relationships. Google fundamentally changed how it approached product development and testing. These weren't just diversity initiatives—they were fundamental changes to how these companies did business.

The data told the story. WarnerMedia found that streaming series with diverse casts achieved 67 percent higher viewership. JPMorgan's community-focused branches opened new markets and customer relationships. Target's private brand portfolio, built with diverse suppliers, grew twice as fast as national brands. Microsoft's more inclusive AI systems captured markets its competitors couldn't reach. Google's more inclusive product development processes led to innovations that served previously overlooked user needs. What had begun as a response to social justice concerns had evolved into a competitive advantage.

But the impact of these transformations wouldn't stop at America's borders. As these companies operated globally, their changed practices rippled outward. Microsoft's AI principles influenced technology development worldwide. WarnerMedia's content changes affected viewing habits from Buenos Aires to Bangkok. JPMorgan Chase's lending practices shaped banking in markets across continents. Target's supplier diversity program created opportunities for entrepreneurs around the globe. Google's inclusive design principles began influencing product development practices internationally.

More importantly, companies beyond American shores were watching and learning. They saw how these US corporations had turned inclusion from a social initiative into a business imperative. They noticed how the companies that adapted most successfully to America's racial reckoning were gaining competitive advantages in unexpected ways. And they began to ask themselves: How do these lessons translate to our own cultural contexts? How can we build more inclusive businesses in our own markets?

The answer to these questions would vary dramatically by region and culture. But one thing was becoming clear: the transformation sparked by George Floyd's murder wouldn't be contained by national boundaries. A new model of business was emerging—one that recognized inclusion not as a program to be managed, but as a fundamental driver of 21st-century business success. The only question was how would this American revolution in corporate practice reshape business around the world?

4

Exponential Expansions

AT 7 AM on a crisp September morning in 2020, I stood on a quiet street in São Paulo, Brazil, staring at an enormous mural of George Floyd's face. I had been out for my usual morning run when the stark black and white image stopped me in my tracks. The words "I CAN'T BREATHE" stretched across the wall in both English and Portuguese. As I caught my breath, my phone buzzed with urgent messages from colleagues across time zones: Singapore, Tokyo, New York.

A month later, I was in London for a series of DEI consultations when I encountered another Floyd mural, this one incorporating elements of British racial justice movements. When I shared my amazement at seeing George Floyd murals abroad with my European colleagues, they soon started texting me photos of similar artwork appearing in Berlin, Paris, and across the globe. In each location, these murals became powerful symbols of local struggles against systemic oppression.[1] In Berlin, artist Jesus Cruz Artiles captured the urgency of the moment, stating that his mural was meant to "raise our voices against police brutality, against racism, because these things keep repeating." In Palestine, artist Taqi Spateen connected Floyd's story to the Palestinian struggle for liberation, painting "I CAN'T BREATHE, I want justice, not O2" on Israel's separation wall in Bethlehem.[2]

These murals represented something profound: the transformation catalyzed by George Floyd's murder wasn't contained to corporate boardrooms or even to the United States. It was sparking changes across every sector of society, in communities around the world. In Brazil, where racial dynamics have historically been complex, Floyd's story resonated deeply with the Black community's ongoing struggle against systemic racism. As protestors in Brazil chanted "Black lives matter here, too," they connected their own experiences of police violence and discrimination to the global movement.[3] The Brazilian police killed nearly six times as many people as in the United States in the previous year, with most victims being Black, highlighting the urgent need for reform.[4]

In European cities, Floyd's image became a catalyst for confronting their own histories of colonialism and present-day systemic inequities. The protests that erupted across Europe weren't simply expressions of solidarity with American activists; they were demands for accountability in their own societies.[5] In Belgium, protesters challenged the country's colonial legacy, leading to the removal of statues of King Leopold II in Brussels and Antwerp. In the UK, demonstrators in Bristol toppled the statue of a 17th-century slave trader, forcing a national conversation about how Britain remembers its imperial past.[6]

This global movement created both unprecedented opportunities and unique challenges. As Rokhaya Diallo, a French filmmaker and journalist, observed, "I've never seen so many people marching against police brutality . . . Even the fact that we are now having this debate, that we are comparing ourselves to the U.S., to me that's new."[7] However, each country faced its own obstacles in addressing systemic racism. In France, for example, the nation's self-image as a color-blind republic has historically hindered efforts to organize around racial identity.[8]

What emerged was a truly global reckoning with racism that transcended national boundaries while remaining deeply rooted in local contexts. As scholar Yassmin Abdel-Magied noted, "The structural racism underlying police brutality in the United States thrives globally . . . The system of white supremacy is alive and well."[9] This awakening forced institutions worldwide to confront their role in either perpetuating or dismantling systemic inequities.

What follows is the story of how that transformation unfolded, and how the urgency for change sparked by one tragedy in Minneapolis rippled through communities around the world. It's a story about how institutions that had long resisted meaningful change were finally forced to confront their role in maintaining systems of oppression. Most importantly, it's a story about why these changes may prove more lasting than any corporate initiative: because when transformation reaches into the heart of how communities learn, create, and understand themselves, there's no easy way to turn back.

The Global Corporate Response

As multinational companies scrambled to respond to George Floyd's murder, they faced unprecedented pressure from employees demanding concrete action. Within weeks, 85.3 percent of companies had discussed Floyd's death with their teams, and 57.7 percent committed to scheduling ongoing discussions about race.[10]

The corporate response revealed both the urgency of the moment and the limitations of conventional approaches. Many organizations discovered that their existing diversity frameworks, which often prioritized gender equity and broad inclusion goals, weren't equipped to address the specific challenges of racial justice on a global scale. This was particularly evident in regions where discussions of race had rarely been explicit. In India, for example, while companies proudly displayed their commitment to gender and disability inclusion on their websites, many carefully avoided mentioning caste, despite it being a fundamental axis of discrimination affecting hundreds of millions.[11]

The disparity was stark: while upper-caste groups, comprising roughly 20 percent of India's population, owned about 55 percent of the country's wealth, companies rarely tracked caste representation in their workforce. As one CEO of an investment firm tellingly remarked, he did not feel bad about the caste imbalance at his firm because, "Dalits have the quota system for their jobs." This comment reveals how corporate India often deflected responsibility for addressing caste discrimination to government quotas.[12] DEI experts in India began pushing to "Indianise" global diversity models to incorporate caste at a high level, arguing that companies needed to rethink traditional definitions of merit that often privileged upper-caste candidates through requirements like "good spoken English" and "social confidence."[13]

One of the most significant innovations to emerge from this period was the broader adoption and adaptation of what became known as the "Embassy Model." This is one key approach used by international companies to handle sensitive DEI issues across cultural boundaries. Originally developed to create safe spaces for LGBTQ+ employees in countries with restrictive laws, the Embassy Model provided a framework that companies could adapt for addressing racial equity globally. This approach allows a large corporation to treat their offices, warehouses, and factories in various countries as little bubbles, in which the policies of the company will be observed, regardless of what the local customs are in the area.[14]

Companies like Maersk demonstrated how the Embassy Model could be effectively implemented, creating protected spaces where employees could engage in open DEI discussions while respecting local cultural contexts. As Maersk noted, "The embassy model creates safe, inclusive workplaces for all employees . . . allowing us to enforce our corporate policies regardless of local context."[15] This approach was particularly crucial in jurisdictions where certain identities and discussions weren't legally protected. Research has shown the business impact of such inclusive spaces: 84 percent of LGBTQ+ employees at supportive companies reported being proud to work for their employer, compared to just 68 percent at unsupportive companies.[16] Moreover, 82 percent of ally respondents and 71 percent of LGBTQ+ individuals indicated they were more likely to purchase goods or services from companies that supported equality.[17]

The transformation wasn't limited to internal policies. Major corporations made substantial financial commitments to advance racial equity. Cisco's response exemplified this comprehensive approach, beginning with an immediate $5 million pledge to nonprofits promoting social justice. But rather than simply writing checks, the company developed a "Social Justice Beliefs and Actions" framework that included both direct support and systemic change. Through their Black Equity Grant Program, they built two-way partnerships with organizations working on issues from police reform to economic empowerment, combining financial support with volunteer engagement, product donations, and expertise sharing.[18]

Unilever similarly committed to systemic change, pledging €2 billion annually by 2025 to suppliers owned and managed by underrepresented groups.[19] But they went beyond procurement, addressing fundamental economic inequities by committing to ensure everyone who directly provided goods and services to Unilever would earn at least a living wage by 2030. The company recognized that living wages stimulated broader economic growth, creating "a virtuous cycle" that helped break cycles of poverty. They also committed to helping 5 million small and medium-sized enterprises grow through access to skills, finance, and technology.[20]

Some organizations took unprecedented steps toward transparency and accountability. HSBC UK, for instance, published their diversity data publicly for the first time, acknowledging they had "a lot of work to do, particularly with respect to the representation of Black colleagues at senior levels."[21] The bank established an ethnicity framework based on the UK's Race at Work Charter, creating a new Ethnicity Steering Committee chaired by an executive sponsor. They committed to reviewing recruitment and career development practices, with particular focus on supporting Black colleagues, while reinforcing a zero-tolerance approach to racism.[22]

Their African Heritage Employee Resource Group played a role in facilitating change, organizing panel discussions that encouraged frank conversations about racial issues. As Louise Sherman, National Co-Chair of the ERG, noted, "After George Floyd's death, we had a panel discussion on a range of topics and encouraged participants to really open up and speak frankly." The ERG also collaborated with other employee resource groups, demonstrating how intersectional approaches could strengthen diversity efforts.[23]

Yet this period also revealed the limitations of corporate-led change. While companies could create safe spaces for conversations about race and equity, they couldn't easily resolve centuries of cultural and systemic inequities. In India, for example, despite corporate DEI initiatives, studies showed that candidates with high-caste Hindu names were still 60 percent more likely to be called for interviews than those with low-caste names when identical CVs were submitted.[24] DEI experts noted that most companies didn't even track caste representation in their workforce, making it impossible to measure progress. As Christina Dhanuja, a DEI-caste strategist in Chennai observed, companies that ignored caste were "just exposing themselves to lawsuits and reputational damage."[25]

The challenges of measuring progress varied by region. While some markets had established frameworks for tracking racial and ethnic diversity, others lacked basic demographic data. Companies had to balance global standards with local realities. In some regions, collecting certain demographic data was illegal or culturally sensitive. This forced organizations to develop alternative metrics for measuring inclusion and equity, from employee engagement scores to supplier diversity statistics to community impact assessments.

What emerged was a more nuanced understanding of how global organizations could support social transformation while respecting local contexts. The Embassy Model and similar frameworks provided a structure for this balance, creating protected spaces for progress while acknowledging that change would look different in different places. As HSBC UK's CEO Ian Stuart noted, companies needed to "use our position as a global organisation to support diversity and inclusion, both in the UK and internationally," while recognizing that improving representation required sustained, locally relevant efforts.[26]

For many organizations, this period marked a transition from viewing diversity as a compliance issue or business imperative to understanding their role in broader societal transformation. As Unilever CEO Alan Jope explained, "The two biggest threats that the world currently faces are climate change and social inequality . . . Without a healthy society, there cannot be a healthy business."[27] This recognition that corporate success was inextricably linked to social equity would prove crucial as organizations continued to navigate the challenges of building truly inclusive global operations.

Cultural Institutions Transform

The global media industry's transformation in the wake of George Floyd's murder revealed both the universal resonance of racial justice issues and the distinct ways they manifested in different cultural contexts. In Europe, news organizations that had long prided themselves on objectivity were forced to confront their role in perpetuating colonial narratives. As French filmmaker and journalist Rokhaya Diallo noted, when she attempted to discuss race on television, she was often "assaulted by the others around the table" simply for trying to "tackle race" in a country that clung to the "fallacy of universalism of a country that would be colorblind."[28]

The BBC took concrete steps toward transformation, expanding their groundbreaking 50:50 Project beyond gender to include ethnicity and disability representation. The initiative, which began as a grassroots effort in the BBC's London newsroom, had already demonstrated remarkable success using a data-driven methodology. By March 2020, 66 percent of BBC content featured 50 percent women contributors, up from just 34 percent when teams first began monitoring. Programs like Radio 4's *The World This Weekend*, *BBC Breakfast*, and *The Andrew Marr Show* all achieved gender parity.[29]

The impact was measurable: nearly 40 percent of audience members reported noticing an increase in women's representation in BBC online content. Among younger viewers, the changes had an even stronger effect: 40 percent of those aged 16–34 reported greater enjoyment of BBC content due to increased female representation.[30]

In the aftermath of George Floyd, the BBC set new targets: 20 percent Black, Asian, and Minority Ethnic representation and 12 percent disability representation across all genres. The organization also partnered with Media Trust to launch the Reframing Disability program, which coached disabled experts and trained journalists on working with disabled contributors.[31]

In the film industry, the changes were equally profound but met with varying degrees of resistance. The Cannes Film Festival, which had already faced criticism for its historical exclusion of diverse voices, was pushed to confront its track record. A 2018 protest led by 82 women, including Cate Blanchett and Ava DuVernay, highlighted the stark gender disparity: only 82 female directors had been featured at Cannes since its inception in 1946, compared to 1,688 male directors. The protesters declared, "Women are not a minority in the world, yet the current state of our industry says otherwise."[32]

The racial disparities were even more pronounced. Between 2017 and 2019, only 35 percent of films accepted to major film festivals were directed by people of color. The problem was systemic—research showed that most festivals relied heavily on recommendations from current board members or recruitment from within the same industry circles, perpetuating homogeneous networks. Even more troubling, while 95 percent of respondents believed they needed diverse candidates, only 16 percent rated lack of diversity as a top problem in recruitment.[33]

In the wake of George Floyd, Cannes finally agreed to make concrete changes. In 2022 they launched "AfroCannes" specifically to promote diversity and inclusion in the film industry, featuring panel discussions, screenings, and efforts to connect creatives from across the global film ecosystem.[34] The 77th Cannes Film Festival in 2024 demonstrated tangible progress, featuring over 20 African films, with directors like Mo Harawe and Rungano Nyoni premiering works in prestigious categories.[35]

In India, the entertainment industry was forced to confront its own complex relationship with racial and caste-based discrimination. Bollywood celebrities who spoke out in support of Black Lives Matter faced immediate backlash for their past promotion of skin-whitening products.[36] The criticism highlighted how the industry had long perpetuated colorism through both product endorsements and casting practices. Research showed that Bollywood films consistently associated fair skin with positive attributes while darker skin was linked to negative roles, reinforcing harmful stereotypes related to both caste and color.[37]

In European media, the transformation extended beyond representation to questioning fundamental assumptions about objectivity and neutrality. As journalist Gary Younge noted, there was a "selective amnesia" in Europe about its imperial legacy and a "toxic nostalgia that to this day taints their misunderstanding of that history."[38] The challenge was particularly acute in France, which had "largely failed to grapple with their bloody legacies" of colonialism, and Belgium, where media coverage of racial issues often missed the mark. When Adil, a 19-year-old Belgian man of Moroccan descent, was killed in a police chase, most local outlets focused on the riots that followed rather than examining the underlying issues of police violence and racial profiling.[39]

The structural barriers to change were significant. As Ojeaku Nwabuzo of the European Network Against Racism explained, most European governments didn't systematically collect data on how race affected employment, housing, healthcare access, or police interactions. This lack of data made it difficult for media organizations to effectively cover systemic racism: "You have research studies by universities every once in a while, but it's not systematic."[40] Additionally, Europe lacked the decades of civil rights imagery and role models that American media could draw upon, making it harder to create a common visual language for discussing racism.

The process revealed how differently racial issues manifested across cultures. In France, where the government maintained a strictly "color-blind" approach, media organizations struggled to discuss racism explicitly. The European Network Against Racism noted that "European media is not used to talking about discrimination and police brutality," often focusing on peripheral issues rather than addressing systemic racism directly.[41] This reluctance to confront racial issues head-on meant that when incidents of discrimination occurred, media coverage often missed the broader context.

Yet amid these challenges, there were signs of genuine transformation. Young journalists and media professionals pushed for change from within their organizations. French journalist Rokhaya Diallo observed, "I've never seen so many people marching against police brutality. ... Even the fact that we are now having this debate, that we are comparing ourselves to the U.S., to me that's new." This shift meant people could no longer "take for granted that nothing is happening here."[42]

The pressure from younger generations was particularly effective in challenging traditional practices. As activist Sihame Assbague noted of the protests in Paris, "A lot of young people are saying, we're fed up with police brutality, with structural racism and we are not going to keep silent anymore."[43] In the Netherlands, this generational pressure led to concrete change. After years of defending the traditional Zwarte Piet (Black Pete) character, Dutch Prime Minister Mark Rutte finally acknowledged the practice as discriminatory after speaking with young

Black children about their experiences.[44] This generational shift suggested that while institutional change might be slow, new voices were emerging to challenge longstanding narratives.

What made these changes particularly significant was their potential to reshape cultural memory and understanding. When media organizations transformed their practices, they didn't just alter their current coverage; they reframed how societies understood themselves and their histories. This transformation, while uneven and often contested, represented a fundamental shift in how cultural institutions approached issues of race, representation, and power.

Regional Perspectives and Responses

While George Floyd's murder sparked global outrage, each society interpreted and responded to it through the lens of their own cultural and historical experiences with oppression and resistance. In Brazil, the Black Coalition for Rights, comprising over 150 entities of the Brazilian Black movement, launched a powerful manifesto declaring "As long as there is racism, there will be no democracy." The Coalition used Brazil's Law on Access to Information to demand transparency about COVID-19's impact on Black communities, recognizing how the pandemic had exposed and exacerbated existing racial inequities.[45] Their manifesto made "a broad call for democratic sectors, institutions and organizations of Brazilian society to position themselves against the ills highlighted by the racism historically faced by the black population."[46]

The Brazilian response revealed how racism operated differently there, often through economic exclusion rather than explicit discrimination. The statistics told a stark story: more than 50 percent of Brazil's 209.5 million people were Afro-Brazilian, yet they fared worse in every economic measurement. Police brutality was rampant as well. In 2019, Rio de Janeiro alone had more than 1,800 victims of state violence, with 80 percent being Black and economically marginalized. As Tracy Devine Guzmán, associate professor of Latin American Studies at the University of Miami, explained, "Racism is so deeply rooted that it is hard to dissect with precision."[47] Another expert noted, "A killing in a favela happens all the time and it does not even make the news."

The impunity was nearly complete, with affected families often hesitant to speak out for fear of violent retribution.

In Europe, Floyd's death forced confrontation with colonial legacies that many countries had long avoided addressing. In Germany, approximately 15,000 people gathered at Berlin's Alexanderplatz, holding signs that declared not only "Black Lives Matter" but also "Germany is not innocent." The protests led authorities to actively discourage more people from joining as the square reached capacity, with organizers calling for moments of silence lasting 8 minutes and 46 seconds, the time Floyd was pinned down.[48]

The public reckoning sparked intense debate about systemic racism in German institutions. When Saskia Esken, co-leader of the SPD party, claimed there was "latent racism in the ranks of security forces," it prompted the Interior and Justice Ministries to launch a study examining racial profiling by police. The controversy revealed deep divisions. While Justice Minister Christine Lambrecht argued she didn't see "a particular, structural racism problem," others insisted that examining such biases was crucial for institutional reform.[49]

The resonance of Floyd's case with local incidents became tragically clear in June 2021, when Stanislav Tomáš died in Teplice, Czech Republic, after police officers restrained him with one kneeling on his neck. While authorities rushed to tweet "No Czech George Floyd" and defend the officers, the Czech Deputy Public Defender of Rights found that police had "delayed calling an ambulance and neglected to monitor Stanislav's health condition." The case highlighted systemic issues. As ERRC President Đorđe Jovanović noted, "Prime Minister Babiš was congratulating the police officers for a job well done long before any investigation had been concluded. ... The investigators willfully ignored the testimony of paramedics, and the victim's guilt was all but decided before the facts were known."[50]

In Australia, Floyd's words "I can't breathe" carried particular resonance, echoing the final words of David Dungay Jr., an Aboriginal man who died in a Sydney prison in 2015 under similar circumstances. The parallels were haunting: Dungay had also pleaded "I can't breathe" 12 times while being pinned down by officers. Five years after his death, his mother Leetona Dungay watched the conviction of Derek Chauvin for Floyd's murder with mixed emotions: "I feel very happy for the [Floyd] family, they've got justice and they've fought really hard to get where they are today. ... We have seen some kind of justice in the USA, when will we see justice in Australia?"[51]

Despite attempts by law enforcement to shut down rallies due to COVID-19 risks, tens of thousands of Australians marched in protests across the country. In Sydney, demonstrator Sarah Keating captured the urgency of the moment: "I thought Australians were resting on their laurels. Just because we're not as bad as America doesn't mean we're good enough . . . 432 Aboriginal deaths in custody is atrocious. That number should never have gotten that high. It should just be zero."[52] The protests drew explicit connections between Floyd's murder and Australia's own history of racial injustice. Protesters chanted "Always was, always will be Aboriginal land" alongside "Too many coppers not enough justice."[53]

In Africa, the response revealed both solidarity and a challenge to examine local conditions. Outside the US Embassy in Pretoria, South Africa's Economic Freedom Fighters organized a powerful demonstration where protesters knelt in silence for the exact duration of Floyd's suffering. "Enough with police brutality on our black bodies," EFF leader Julius Malema told the crowd, connecting Floyd's death to recent killings by South African security forces enforcing COVID-19 lockdowns.[54]

Across the continent, African leaders spoke out forcefully. Ghana's President Nana Akufo-Addo declared it "cannot be right that, in the 21st century, the United States, this great bastion of democracy, continues to grapple with the problem of systemic racism." Niger's President Mahamadou Issoufou called Floyd's death "the symbol of the old world that must be changed." The African Union Commission chair Moussa Faki Mahamat explicitly linked the murder to the Organization of African Unity's 1964 resolution on racial discrimination in America, connecting contemporary struggles to historical pan-African solidarity.[55]

Yet these official statements prompted pushback from intellectuals demanding attention to local abuses. Cameroonian economist Célestin Monga acknowledged the legitimacy of African leaders' anger over Floyd's murder but challenged them to show equal outrage "when our police and soldiers are martyring our citizens on a daily basis." In

Kenya, this tension between international solidarity and local account-ability played out in the streets of Nairobi, where protesters in the Mathare slum carried signs with names of friends and family killed by police. Human Rights Watch had documented how Kenyan police enforced COVID-19 curfews "in a chaotic and violent manner," including the killing of 13-year-old Yassin Hussein Moyo, shot while standing on his balcony.[56]

What emerged across these responses was not a single global move-ment, but rather a constellation of local transformations, each drawing inspiration from Floyd's story while remaining rooted in their own cul-tural contexts and historical experiences. The phrase "I can't breathe" became a universal expression of the experience of systemic oppres-sion, but the specific meaning and response varied by region. In Brazil, it catalyzed challenges to economic exclusion. In Europe, it forced confrontation with colonial legacies. In Australia, it amplified long-standing calls for justice for Indigenous deaths in custody. In Africa, it sparked both solidarity with African Americans and examination of local police violence.

This diversity of responses demonstrated both the universal power of Floyd's story and the necessity of translating calls for justice into locally resonant action. As one hundred African writers expressed in an open letter, the repercussions of Floyd's murder could lead to a revival of pan-African dreams, calling for Africa to be a "refuge" for its diaspora.[57] Yet even this vision had to be translated through local reali-ties and struggles, showing how global movements for justice must always speak through local voices and experiences.

Lessons in Transformation

As I reflected on the transformations I witnessed across continents and institutions in the wake of George Floyd's murder, several patterns emerged about how meaningful change occurs. These insights came not from any single organization or region, but from observing the commonalities across seemingly disparate responses.

The most striking realization was how Floyd's murder became a catalyst precisely because it occurred at a moment when the world was already at a breaking point. The pandemic had forced millions into isolation, creating both a collective restlessness and an unavoidable confrontation with societal inequities. As one Brazilian activist noted, the pandemic context "intensified the claims about the eradication of racism and genocide of the black population."[58] In Kenya, COVID-19 curfew enforcement had itself become a deadly demonstration of police brutality, claiming at least 15 lives.[59]

The video of Floyd's murder, viewed by people confined to their homes during lockdown, became impossible to ignore or dismiss. The moment felt different because it was different. It was a convergence of long-simmering grievances, pandemic-exposed inequities, and a shared sense that returning to "normal" was no longer acceptable.

The second key lesson was that authentic transformation often began with local pain finding global resonance. When Floyd said, "I can't breathe," those words echoed differently in each context, recalling David Dungay Jr.'s identical plea in an Australian prison, amplifying the Black Coalition for Rights' demands in Brazil, and galvanizing Roma activists after Stanislav Tomáš's death in the Czech Republic. Real change started not when institutions imported American frameworks wholesale, but when they recognized how Floyd's story illuminated their own unaddressed injustices.

A third insight was that surface-level diversity initiatives often accidentally exposed deeper structural issues that required more fundamental solutions. We saw this in India, where corporate DEI efforts stumbled into entrenched questions of caste privilege. The vulnerability to COVID-19 itself exposed these structural inequities too. In Brazil, the Black Coalition demanded data on how the pandemic affected Black communities precisely because they knew who was most at risk. The organizations that achieved lasting change were those willing to follow these exposures to their logical conclusions rather than retreat to comfortable superficiality.

The fourth lesson was that meaningful transformation required institutions to expand their understanding of their own purpose. This wasn't just about doing existing things more inclusively, it was about fundamentally reimagining institutional roles. Media organizations had to move beyond simply diversifying their newsrooms to questioning whose perspectives shaped the very definition of news.

Cultural institutions had to shift from displaying diverse art to reconsidering their entire relationship with the communities they served.

Perhaps most importantly, the examples revealed that real change happened not through grand initiatives but through sustained attention to specific, local realities. The manifesto of Brazil's Black Coalition for Rights worked because it connected abstract principles to concrete demands for COVID-19 data. The protests in Berlin succeeded because they linked global solidarity to specific calls for examining police practices. The Australian Indigenous justice movement gained momentum by connecting Floyd's story to precisely documented patterns of deaths in custody.

This attention to specificity did not minimize the global nature of the movement; rather, it gave it genuine power. This suggested a fundamental truth about institutional transformation: it happens not through importing universal solutions but through the careful work of translation. This requires finding how global principles can animate local change while allowing local realities to enrich global understanding. The institutions that succeeded were those willing to engage in this complex dialogue between the universal and the particular, the global and the local, the immediate and the historical.

The Path Ahead

In early 2024, I found myself back in São Paulo, retracing the morning running route where I'd first encountered that stark black and white mural of George Floyd. The image was still there, but now partially obscured by graffiti, its edges fading under layers of weather and wear. Nearby, someone had spray-painted in Portuguese, "Stop Importing American Problems" across another racial justice mural.

These altered images seemed to capture something essential about this moment in the global movement for institutional change. The initial wave of transformation had achieved real progress, from the BBC's data-driven approach to representation, to the Brazilian Black Coalition's concrete policy demands, to Australian Indigenous activists finally being heard on the world stage. Organizations across sectors had begun the difficult work of examining their fundamental assumptions and practices.

But like all movements for profound social change, this one was beginning to encounter resistance. The very visibility of these initiatives—the murals, the protests, the institutional commitments—had made them targets. Some of the same institutions that had embraced transformation were now facing mounting pressure to retreat to what critics called a more "measured" approach.

As I studied those fading murals, I realized they told a story about both progress and pushback. The original images represented a moment of awakening and possibility. Their defacement marked the inevitable resistance to change. But their continued presence, even in altered form, testified to something more lasting: the conversations they sparked couldn't simply be painted over.

The coming years would test how deeply the changes of this period had taken root. Some institutions would likely retreat in the face of opposition. Others would find ways to maintain their commitment to transformation while navigating resistance. But one thing was becoming clear: the movement sparked by Floyd's murder had fundamentally shifted how organizations around the world understood their responsibilities to their communities. What remained to be seen was how they would respond when that understanding was challenged.

5

The Backlash Begins

"I don't want to hire any more Black people."

THE WORDS HUNG heavy in the Virgin Hotel's conference room, cutting through the usual buzz of corporate meetings in midtown Manhattan. The diversity recruiter's voice trembled as he shared what his client had told him. Around the table, other DEI professionals shifted uncomfortably in their seats, but I sat perfectly still, letting the weight of that statement sink in.

After three decades in this work, I'd heard plenty of coded language about diversity. Companies would talk about "cultural fit" or "maintaining standards" (subtle ways of maintaining exclusion while preserving deniability). But this raw hostility was something new. Or perhaps more accurately, something old reemerging in a new context.

By 2023, the landscape of corporate diversity efforts was shifting dramatically. A report from the consulting firm Paradigm revealed a concerning trend: the percentage of organizations with a DEI budget had dropped from 58 percent in 2022 to 54 percent in 2023, while those with a DEI strategy fell from 80 percent to 71 percent during the same period.[1] Companies cited various factors, including economic uncertainty and an increasingly complex legal landscape.

The numbers painted a stark picture. According to Lightcast, a labor market analytics firm, demand for diversity roles declined by approximately 43 percent from its peak in August 2022 through July 2024.[2] Even more telling was the instability within these roles: only 36 percent of people who held director or manager positions in DEI departments between 2020 and 2022 remained in those roles by mid-2024.

Major corporations began quietly revising their diversity commitments. Companies like Brown-Forman and John Deere reversed the DEI commitments they had made following George Floyd's murder.[3] The changes weren't just about budget cuts; they represented a fundamental shift in how corporate America approached diversity initiatives.

This retreat wasn't happening in a vacuum. A sophisticated campaign was under way to reframe DEI itself. Conservative activists and politicians increasingly portrayed diversity initiatives as divisive rather than inclusive.[4] The pressure came from multiple directions: legal challenges, political rhetoric, and social media campaigns all contributed to creating an environment where companies felt increasingly vulnerable about their diversity programs.

The irony wasn't lost on those of us who had been in this field long enough to see the patterns. Progress itself had helped spark the backlash. While the gains hadn't been revolutionary, they were significant enough to trigger resistance. For instance, a study by KPMG and the African American Directors Forum found that by September 2022, 76 percent of public Fortune 1000 companies had at least one African American director on their board, compared to 61 percent at the end of 2020.[5] These incremental but real advances in representation seemed to fuel rather than diminish opposition.

The impact was particularly visible in corporate America's middle management, where the day-to-day work of building inclusive workplaces happened. According to Paradigm's research, companies were actively pulling back from even basic diversity metrics and analytics. Only 26 percent of companies were examining their hiring outcomes by race or ethnicity, while just 33 percent analyzed promotions through this lens.[6] This retreat from data-driven accountability marked a significant shift from the bold commitments of 2020.

Some of this retrenchment was driven by legal concerns. In *Students for Fair Admissions v. Harvard*, the Supreme Court ruled that affirmative action programs in college admissions processes violated the Equal Protection clause of the 14th Amendment.[7] In the wake of this decision, many companies feared their diversity programs could become targets for similar challenges. As one report noted, "HR leaders are de-emphasizing data and analytics as a part of their DEI efforts, in response to the changing legal landscape and increased scrutiny on DEI efforts."[8]

The opposition was becoming increasingly coordinated. Social media influencers targeted specific companies, pressuring them to roll back their diversity initiatives. Companies with strong consumer bases in rural and conservative areas found themselves particularly vulnerable to these campaigns.[9] The pressure often worked: major retailers and manufacturers began revising or rebranding their diversity programs, trying to find ways to maintain some semblance of inclusion while avoiding political controversy.

As I sat in that Virgin Hotel conference room, listening to my colleagues share similar stories of resistance and retrenchment, I couldn't help but reflect on the ever-evolving nature of this work. The data showed that DEI positions tend to be cyclical, flourishing during economic booms and contracting during periods of uncertainty.[10] But this time felt different. The sophistication of the opposition, the legal challenges, the political pressure. It all suggested we were entering a new phase in the long struggle for workplace equity.

The Weaponization of Words

The attacks became increasingly brazen as political rhetoric intensified. When Kamala Harris emerged as the Democratic presidential frontrunner in July 2024, multiple Republican representatives publicly dismissed her as a "DEI hire."[11] Rep. Tim Burchett's attacks were particularly pointed, claiming that Biden's commitment to diversity inevitably led to "mediocrity." When pressed about his comments, Burchett doubled down: "When I hear her talk, I just scratch my head and think this is what DEI is really about. ... She checks all the boxes. She'll say she's of Indian descent one day, then she'll say she's of Black descent. It's just box-checking."[12]

The rhetoric spread quickly through Republican ranks. Representative Harriet Hageman of Wyoming joined in, dismissing Harris as "intellectually . . . the bottom of the barrel" and declaring her "a DEI hire" while arguing that Democrats felt trapped with her candidacy "because of her ethnic background."[13] These attacks notably ignored Harris's extensive qualifications, from her service as vice president, to her years as a US senator, to her six-year tenure as California's attorney general, and her time as San Francisco's district attorney.[14]

The backlash against these attacks revealed growing concerns even within Republican circles about the weaponization of DEI as a political tool. Former Speaker Kevin McCarthy broke ranks with his party to condemn the attacks, calling them "stupid and dumb" and warning his colleagues, "I disagree with DEI, but she's the vice president of the United States. ... These congressmen that are saying it, they're wrong in their own instincts."[15]

The weaponization of DEI language reached new extremes following the Baltimore bridge collapse in March 2024. Within hours of the tragic incident that claimed six lives, Utah State Representative Phil Lyman posted on social media: "This is what happens when you have governors who prioritize diversity over the wellbeing and security of citizens."[16] His attack specifically targeted Karenthia A. Barber, a Black woman serving as one of six commissioners overseeing the Port of Baltimore, focusing on her background in diversity consulting while ignoring her extensive experience teaching at the university level and being the first female chair of the Maryland Automobile Insurance board.[17]

The incident became a lightning rod for DEI critics. Conservative media figures jumped in, with Fox Business Host Maria Bartiromo attempting to link the bridge disaster to the Biden administration's border policy, while American Conservative Union chairman Matt Schlapp blamed "drug-addled workers" and COVID lockdowns.[18] These claims seem all the more strange considering that the reason the bridge collapsed had nothing to do with flawed engineering. It turns out a massive cargo ship had lost power, eliminating the crew's ability to control navigation. The ship crashed into the bridge at full speed, tearing it into fragments. Moreover, the quick thinking of the crew in sending a distress signal had likely saved lives by allowing authorities to stop traffic to the bridge.[19]

The response from Maryland's leadership was swift and unequivocal. Governor Wes Moore, when asked about the DEI accusations, responded with barely contained frustration: "I have no time for foolishness. I'm locked in on making sure that we can bring closure and comfort to these families and making sure that we're going to keep our first responders safe or doing heroic work."[20] Baltimore Mayor Brandon Scott was more direct, arguing that "DEI" had become a substitute for racial slurs: "We know what they want to say, but they don't have the courage to say the N-word. ... The fact that I don't believe in their untruthful and wrong ideology, and I am very proud of my heritage and who I am and where I come from scares them, because me being at my position means that their way of thinking, their way of life of being comfortable while everyone else suffers is going to be at risk."[21]

The politicization of DEI reached new heights in Congress when Senator JD Vance introduced the "Dismantle DEI Act" in June 2024. The sweeping legislation sought to eliminate all federal DEI programs and funding, targeting not just federal agencies but also contractors receiving federal funding, grant recipients, and educational accreditation agencies. The bill would terminate Chief Diversity Officers, close DEI offices, end diversity training, and outlaw mandatory employee DEI pledges. "The DEI agenda is a destructive ideology that breeds hatred and racial division," Vance declared. "It has no place in our federal government or anywhere else in our society."[22]

Throughout this period, one of the most persistent myths driving the backlash was the false equation of diversity with lowered standards. Research consistently showed the opposite: embracing diversity enriched talent pools and enhanced organizational performance. Studies demonstrated that diverse teams were better equipped to drive innovation, improve decision-making, and understand diverse consumer needs. The data showed that DEI initiatives, far from being a "problem to solve," presented significant opportunities for growth and innovation, giving organizations a competitive edge in understanding and serving diverse consumer bases.[23]

Even some conservative commentators began warning about the overuse and weaponization of "DEI" as a political cudgel. As one *Washington Examiner* opinion piece noted, "Conservatives are in the process of overusing the phrase 'DEI' like liberals have done with 'racist' or 'Nazi.' Once the phrase loses its definition and focus, it becomes much easier for ideological adversaries to dismiss it as a meaningless smear."[24]

The Rise of Cancel Culture

When Dictionary.com added "cancel culture" to its database in 2020, it defined the term as "the practice of withdrawing support for public figures and companies after they have done or said something considered objectionable or offensive."[25] But this clinical definition barely captured the transformative power this social phenomenon would have on corporate America. While some criticized it as a form of digital mob justice, others viewed it through the lens of what scholar Meredith Clark termed "digital accountability praxis," a way for marginalized communities to demand change from powerful institutions. As Clark explained, these practices had deep roots in Black communicative traditions, particularly "reading," or giving someone a detailed critique that demonstrated an incisive ability of character assessment. "Not every critique can come wrapped up in niceties and polite speech," Clark noted. "Sometimes, the urgency and weight of oppression require us to immediately cry out." This framework helped explain why social media callouts often felt more like a "critique of systemic inequality rather than an attack against specific, individualistic transgressions."[26]

The impact on business was particularly profound, fundamentally altering how consumers wielded their economic power. According to BusinessBecause, 75 percent of Generation Z consumers reported they would boycott companies that discriminated against race and sexuality across advertisement campaigns. More than 60 percent of Black consumers reported experiencing racial discrimination in retail stores, while approximately one-third of minority consumers reported experiencing racial discrimination from advertisements. For many ethical and socially responsible consumers awakening in the aftermath of the Black Lives Matter movement, traditional corporate responses were no longer sufficient. As Dr. Michele Rogers of Northwestern University's Kellogg School of Management observed, "The younger generation has lived through the fluctuating economy, and they've grown up with 1 percent of the population having the vast majority of the riches, so they have a different perspective on the world today. They perhaps have less to lose in speaking out about inequalities." Millennial and Generation Z consumers, forming the most ethnically and racially diverse adult group in US history, began pushing brands to reflect their values in unprecedented ways.[27]

The transformation was particularly visible in how quickly corporate missteps could escalate into existential crises. As University of Michigan marketing lecturer Marcus Collins noted, "Where consumers spend their money becomes votes for what they feel is legitimate. And when the retailer is discriminatory, individuals may behave accordingly and choose not to spend their dollars there." This new dynamic fundamentally changed how companies approached diversity and inclusion initiatives.[28]

Several high-profile incidents in 2020 exemplified this new reality, none more dramatically than the case of L'Oréal Paris in June of that year. After posting a statement supporting Black Lives Matter, the company faced immediate backlash when transgender model Munroe Bergdorf called out their hypocrisy, objecting that L'Oréal had previously dropped her from a campaign in 2017 for speaking out about racism. The public pressure led to swift action: L'Oréal's new president reached out directly to Bergdorf, offered a public apology, and appointed her to the company's UK Diversity and Inclusion Advisory Board. The company also announced €50,000 in donations to transgender youth and Black Pride organizations.[29]

This new reality manifested dramatically in corporate advertising. In September 2020, South African retail chain Clicks faced intense backlash over an advertisement for TRESemmé hair products that depicted Black women's hair as "dry, damaged, frizzy and dull" while showing white women's hair as "normal." The controversy sparked immediate outrage, with the Economic Freedom Fighters (EFF) threatening to close all Clicks stores if the company didn't comply with demands to reveal everyone involved in the ad's creation. When Clicks opened its stores despite the threats, 37 locations were vandalized, looted, and, in some cases, petrol-bombed, forcing the company to temporarily close all 880 locations. Despite seeking urgent court relief to prevent protests outside their stores, Clicks's request was denied. The incident highlighted how quickly social media outrage could escalate into real-world consequences.[30]

In March 2021, television host Sharon Osbourne found herself at the center of a firestorm. After defending broadcaster Piers Morgan's criticism of Meghan Markle's interview with Oprah Winfrey, she faced immediate backlash on social media. During a heated on-air exchange with co-host Sheryl Underwood on *The Talk*, Osbourne became defensive when challenged about her support of Morgan, saying "I feel like I'm about to be put in the electric chair because I have a friend who many people think is racist, so that makes me a racist." Within weeks, CBS announced her departure from *The Talk* after 11 seasons, stating that her behavior did not "align with our values for a respectful workplace."[31]

Just days earlier, Morgan himself had left ITV's *Good Morning Britain* following his own controversy. After claiming he didn't "believe a word" of Meghan Markle's discussion of mental health struggles, Morgan faced over 41,000 complaints to media watchdog Ofcom. When challenged on air by weather presenter Alex Beresford about "continuing to trash" the duchess, Morgan walked off the set. ITV later announced his immediate departure from the show.[32]

This created what legal scholars termed "continuous accountability," the understanding that any action or statement could face instant, global scrutiny. The dynamics fundamentally changed how businesses approached corporate social responsibility (CSR). As legal scholar Gabrielle Brill noted, while traditional CSR focused on voluntary actions, this new era of corporate accountability focused on "establishing institutional mechanisms that hold companies accountable rather than merely urging companies to act toward a socially desirable end voluntarily." The transformation was particularly evident in how companies responded to social justice issues. A 2016 Public Affairs Council study found that "more than three-quarters" of companies "experienced increased pressure to weigh in on social issues," and from 2013 to 2016, not a single respondent reported that pressure to engage with social issues had decreased. As detailed in the *University of Richmond Law Review*, "Corporate executives used to fear a bad newspaper story; today, they dread a bad viral video or negative trending hashtag that can hurt their brands or stock prices more than a bad newspaper story."[33]

Corporate Retreat and Missteps: When Cancel Culture Turned on DEI

The evolving dynamics of cancel culture became particularly evident in June 2023, when Starbucks found itself caught between competing social movements. The controversy emerged amid a broader wave of conservative pushback against companies expressing support for LGBTQ+ rights, which had already impacted Target's Pride merchandise and led to boycotts against brands like Bud Light, The North Face, Kohl's, Lego, and PetSmart. When Starbucks Workers United claimed the company was banning Pride decorations, the response was immediate and polarized. Conservative commentator Charlie Kirk celebrated on Twitter: "BREAKING: Starbucks has banned Pride decorations in its stores halfway through Pride Month. ... Good! Keep the pressure on, folks." Meanwhile, LGBTQ+ advocates and employees expressed betrayal, with Democratic congressional candidate Nick Autiello noting "Starbucks choosing an extremist, hateful minority over its LGBTQ+ staff, employees, and customers is wrong."[34]

The complexity of the situation deepened when workers reported different experiences across locations. According to The New Republic, employees in at least 21 states received varying explanations for Pride decoration restrictions. Some cited labor shortages, others safety concerns following attacks on Target stores, and still others claimed customers felt excluded by the displays. The incident highlighted how companies increasingly found themselves navigating conflicting social pressures with no clear path forward.[35]

This wasn't Starbucks's first experience with cancel culture. In April 2018, the company faced intense backlash when two Black men, Rashon Nelson and Donte Robinson, were arrested while waiting for a business meeting at a Philadelphia location. The incident began when Nelson asked to use the restroom and was told it was for paying customers only. The pair then sat down to wait for their business associate, Andrew Yaffe, for a meeting about potential real estate opportunities. Instead, police officers approached their table and insisted they leave. "It was just, 'Get out, you have to leave. You're not buying anything, so you shouldn't be here,'" Nelson later recalled. Despite explaining they were there for a meeting, the men were handcuffed and held in custody for eight hours before the district attorney declined to press charges.[36]

The incident, captured on video by onlooker Melissa DePino, quickly went viral and sparked protests outside the Starbucks location. While Philadelphia Police Commissioner Richard Ross initially defended his officers' actions, saying they "did absolutely nothing wrong," Philadelphia Mayor Jim Kenney saw it differently, stating the incident "appears to exemplify what racial discrimination looks like in 2018." For Nelson and Robinson, the experience was deeply traumatic. "Anytime I'm encountered by cops, I can honestly say it's a thought that runs through my mind," Nelson said. "You never know what's going to happen."[37]

The company's response evolved as public pressure mounted. CEO Kevin Johnson issued an apology, calling the incident "reprehensible" and acknowledging that the company's "practices and training led to a bad outcome." Starbucks then announced it would close more than eight thousand company-owned stores for racial bias training, a decision *TIME* magazine estimated could cost around $8.8 million in lost revenue. The closure sparked varied reactions on social media, with some praising it as a "progressive step forward" while others used the opportunity to highlight Black-owned coffee shops. The company emphasized this was "only the beginning," announcing plans to deepen its diversity and inclusion efforts in the months ahead.[38]

Other major brands faced similar challenges navigating cancel culture's evolving expectations. In May 2019, Gucci sparked outrage by selling a $790 "Indy Full Head Wrap" that resembled the Sikh dastaar, a sacred religious article. The backlash was swift and intense. "Did someone at @gucci even bother to figure out what a dastaar (turban) means to Sikhs? Did it cross your minds to consider the history behind our identity? My people are discriminated against, even killed, for wearing a turban," wrote Aasees Kaur on Twitter. Despite having previously established a diversity council following other controversies, the company had failed to consult with Sikh communities. As Simran Jeet Fingh, senior fellow at the Sikh Coalition, explained, the issue wasn't just about cultural appropriation but about corporate structure: "If these companies had diverse communities represented within their corporate structures, there is no way that something as insensitive as this would pass through and make it to the market."[39]

These and other similar experiences revealed how cancel culture had evolved beyond simple calls for accountability into complex negotiations between competing stakeholder interests. Companies increasingly found that surface-level responses or quick fixes could backfire, while meaningful change required deeper engagement with affected communities and careful consideration of unintended consequences.

The challenge wasn't just avoiding controversy, it was building authentic relationships and implementing structural changes that could withstand scrutiny from multiple directions simultaneously.

By early 2024, a striking reversal was under way in how cancel culture shapes corporate behavior. Target, which had previously earned praise for its diversity initiatives, found itself facing intense backlash over its Pride Month merchandise collection. Conservative activists posted threatening videos from inside stores, with some even vandalizing displays, leading to bomb threats at stores in five different states.

The first signs of trouble came in May 2023, when Target's Pride Month merchandise collection sparked an intense backlash. The controversy intensified in 2024, when Target announced it would reduce the number of stores carrying Pride-themed merchandise and modify its product offerings. To many observers, it looked like a retreat from the company's post-Floyd commitments to diversity and inclusion.[40]

Store traffic dropped 13.9 percent in the final week of May, and analysts noted this decline coincided with the Pride controversy making national headlines. The pressure intensified when shareholders filed a lawsuit claiming that Target's focus on diversity initiatives, particularly the Pride campaign, had led to financial instability and declining stock value. The lawsuit alleged that the board had prioritized activist calls for diversity, equity, and inclusion without adequately considering potential negative responses.[41]

Three major Wall Street firms downgraded the company's shares, with Citi analyst Paul Lejuez noting, "Despite the recent stock pressure, we cannot recommend investors buy the stock given these dynamics and now believe the risk, reward is more balanced, but risk is more to the downside near term." The controversy ultimately contributed to a $15.7 billion drop in market value.[42]

This wasn't an isolated incident. Bud Light faced similar pressures after partnering with transgender influencer Dylan Mulvaney for a promotional campaign featuring a personalized beer can celebrating Mulvaney's "365 Days of Girlhood." The backlash was immediate and intense, with some critics, like Kid Rock, literally shooting cases of Bud Light with automatic weapons in protest videos. Within weeks, the controversy had wiped more than $4 billion off Anheuser-Busch's value, with JPMorgan forecasting a 26 percent drop in 2023 earnings, noting "there is a subset of American consumers who will not drink a Bud Light for the foreseeable future." The company's initial response was muted, with CEO Brendan Whitworth stating, "We never intended to be part of a discussion that divides people. We are in the business of bringing people together over a beer." Two marketing executives, including Alissa Heinerscheid, who had become the first woman in the brand's history to lead marketing just months earlier, subsequently took leaves of absence.[43]

The human cost of these controversies often went unacknowledged. Mulvaney herself remained silent for weeks before finally addressing the backlash in a TikTok video. "I've been offline for a few weeks," she explained, "and a lot has been said about me, some of which is so far from my truth that I was like hearing my name, and I didn't even know who they were talking about sometimes." She described being followed "on and off for the past two months" and struggling with the cruelty of the response. "I've always tried to love everyone," she said, "but what I'm struggling to understand is the need to dehumanize and to be cruel."[44,45]

The impact on corporate diversity efforts proved particularly profound. By mid-2023, major media companies including Disney, Warner Bros. Discovery, Netflix, and the Academy of Motion Picture Arts and Sciences all saw the departure of their diversity leaders. Disney's chief diversity officer Latondra Newton left after six years of overseeing the company's "commitment to producing entertainment that reflects a global audience." Netflix's first-ever head of inclusion strategy Verna Myers announced her departure after launching strategic interventions and creating a curriculum that saw more than 600 executives globally participate in workshops on inclusive leadership. Warner Bros. Discovery removed diversity officer Karen Horne, claiming it was due to reorganization rather than cost-cutting. As Brian Brackeen, a managing partner at Lightship Capital observed, "DEI's out of style now." The timing was notable. As one observer pointed out on social media, "Not to put too fine a point on it, but all of them being Black women, and all of this happening during the WGA strike and leading up to a possible SAG strike, is very telling."[46]

The transformation of Employee Resource Groups (ERGs) provided another striking example of this corporate repositioning.

Companies like Harley-Davidson, following pressure from conservative activists, rebranded their ERGs as "Business Resource Groups" (BRGs), emphasizing that they would "exclusively be focused on professional development, networking, mentoring, and supporting talent recruitment efforts."[47] Brown-Forman, the maker of Jack Daniel's, similarly narrowed the scope of their employee groups, moving away from broader cultural awareness goals to focus solely on professional development and networking.

Perhaps the most significant shift came from the Society for Human Resource Management (SHRM), the leading organization for HR professionals. In July 2024, SHRM president Johnny C. Taylor, Jr. announced they would no longer use the term "equity," adopting "I&D" (Inclusion and Diversity) instead of DEI. Taylor argued that "DEI programs in their current form are not working" and cited "societal backlash and increased polarization" as key factors in the decision.[48]

The decision sparked immediate controversy within the HR community. Critics argued that removing "equity" fundamentally undermined efforts to address systemic workplace disparities. As one HR executive noted on LinkedIn, "Without it, can we genuinely claim to be advancing DEI(B) work?"[49]

The rebranding trend extended to the very concept of belonging itself. Walmart made headlines by appointing Denise Malloy as its first Chief Belonging Officer, changing the wording away from calling her a Chief Diversity Officer. The company positioned this change as a way to create "a welcoming environment for all types of customers," implementing initiatives like sensory-friendly shopping hours.[50]

The scale of this corporate repositioning became clear in a Conference Board survey of executives, which revealed that 50 percent of companies had adjusted their DEI terminology to reduce emphasis on racial diversity, with another 20 percent considering similar changes. "Companies are trying to minimize exposure to scrutiny, legal challenges, and salacious headlines," explained Andrew Jones, a senior researcher at the Conference Board's ESG Center.[51]

A comprehensive study by The Heritage Foundation found that while 486 out of the top 500 Fortune companies still maintained some form of DEI commitment on their websites, the nature of these commitments had changed significantly. Many companies were quietly moving their diversity functions under different departments and stopping the publication of detailed diversity data.[52]

The tech industry emerged as a particular flashpoint in this debate when Scale AI's CEO Alexandr Wang introduced the idea of "MEI" (Merit, Excellence, Intelligence) as an alternative to DEI. Wang argued that "Scale is a meritocracy, and we must always remain one," positioning MEI as a framework focused purely on merit-based hiring.[53] However, this approach drew sharp criticism from diversity experts. As Mutale Nkonde, a founder working in AI policy, pointed out, "The post is misguided because people who support the meritocracy argument are ignoring the structural reasons some groups are more likely to outperform others."[54]

The debate over meritocracy versus diversity revealed a deeper paradox in corporate America's approach to inclusion. Research consistently showed that organizations focusing too heavily on meritocracy saw an increase in bias, as it freed people from feeling they needed to try hard to be fair in their decision-making. As Natalie Sue Johnson, co-founder of the DEI consulting firm Paradigm, explained, "They think that meritocracy is inherent, not something that needs to be achieved."[55]

The consequences of this corporate repositioning were particularly visible in the tech sector's hiring practices. Indeed.com reported that DEI-related job listings had plummeted by 44 percent in 2023, while the data industry saw new women recruit levels drop dramatically from 36 percent in 2022 to just 12 percent a year later. The representation of Black, Indigenous, and professionals of color in VP or above data roles remained stagnant at 38 percent.[56]

The corporate retreat manifested differently across industries. At Brown-Forman, the changes were sweeping: the company not only rebranded its employee groups but also canceled its supplier diversity goals and ended its participation in the Human Rights Campaign index for LGBTQ+-friendly workplaces. The company's spokesperson, Elizabeth Conway, explained this shift by noting, "Since then, the world has evolved, our business has changed, and the legal and external landscape has shifted dramatically, particularly within the United States."[57]

The legal landscape played a role in driving these changes. As one article in the *Harvard Business Review* noted following the Supreme

Court's affirmative action decision, "When the right case reaches the court, the same justices who just endorsed a 'colorblind' approach to higher education could also hold that private employers cannot consider race, sex, or other protected characteristics in workplace decisions." This led many companies to pre-emptively modify practices like "reserving hiring or promotion slots for underrepresented groups" or "setting strict demographic targets tied to manager compensation."[58]

The generational aspect of this debate added another layer of complexity. Younger workers increasingly prioritized personal well-being and were willing to leave employers who didn't align with their values. As consumers, they had already demonstrated they would avoid products and services from brands that didn't match their principles. This created a challenging balancing act for companies trying to navigate between external pressure to reduce DEI initiatives and internal pressure to maintain them.[59]

In the tech industry, the debate over meritocracy versus diversity revealed troubling inconsistencies. While Scale AI championed MEI and meritocracy, an investigation revealed that their data annotators (many living in economically depressed countries) worked multiple eight-hour days without breaks for as little as $10 per day. This highlighted the disconnect between rhetoric about merit and actual practices affecting vulnerable workers.[60]

The impact on women in tech was particularly stark. A Deloitte survey found that over half of women in AI had left at least one employer due to gender-based treatment differences, while 73 percent had considered leaving the tech industry altogether due to unequal pay and limited advancement opportunities. These statistics suggested that the retreat from formal DEI programs was having real consequences for workplace equity.[61]

The Heritage Foundation's comprehensive analysis revealed the extent of corporate America's linguistic gymnastics around diversity initiatives. Companies increasingly adopted vague terminology, with Oracle's senior leadership offering seven different definitions of DEI in a single blog post. As one vice president admitted, "The real challenge is the definition of diversity in the workplace."[62]

The tension between public positioning and private practice became particularly evident in companies' handling of demographic data. The Conference Board's research showed that while companies were pulling back from public diversity metrics, many maintained internal tracking systems. "The core work is ongoing, as companies recognize the tangible benefits of inclusive work environments," noted Andrew Jones, though he acknowledged that "by removing specific group references, companies risk diluting the progress that has been made in creating opportunities for underrepresented groups."[63]

The Path Forward

Looking back at that conference room where our story began—where a diversity recruiter shared her client's stark refusal to hire Black candidates—I realized we were witnessing more than just individual resistance. The landscape of corporate diversity efforts had shifted dramatically since 2020. The numbers told a stark story: declining DEI budgets, disappearing diversity roles, and companies quietly revising or abandoning their commitments.

The sophistication of the opposition was striking. Legal challenges inspired by the Supreme Court's affirmative action ruling created a chilling effect. Political figures weaponized DEI language, cynically blaming diversity for everything from bridge collapses to perceived incompetence. Social media campaigns coordinated pressure on companies, particularly those with consumer bases in conservative regions. Even the terminology itself became contentious, with organizations scrambling to rebrand their initiatives and distance themselves from certain words.

The corporate response often seemed like pure retrenchment. Major brands pulled back from Pride displays in the face of boycotts. Companies rebranded their ERGs to emphasize business rather than culture. Organizations stopped publishing detailed diversity metrics. The SHRM even dropped "equity" from its framework entirely.

But beneath this apparent retreat, something more complex was happening. While companies might publicly distance themselves from DEI terminology and explicit programs, many were quietly maintaining their internal efforts. The Conference Board's research revealed organizations continuing to track demographic data and inclusion metrics, even as they changed their public language. When pressed about program changes, corporate leaders often spoke of "evolution" rather than abandonment.

This suggested that what looked like retrenchment on the surface might be something else entirely. Perhaps, rather than truly retreating from diversity and inclusion, corporate America was finding new ways to weave these principles into their fundamental business practices. The story of how this transformation unfolded—and what it meant for the future of workplace equity—would prove far more nuanced than the headlines suggested.

6

Behind the Curtain—Corporate Evolution within the Backlash

IN THE AFTERMATH of 2020's racial reckoning, corporate America found itself caught between competing pressures. On one side, mounting backlash threatened to unravel years of diversity initiatives. Conservative activists coordinated sophisticated campaigns against companies perceived as "too woke." Legal challenges inspired by the Supreme Court's affirmative action ruling created a chilling effect on diversity programs. Even the language of inclusion itself became contentious, with terms like "DEI" becoming increasingly weaponized in political discourse.

Yet beneath the surface, a more complex story was unfolding. Despite headlines proclaiming the "end of DEI," reality painted a more nuanced picture. According to the Conference Board's December 2023 survey of human resources officers, there was "unanimous support for maintaining, if not intensifying, DEI efforts into 2024, with 63 percent actively seeking to further diversify their workforce".[1] The Congressional Black Caucus's September 2024 corporate accountability report revealed telling patterns: of the 189 organizations that responded to their survey, companies weren't abandoning their commitments; they were evolving their approach. The manufacturing (31 percent), finance and insurance (25 percent), and information (16 percent) sectors showed particularly strong engagement, with most companies providing detailed documentation of their ongoing initiatives.[2]

Despite the pullback in formal DEI programs, some measures of diversity continued to show progress. For instance, Paradigm's data revealed a 6-point increase in the number of companies with senior DEI leaders and an 8-point increase in organizations that had goals related to representation for women in leadership from 2022 to 2023.[3] This suggested that while companies might be retreating from public DEI commitments, many were still quietly working to build more inclusive workplaces.

In Chapter 3, we explored how companies like Target, Microsoft, WarnerMedia, and JPMorgan made unprecedented commitments following George Floyd's murder. Their initial responses—from Target's $10 million pledge to Microsoft's facial recognition moratorium—seemed to signal a fundamental shift in corporate America. But as these organizations faced growing pressure to retreat from these commitments, their responses would reveal a more complex story about how corporate America was learning to navigate between public pressure and private transformation.

The main reason the backlash was not complete is the economic argument for diversity remained compelling, even in the face of political pushback. Research consistently showed that employees who felt their company valued diversity were 150 percent more likely to be engaged at work.[4] Companies that maintained diverse leadership continued to demonstrate stronger financial performance, particularly those with gender diversity on their boards.

However, the disconnect between corporate rhetoric and reality was becoming increasingly stark. While 98 percent of business leaders believed their companies were inclusive, only 80 percent of employees reported feeling included at work.[5] This gap between perception and experience highlighted one of the continuing challenges facing DEI work: the tendency for leadership to overestimate their progress while underestimating the ongoing need for sustained commitment.

The question wasn't whether some companies would retreat from their diversity commitments. That was already happening. The real question was whether the fundamental changes in how business approaches diversity and inclusion could survive this period of retrenchment. The evidence suggested a mixed picture: while formal DEI programs might be scaled back, the underlying push for more inclusive workplaces continued, albeit in different forms and through different channels.

Not Complete Retreat

The corporate retreat from DEI manifested in increasingly sophisticated ways throughout 2024. Rather than outright abandonment, many organizations opted for strategic rebranding of their diversity initiatives. At Levi Strauss & Co., this evolution was clearly visible. In 2020, they had proudly appointed Elizabeth A. Morrison as Chief Diversity, Inclusion and Belonging Officer, emphasizing their commitment to "creating a more diverse and equitable company and culture."[6] By 2024, however, the company had shifted to a new integrated role of "Chief DE&I and Talent Officer," combining diversity responsibilities with broader talent management functions.[7]

Some companies found innovative ways to rebrand while deepening their commitments. At Eli Lilly, while DEI references dropped from 48 mentions in their 2023 shareholder letter to zero in 2024, the company maintained its practice of tying executive compensation to diversity goals and continued citing workforce diversity as a core priority.[8]

Even companies perceived as retreating from DEI often maintained their core programs while adjusting terminology and implementation. For example, 91 percent of executives surveyed by Littler Mendelson reported that the Supreme Court's affirmative action ruling had not lessened their prioritization of DEI. In fact, 57 percent said they had expanded their programming in the past year.[9]

Corporate consultants noted this shift in approach while maintaining substance. Rhonda Moret, founder of Elevated Diversity, observed increased demand for employee resource groups, particularly those focused on caregivers, veterans, and first-generation Americans. While unconscious bias training requests declined, companies sought more nuanced approaches to inclusion. As Moret explained, many consultants were reframing their work as "L&I" (Leadership and Inclusion) while maintaining their core mission.[10]

Diana Scott, who leads the Conference Board's US Human Capital Center, emphasized that about 90 percent of organizations remained committed to their diversity initiatives after reviewing them. "Most organizations are trying to stay the course because they want to create an inclusive, diverse, vibrant culture in the organization," she explained. "Because they know that contributes to employee engagement, which contributes to employee productivity, which contributes to bottom-line business results. You don't do DEI because you're trying to be 'woke.' You do DEI because it's actually serving your business."[11]

Many companies were discovering that skills-based hiring could achieve diversity goals while sidestepping political controversy. As Spring Lacy, global head of talent acquisition and DEI at Verizon noted, "It dismisses this notion that you have to lower the bar if you want diversity in your organization. ... We've got lots of super smart, super skilled people of color, women, people with disabilities, LGBTQI community, who just aren't seen for all of the biases."[12]

Harvard Business School's research on inclusive interviewing showed how leading companies were redesigning their entire recruitment process. This included rewriting job descriptions to eliminate unconscious bias, standardizing interview processes, and expanding recruitment sources. Most importantly, these weren't special accommodations—they were recognized as better practices that improved the quality of all hires.[13]

The most significant shift was in how companies integrated these initiatives into their core operations. Indeed's approach exemplified this trend. Rather than maintaining a separate DEI team working parallel to HR, they embedded diversity and inclusion principles throughout their business processes. As Maggie Hulce, Indeed's chief revenue officer, explained, "It's almost an impossible task to ask a separate group to influence everybody else unless it's built into core processes."[14]

Integration vs. Isolation

By early 2024, research showed a clear pattern in how successful organizations were approaching diversity and inclusion. According to The Diversity Movement's comprehensive analysis of hundreds of organizations, companies achieving the strongest results weren't treating DEI as a separate function—they were embedding it into their core business strategies.[15]

This evolution was particularly evident in how companies approached supplier diversity. According to supplier.io's 2023 benchmarking study of over 1.4 trillion dollars in spend data across 466 companies, the most successful organizations weren't just adding minority-owned businesses to vendor lists—they were transforming their entire procurement approach. Top-performing companies in supplier diversity achieved nearly triple the diverse spend of industry averages, with best-in-class organizations reaching 17.8 percent compared to the overall average of 7.5 percent.[16]

McKinsey's research provided compelling evidence for this integrated approach. Their analysis of 1,200 companies worldwide found that organizations with the highest racial, ethnic, and gender representation were 39 percent more likely to financially outperform their peers.[17] This wasn't just about hitting diversity goals—it reflected fundamental changes in how companies operated.

The demographic realities made this integration increasingly urgent. By 2025, Generation Z will comprise a quarter of the workforce, and they are the most ethnically diverse generation in history.[18] For companies hoping to attract and retain this talent, inclusion couldn't be a separate initiative—it had to be fundamental to how they operated.

The results of these integrated approaches were measurable. According to The Diversity Movement's analysis, employees who felt their company valued diversity were 150 percent more likely to be engaged at work. Glassdoor found that diversity was crucial for job seekers, with a third of underrepresented employees saying they wouldn't even apply to companies lacking a diverse workforce.[19]

This transformation from isolation to integration is best understood through the experiences of major companies that were forced to evolve their approach in response to mounting pressure. In Chapter 3, we examined their initial responses to George Floyd's murder. Now, we'll see how these same organizations navigated the complex terrain between public backlash and private transformation, revealing different paths toward embedding inclusion into their core operations.

How the Target Story Played Out

When we encountered Target in Chapter 3, the company was still in the early stages of responding to George Floyd's murder, which had occurred just three miles from their corporate headquarters. Their initial $10 million pledge and establishment of the Racial Equity Action and Change committee represented traditional corporate responses to crisis. But beneath Target's headline-grabbing controversies, including intense backlash to their Pride merchandise in 2023, a different story was unfolding.

Even as Target adjusted its Pride merchandise strategy in response to public pressure, the fundamental transformation of its business model continued apace. The company's private brand portfolio, which included numerous products from diverse suppliers, was growing at twice the rate of national brands. The Forward Founders program, which had begun as an accelerator to help Black entrepreneurs navigate the retail industry, had expanded beyond its initial scope, supporting more than 30 Black entrepreneurs and 60 diverse founders through two classes.[20]

The reimagined store formats, first tested at the Lake Street location—where Target had conducted extensive community listening sessions following the George Floyd protests—were proving that inclusion could drive growth. The changes weren't superficial: the Lake Street redesign had responded directly to community needs, from making the pharmacy more accessible for elderly customers to stocking the grocery section with culturally relevant foods. Target's multi-category offerings and community-centered approach were creating what Chief Growth Officer Christina Hennington described as "an emotional connection to that consumer." The company wasn't just selling products—it was building relationships with communities that had long felt ignored by major retailers.[21]

Target had invested more than $100 million through its private foundation to advance racial equity,[22] expanded its supplier diversity program, and was on track to meet its $2 billion commitment to Black-owned businesses. The company had also transformed its approach to product development, with its own brands becoming part of its "secret sauce" for growth.

"Value is top of mind, but we have to think about value more holistically than just price," explained Rick Gomez, Target's Chief Food and Beverage Officer, pointing to how the company's post-Floyd transformation had changed even its approach to everyday retail. The focus wasn't just on offering lower prices—it was about understanding and serving communities in ways that traditional retailers had never attempted.[23]

For Target, the journey from the damaged Lake Street store to its new model of inclusive retail represented more than just a response to the crisis. It demonstrated how one of America's largest retailers had fundamentally reimagined its relationship with diverse communities. While controversies like the Pride merchandise backlash might force tactical adjustments, the deeper changes—to store formats, supplier relationships, product development, and community engagement—had become integral to how Target did business. The company that emerged from Minneapolis's moment of crisis would never be the same.

Where Microsoft Ended Up

When we saw Microsoft in Chapter 3, the company had made a decisive break with its past, barring facial recognition sales to police departments and acknowledging the systemic biases in its AI systems. The journey had begun with MIT researcher Joy Buolamwini's discovery that Microsoft's facial recognition software worked nearly perfectly for light-skinned males but failed dramatically for darker-skinned females. Now, in mid-2024, a development seemed to signal a retreat from this commitment to addressing bias: the company disbanded its dedicated diversity and inclusion team, with internal communications suggesting that "DEI programs everywhere are no longer business critical or smart as they were in 2020." The move sparked immediate controversy, appearing to confirm fears that corporate America's commitment to racial equity had been merely a temporary response to George Floyd's murder.[24]

Although it appeared ominous to some, the reality was more complex. Even as Microsoft dismantled its formal DEI structure, the company was quietly revolutionizing how it approached inclusion— moving from isolated initiatives to embedding inclusive principles directly into its core product development process. This transformation became evident just months later, in October 2024, when Microsoft announced a groundbreaking partnership with Be My Eyes, an initiative to improve AI systems for the 340 million people worldwide who are blind or have low vision.

The Be My Eyes partnership revealed a fundamental shift in Microsoft's approach. Rather than treating accessibility as a separate consideration or an afterthought, the company was now tackling it as a core engineering challenge. The project acknowledged that AI systems were often failing not just because of biased data, but because they weren't being built with diverse perspectives from the start.

"AI requires large amounts of data for training and utility but too often disability is underrepresented or incorrectly categorized in datasets," Microsoft explained. The company's research had revealed that disability-related objects were included less frequently in popular image-text datasets, leading to approximately 30 percent less accurate recognition of these items. This "disability data desert," as they termed it, wasn't just a technical oversight—it was effectively encoding exclusion into AI systems.[25]

The contrast between disbanding the DEI team and deepening inclusion work through initiatives like Be My Eyes highlighted an evolution in how major tech companies approach diversity and ethics in AI development. The focus had shifted from treating bias as a problem to be solved with better algorithms or dedicated DEI initiatives, to recognizing it as a fundamental challenge requiring transformation in how AI is conceived, developed, and deployed.

"We are committed to building inclusive AI that is representative of all who use it," declared Jenny Lay-Flurrie, Microsoft's Chief Accessibility Officer, "while also protecting marginalized members of society from proliferated bias that could impact education, employment, and civic engagement." This wasn't just another corporate statement—it represented a new understanding that true inclusion couldn't be achieved through separate DEI programs, but only by embedding inclusive principles into the very fabric of product development and business strategy.[26]

Microsoft's 2024 transformation exemplifies the broader pattern of "boom to backlash" that characterized corporate America's response to George Floyd's murder. The initial boom was evident in Microsoft's sweeping commitments: barring facial recognition sales to police, establishing new AI ethics frameworks, and expanding diversity initiatives. Then came the apparent backlash, symbolized by the dissolution of the formal DEI team—a move that seemed to signal retreat from those commitments.

But Microsoft's story reveals something more nuanced than simple progress and regression. While the company appeared to be stepping back from public DEI commitments, it was simultaneously embedding the principles of diversity, equity, and inclusion more deeply than ever into its core operations. The Be My Eyes partnership demonstrated how inclusion had evolved from a separate initiative into a fundamental engineering priority. This wasn't just about optics or compliance—it was about building better products that served a truly global market.

This transformation has yielded unexpected benefits. By integrating inclusive design principles directly into product development, Microsoft has positioned itself to attract top talent from underrepresented groups worldwide. Engineers, designers, and researchers who might once have been skeptical of tech industry commitments to diversity can now see their perspectives valued not just in HR initiatives but in the actual products they'll help create.

The question was no longer just about fixing biased algorithms or maintaining dedicated DEI teams—it was about transforming the entire process of technological innovation to ensure it served humanity in all its diversity. In this way, Microsoft's evolution suggests that the most effective response to the DEI backlash isn't to double down on separate initiatives, but to weave the principles so thoroughly into business operations that they become indistinguishable from the pursuit of excellence itself.

WarnerMedia's Act 3

In Chapter 3, we saw WarnerMedia undertake one of the entertainment industry's most comprehensive diversity transformations, creating "The Red Book" catalog of diverse suppliers and launching ambitious pipeline programs across every sector from animation to news. By 2024, however, the entertainment industry was showing signs of retreat. As writer-producer Hilliard Guess observed, despite growing evidence that diverse content performed well, "there's still a lot of very mediocre [white] people who are successful in Hollywood. If they looked like us, they wouldn't be in that position."[27]

As Julie Ann Crommett, founder of the DEI organization Collective Moxie, noted with frustration: "What is wild is that in a moment of great economic shift, contraction and change in the actual mechanisms of Hollywood content making and distribution, this idea has not taken hold that inclusive storytelling could help reinvent this business." She added, "That's mind-boggling—that the business itself is not shifting to meet what the data is telling us."[28]

As the industry began dismantling DEI teams, Karen Horne, who had risen to become Warner Bros. Discovery North America's senior vice president for DEI, was laid off as part of the company's restructuring. "The systems that are in place don't support success," Horne observed after her departure.[29] It appeared to be a classic setback in the face of political pressure.

The data, however, continued to validate the importance of diverse storytelling. According to 2024 research, streaming series with diverse casts consistently outperformed less representative shows. Among the Top 20 streaming series, those featuring diverse casts achieved 67 percent higher viewership. In film, comedies with diverse casts showed a remarkable 73 percent success rate.[30]

The transformation manifested differently across the company's divisions. DC Comics' Milestone Initiative specifically targeted Black writers, creators, and artists, recognizing that "comics are one of the first things that children consume, and they're often not diverse or they're drawn in a way that marginalizes people, especially women."[31]

Internal voices revealed how deeply the changes had penetrated. "When I think of initiatives like our equity and inclusion report, I'm so motivated by the fact that it keeps us accountable," explained

Ramon Torres, senior project manager of equity and inclusion for content. "The only way you truly do that is by putting yourself out there to be scrutinized. That's the only real way that you can create systemic change and instill a sort of reflective mirror for an organization where people come and go. Numbers won't lie over time."[32]

The pressures of the market were pushing some creators to look beyond traditional studio structures. "Why not look towards the Kevin Harts, the Issa Raes, the Lena Waithes and say, 'Let's come up with our own way of distributing, creating, and marketing things?'" proposed writer-filmmaker Thembi Banks, pointing to Tyler Perry's independent studio as inspiration. "People were scratching their heads looking at this man like, What is this and why would I want it? You know why you want it? Because there's an audience out there for it!"[33]

What began as a crisis response to racial injustice had evolved into something more fundamental: a recognition that the audience itself was changing. As one industry veteran observed in the McKinsey report, looking back on three decades of evolution: "When I started out in the industry some 30 years ago, it wasn't a desert. I had many Black colleagues who seemed to be on the path to success—studio vice presidents and producers of top shows. But at some point, they hit a wall and ultimately left the industry. Each was a real loss."[34]

The difference now was in the numbers themselves. Even as companies dismantled their DEI departments, audience preferences spoke clearly through viewership data. The success wasn't accidental—it was the direct result of transformed business practices, from development through distribution. WarnerMedia's journey suggested that true inclusion wasn't achieved through separate programs or departments, but by fundamentally reimagining how stories are told and who gets to tell them.[35]

What Happened to JPMorgan?

In Chapter 3, we left JPMorgan Chase at a pivotal moment. The nation's largest bank, which previously paid millions to settle racial discrimination lawsuits, had just announced an unprecedented $30 billion commitment to racial equity. By December 2023, as conservative legal groups threatened lawsuits against companies over their diversity initiatives, JPMorgan Chase found itself making adjustments. The descriptions of programs like "Advancing Hispanics and Latinos" and "Advancing Black Pathways" were modified to invite applications from all students, "regardless of background." It was the kind of change that, to casual observers, might have suggested a retreat from the bank's post-Floyd commitments.[36]

But a closer look revealed a different story. Even as the bank adjusted the language of some programs, it was quietly revolutionizing how inclusion was embedded in its core business model. A third-party audit conducted by PricewaterhouseCoopers confirmed the bank was not just meeting its racial equity commitments—it was fundamentally transforming how it operated in underserved communities.[37]

The Anacostia branch offered a perfect example of this deeper transformation. Rather than just providing traditional banking services, the location was designed as a community hub, complete with space for financial education workshops and small business mentoring. The bank hired staff locally and engaged local artists to ensure the branch complemented its neighborhood. This wasn't charity—it was smart business. As Peter Scher explained, "When communities thrive, our business thrives."[38]

This philosophy was evident in how JPMorgan approached small business lending in historically underserved areas. Rather than simply setting diversity goals, the bank created a special purpose credit program that fundamentally changed how credit decisions were made in majority-minority communities. The bank hired 45 local senior business consultants to provide one-on-one coaching and host educational events across 21 US cities.[39]

By 2024, it had become clear that JPMorgan's post-Floyd transformation wasn't just window dressing—it represented a fundamental shift in how America's largest bank thought about the relationship between inclusion and growth. In fact, even as the bank made superficial adjustments to program descriptions in response to legal pressures, it was deepening its commitment to inclusive banking practices. The reason was simple: it was good for business.

This wasn't just about one neighborhood. Across the country, JPMorgan was demonstrating how inclusive practices could drive business growth. In Ohio alone, the bank's racial equity commitment had channeled more than $260 million into underserved communities, including over $163 million in loans for Black, Hispanic, and Latino households to purchase or refinance homes. Far from being acts of charity, these investments were helping the bank expand its customer base and strengthen its market position.[40]

The transformation was perhaps most evident in how JPMorgan approached small business lending. The bank's own research had shown that businesses in majority Black and Latino communities typically operated with minimal cash reserves, making them especially vulnerable to economic shocks. Rather than seeing this as a reason to avoid these markets, JPMorgan recognized it as an opportunity to create new products and services tailored to these communities' needs. By combining lending with education and support services, the bank wasn't just making loans—it was building lasting customer relationships.[41]

Jamie Dimon made the business case explicit: "By driving inclusive economic growth, we can help create a brighter future for all, no matter where people live or the circumstances they're born into." This wasn't just rhetoric—it was a recognition that in an increasingly diverse America, inclusion wasn't optional. It was essential to future growth.[42]

The journey from the discriminatory practices that led to the 2017 settlement to the transformation witnessed in the years following George Floyd's murder represented more than just a change in corporate policy. It demonstrated how one of America's most powerful financial institutions had come to understand that addressing racial inequity wasn't just a moral imperative—it was a business necessity. In the process, JPMorgan Chase had helped create a new model of inclusive banking that suggested diversity and inclusion weren't just surviving the backlash—they were becoming more deeply embedded in how America does business.

Beyond the Backlash: Building Sustainable Change

The transformation of corporate diversity efforts in the wake of George Floyd's murder reveals much about both the power and limitations of social media–driven change. What began with public statements and hasty commitments evolved through waves of cancellation and backlash into something more fundamental: a recognition that sustainable diversity and inclusion require more than superficial changes or defensive posturing.

The journey from initial crisis response to lasting transformation is clearly visible in the stories of our four companies. Target evolved from a simple $10 million pledge to fundamentally reimagining how stores serve diverse communities. Microsoft moved beyond merely restricting facial recognition sales to embedding inclusion directly into AI development. WarnerMedia transformed not just who told stories, but how stories were developed, funded, and distributed. JPMorgan Chase progressed from settling discrimination lawsuits to revolutionizing community banking.

The most successful companies found ways to make inclusion inseparable from operational excellence. Target discovered that community-centered store designs and diverse supplier relationships could drive growth in urban markets. Microsoft learned that inclusive AI development produced better products for everyone. WarnerMedia's data showed that diverse content consistently outperformed less representative shows. JPMorgan found that inclusive banking practices opened new markets and strengthened customer relationships.

This evolution required fundamentally rethinking how organizations approach diversity and inclusion. Rather than treating DEI as a separate initiative vulnerable to political crosswinds, leading organizations began embedding it so deeply into their operations that it became inseparable from business success. This transformation manifested in several key ways, supported by growing evidence that diversity and inclusion were essential components of a company's resources and capabilities that could create sustainable competitive advantages.

One of the most striking examples came from IBM's transformation of its talent development approach. Rather than maintaining separate diversity recruitment programs, the company eliminated degree requirements from over 50 percent of their positions, implemented skills-based assessments, and created multiple pathways for career advancement. As Obed Louissaint, Senior Vice President of Transformation and Culture at IBM explained, they found success hiring "individuals who were baristas, truck drivers, nurses, teachers—all of whom were redefining who they were and had a tech curiosity." The results were compelling. After implementing skills-based hiring, IBM saw increased diversity, improved performance ratings, and better retention across all demographic groups.[43]

The World Economic Forum's research identified several companies achieving remarkable results through systematic approaches to inclusion. Heineken's Women in Sales program increased female senior managers in sales from 9 percent in 2020 to 19 percent in 2022 through targeted recruitment and development. Hong Kong Exchanges and Clearing Limited (HKEX) used its regulatory power to require listed companies to have at least one female director, leading to an increase in female directors from 14.6 percent to 17.3 percent and a decrease in companies with no female directors from 31.5 percent to 21.4 percent.[44]

The most successful organizations discovered that authentic inclusion served as its own defense against social media pressure. Research consistently showed that companies with deeply integrated diversity practices showed stronger financial performance across multiple metrics. A 2024 study of over eight thousand firm-years across global companies found that organizations with higher diversity and inclusion scores demonstrated significantly better performance as measured by both Tobin's Q and Return on Assets (ROA). The researchers found this relationship held true even when controlling for firm size, leverage, age, and other factors, suggesting that diversity and inclusion were fundamental drivers of business success rather than mere correlations.[45]

Perhaps most importantly, successful organizations learned to separate political rhetoric from practical impact. According to MIT Sloan Management Review's Strategy Forum, corporations faced increasing pressure to take positions on social issues, with 71.5 percent of experts arguing that silence itself could be risky in today's environment. As Joshua Gans of the University of Toronto noted, "If there is one thing corporations should be allowed to speak on, it is on policies that impact their employees or customers, regardless of political consequences."[46]

This suggests a path forward for organizations committed to authentic inclusion. Rather than engaging in social media battles or retreating from diversity commitments, successful companies are focusing on demonstrable impact. They're building inclusion so deeply into their operations that it becomes indistinguishable from business excellence. The evidence increasingly shows that this approach not only helps weather political storms but drives superior business performance.

The lessons of this era will likely shape corporate practice for years to come. While social media pressure can spark change, lasting transformation requires moving beyond both performative activism and defensive retreat to build organizations where inclusive excellence is simply how business gets done. The companies that master this transition won't just survive the current backlash—they'll help create a new model of business that better serves an increasingly diverse world.

7

The Power of Courageous Conversations

ONE OF THE first calls I received in the moments after George Floyd was pronounced dead came from Jason, a manufacturing leader I'd placed years ago. As one of the few Black executives in his division, he was grappling with an impossible balance: leading his team through their daily operations while processing his own trauma. When we connected again early the next morning, he walked me through the challenges ahead: 40 faces would be looking at him in the morning standup, each expecting different things. I reminded him that while his perspective as a Black leader was valuable, his primary responsibility was to lead everyone through this moment.

As Director of Operations, Jason knew every eye would be on him this morning. The familiar faces in their Brady Bunch–style Zoom boxes would be looking to him for... what exactly? Guidance? Absolution? Permission to pretend nothing had happened? His cursor hovered over the "Join Meeting" button as he wrestled with questions no management training had prepared him for. How do you lead a discussion about production quotas and safety metrics when your social media feeds are filled with images of someone who looks like you, like your brother, like your son, dying under a police officer's knee? What do you say to the young Black supervisor who texted you at midnight, saying she couldn't focus on quality control reports while processing her grief?

Rebecca's call came through while I was juggling multiple conversations that morning. We'd first met in an airport lounge years earlier when I was returning from Japan en route to speak at a LinkedIn conference about DEI and talent acquisition. Based in the Bay Area, she'd always been thoughtful about cross-cultural leadership, and now she was reaching out with an urgent need to get her response "right." Her stream of text messages reflected a broader truth I was witnessing: George Floyd's murder had affected everyone, but some leaders, like Rebecca, were determined to move beyond emotional reactions to create meaningful dialogue.

As a white senior manager at a national restaurant chain, Rebecca had spent the morning reading and re-reading drafts of an email to her regional teams. Her inbox overflowed with corporate statements about racial justice, each one feeling more carefully crafted and less genuinely human than the last. The team chat groups, usually bustling with updates about menu changes and customer feedback, had fallen eerily silent. Her district managers were sending private messages asking for guidance about how to support their predominantly Black kitchen staff, while her two Black assistant managers, usually among the most engaged voices in meetings, hadn't spoken in yesterday's operations call.

The calls kept coming. "I know I need to say something," one manufacturing plant manager told me, his voice shaking. "But I'm terrified of making things worse." A university dean, known for fearlessly tackling the toughest academic challenges, confessed within minutes of our call: "I've never felt so unprepared for a conversation in my life."

What these leaders were discovering was that their traditional playbooks for handling crisis communications were woefully inadequate for this moment. The carefully crafted corporate statements and HR-approved talking points that had served them through previous challenges now felt hollow and insufficient. Their employees weren't looking for platitudes or carefully worded memos—they were demanding real dialogue about issues that had been simmering beneath the surface for years.

This is where the concept of "courageous conversations" emerged as a tool for organizational transformation. But let's be clear about what makes a conversation truly courageous. It's not just about having difficult discussions or addressing sensitive topics. Courageous conversations require something more fundamental: the willingness to be uncomfortable, to risk saying the wrong thing in pursuit of genuine understanding, and most importantly, to listen with the intent to learn rather than respond.

What made this moment different was its unavoidable nature. As one retail executive told me, "Before George Floyd, talking about race at work was optional. After Floyd, silence wasn't an option anymore." The challenge wasn't just finding the right words—it was creating spaces where people could speak honestly about experiences many had spent years carefully compartmentalizing, while also ensuring these conversations led to meaningful change rather than just shared trauma.

The transformation was remarkable. Before Floyd's murder, conversations about race in corporate America followed predictable patterns. They happened in designated spaces—diversity training sessions, employee resource group meetings, or carefully curated panel discussions. These conversations were often optional, carefully scripted, and designed to minimize discomfort. Many organizations prided themselves on having "difficult conversations," but these discussions typically focused on safe topics like unconscious bias or cultural celebration rather than addressing systemic inequities head-on.

The landscape shifted dramatically in those early weeks of June 2020. Employee Resource Groups that had struggled to get 20 people to attend their monthly meetings suddenly found hundreds logging into their virtual sessions—most of them employees who had never engaged with ERGs before. They weren't there to celebrate diversity or check a box on their annual training requirements. They came because they wanted to understand, to help, and to be part of the solution.

The timing of Floyd's murder during the pandemic created unique opportunities for these conversations. Companies had already adapted to virtual platforms for COVID-related check-ins and "virtual happy hours." These same digital spaces became venues for authentic dialogue about racial justice. The virtual format, somewhat counterintuitively, often made it easier for people to engage in difficult conversations, allowing them to participate through chat functions or anonymous questions when speaking up felt too vulnerable.

Most importantly, these conversations transcended traditional diversity and inclusion silos. This wasn't just a "Black issue" anymore. Everyone—Black, white, Asian, Latino, LGBTQ+, veterans, people with disabilities—wanted to be part of the conversation and part of the solution. The intersectional nature of the response created unprecedented momentum for change.

The stakes couldn't have been higher. In those early days, I witnessed both powerful breakthroughs and painful missteps. Organizations that got it right created lasting transformations in their culture and relationships. Those that fumbled the moment often damaged trust in ways that would take years to repair. The key difference? Understanding that authenticity mattered more than perfection. As I told countless leaders during those weeks, "It's okay to make mistakes as long as you're not being purposefully offensive. What's not okay is staying silent because you're afraid of saying the wrong thing."

In this chapter, we'll explore how to structure and facilitate these conversations, drawing from both successful examples and cautionary tales. We'll examine the key principles that make these discussions productive rather than performative and provide practical frameworks for leaders at all levels to engage in meaningful dialogue about challenging issues. Most importantly, we'll look at how these conversations, when done right, can transform not just individual understanding but entire organizational cultures.

Creating a Brave Space

The distinction between a "safe space" and a "brave space" is crucial for understanding how to facilitate meaningful dialogue about race and equity. A safe space focuses primarily on protecting people from discomfort or conflict. While well intentioned, this approach can inhibit genuine dialogue by making people so worried about causing offense that they don't engage authentically. A brave space, by contrast, acknowledges that discomfort is not only inevitable but necessary for growth. It provides support and structure while encouraging participants to push beyond their comfort zones.

Setting clear expectations forms the foundation of a brave space. As one manufacturing plant manager I worked with put it, "People aren't afraid of difficult conversations—they're afraid of unexpected conversations." This means being explicit about why you're gathering, what topics you'll discuss, how people can participate, and what agreements exist around confidentiality. At a large retail chain I advised, the Chief Human Resources Officer opened their first conversation by establishing this framework: "We're here to understand each other's experiences, share our perspectives honestly, and identify ways we can support each other and create positive change. Some of what we discuss may be uncomfortable, and that's okay. We're not here to blame or shame anyone, but to learn and grow together."

Ground rules for engagement emerge from my experience developing conversation toolkits for organizations, but these aren't just generic meeting guidelines—they're carefully designed frameworks that make difficult conversations possible. Let me break down how these rules function in practice.

The foundation begins with "listen to understand, not to respond." This means more than just staying quiet while others speak. At Moody's, we trained leaders to watch for signs that people were truly listening, like taking notes, asking follow-up questions, and referencing others' comments in their own responses. One leader created a powerful moment by putting down his pen and closing his laptop, saying "I want to focus entirely on hearing what you're sharing." This simple action transformed the dynamic of the conversation.

Speaking from personal experience, using "I" statements serves multiple purposes. It prevents sweeping generalizations that can shut down dialogue while encouraging authentic sharing. We found that modeling this specifically helped. Instead of saying "Black employees feel excluded from advancement opportunities," participants learned to say, "I've encountered these specific barriers in my career progression." This shift from general claims to personal experiences made conversations both safer and more impactful.

The principle that impact matters more than intent required careful explanation and frequent reinforcement. We encouraged participants to practice both giving and receiving feedback about impact. "I know you didn't mean to minimize my experience, but when you said ___, it made me feel ___" became a powerful template for addressing microaggressions without escalating tension. Equally important was teaching people how to receive such feedback: acknowledge the impact, thank the person for sharing, and focus on learning rather than defending.

The acceptance of mistakes proved crucial. We explicitly discussed what constituted a genuine mistake versus intentionally harmful behavior. Using outdated terminology, stumbling over words, or asking awkward questions were treated as learning opportunities. As one retail manager in our program noted, "Once I understood the difference between making a mistake and being malicious, I felt more confident participating in the conversation." We created specific protocols for addressing mistakes: acknowledge it, apologize simply without overexplaining, ask for the correct information or approach, and move forward.

Privacy agreements extended beyond the usual "what's shared here stays here." We developed nuanced guidelines about how insights from these conversations could be used constructively without violating confidentiality. For instance, a leader might say, "I've heard from several team members that our promotion criteria may have unintended barriers" rather than "John shared in our last session that he feels the promotion process is biased." This allowed for action on insights while protecting individual privacy.

The principle of encouraged but not required participation needed careful implementation. We developed multiple ways for people to engage beyond just speaking up in the main discussion. Some wrote reflections in chat, others shared resources in follow-up emails, and some simply nodded or used reaction emojis to show engagement. A university dean I worked with added another powerful principle: "We're not here to be perfect—we're here to be present." This simple statement helped shift the energy from anxiety about saying the wrong thing to commitment to authentic engagement in whatever form felt genuine.

One of the key lessons from the virtual environment was that different people feel comfortable engaging in different ways, and creating a truly brave space means designing multiple pathways for participation. This goes beyond simply offering different formats—it requires understanding how each channel serves different needs and creating intentional flows between them.

Large group discussions serve as anchoring points where shared understanding can be established and collective commitments can be made. However, these need careful structuring to be effective. We found success using a "ripple" format: start with a clear framing question, allow individual reflection time (usually two to three minutes of silence), move to paired sharing, then small groups, before opening to full group discussion. This progressive expansion helps people formulate their thoughts and test their ideas in smaller settings before bringing them to the larger group.

Small group breakouts (typically four to six people) create space for deeper exploration of specific topics or experiences. The key is providing clear prompts and time frames. Rather than general discussion, we give groups specific tasks: share a personal experience related to the topic, identify common themes, and generate potential actions. Groups should be intentionally mixed to include different perspectives while ensuring no one is isolated as the "only" member of their identity group.

Written channels serve multiple purposes beyond just accommodation for those who prefer not to speak. Chat functions can capture real-time reactions and questions without interrupting speakers. Anonymous submission tools allow people to raise sensitive issues they might not feel comfortable attaching their name to. Document sharing spaces let people contribute research, resources, or longer reflections that require more careful composition.

One-on-one conversations play a role in the ecosystem of brave spaces. These aren't just fallback options for those uncomfortable in groups—they're opportunities for deeper connection and understanding. We encourage leaders to schedule "office hours" specifically for these conversations, making it clear that the invitation is open to everyone, not just those directly affected by the issues being discussed.

The art lies in weaving these channels together coherently. At Moody's, we developed what we called a "conversation cascade." This involved starting with large group framing, moving to focused small group work, providing individual reflection and written input opportunities, then bringing insights back to the full group for synthesis and action planning. This wasn't just about offering options—it was about creating a deliberate journey that allowed people to engage in ways that felt authentic while building toward collective understanding and action.

Several common challenges typically emerge when creating brave spaces, but each can be addressed with thoughtful preparation. When faced with silence or limited participation, structured sharing prompts can help break the ice: "Take a moment to reflect on a time when you felt truly seen and heard at work. What made that experience meaningful?" When certain voices begin to dominate, implementing a "step up, step back" principle encourages balanced participation—those who have shared several times should consider creating space for others, while those who haven't spoken might look for opportunities to step into the conversation.

Defensive reactions require establishing a "both/and" framework that allows multiple truths to coexist. We can both acknowledge that everyone here wants to do the right thing and recognize that we may have blind spots or biases to address. Perhaps most importantly, we must be mindful of the pressure often placed on minority employees. Making it clear that no one is expected to be a spokesperson for their identity group helps create genuine choice about participation: "While we value the experiences people choose to share, no one should feel obligated to educate others or represent their entire community."

Leaders play a role in setting the tone for brave spaces, not by dominating the conversation but by modeling the kind of vulnerability and openness they hope to see from others. A powerful example came from a warehouse facility where the site director opened their first conversation by sharing his own journey of understanding: "I grew up thinking I didn't have any biases because I treated everyone the same. But watching the video of George Floyd's murder, I realized I'd never had to have 'the talk' with my kids about how to survive a police encounter. That was a wake-up call for me about my own privilege, and I'm still learning what that means." This kind of authentic sharing helps create permission for others to bring their whole selves to the conversation. It demonstrates that leadership positions don't require having all the answers—they require having the courage to ask difficult questions and engage in genuine dialogue.

A brave space isn't just about having one powerful conversation—it's about creating sustainable channels for ongoing dialogue and action. This means establishing regular check-ins, creating clear accountability for action items, building feedback mechanisms, and developing support systems for continuing difficult conversations. At a national restaurant chain, they created what they called "Courage Corners"—designated times during regular team meetings where people could raise concerns, share experiences, or follow up on previous conversations. This integration into existing structures helped normalize brave conversations as part of their organizational culture rather than treating them as special events.

The ultimate test of a brave space isn't how comfortable people feel—it's how honestly they engage and what actions emerge from the dialogue. As one leader told me, "We know we've created a truly brave space when people start bringing up the things they've been afraid to say for years, and instead of chaos, it creates clarity about what we need to change."

Leading the Conversation

Creating a brave space is just the beginning. The real art lies in guiding the conversation itself—keeping it focused, productive, and meaningful while handling the inevitable challenges that arise. This isn't about controlling the discussion or steering it toward predetermined conclusions. Instead, it's about creating the conditions for authentic dialogue while ensuring everyone feels truly heard.

Opening effectively sets the tone for everything that follows. The most successful conversations begin not with presentations or prepared speeches, but with a moment of genuine acknowledgment. One retail executive I advised started their first conversation by simply saying, "I want to acknowledge that we're all coming to this conversation carrying different experiences, different emotions, and different needs. Some of us are processing deep personal pain. Others are grappling with newfound awareness of systemic issues. All of these perspectives are valid, and all deserve space in our dialogue."

The early moments of the conversation require particular attention to pacing and energy. I teach leaders to use what I call the "widening circles" approach. Start with questions everyone can engage with comfortably, then gradually expand to deeper territory as trust and psychological safety build.

The first circle focuses on presence and intention. Start with questions that acknowledge people's choice to participate: "What made you decide to join this conversation?" or "What's one hope you have for our discussion today?" These opening questions do more than break the ice—they help people articulate why they're there and begin building investment in the dialogue. Watch for signs of engagement like nodding, leaning forward, or using the chat function. If participation is hesitant, you might narrow the question further: "What's one word that describes how you're feeling coming into this conversation?"

The second circle moves to shared experiences and observations. Questions here might include: "What changes have you noticed in our workplace conversations since George Floyd's murder?" or "Where do you see our company's values showing up—or not showing up—in our daily work?" These questions invite people to share observations without requiring personal disclosure. Pay attention to whether people reference their own experiences or speak only in generalities. If responses stay very general, you might need to model going a bit deeper yourself: "I've noticed that our team meetings feel different now—there's more willingness to acknowledge when we're struggling with something."

The third circle explores impact and emotions. This is where you begin asking questions that invite people to share how events or practices affect them personally: "How have recent events influenced your experience at work?" or "When do you feel most included—or excluded—in our workplace?" Watch for shifts in energy as the conversation deepens. Some participants might become more engaged while others pull back. Create space for both reactions: "I notice this topic is bringing up strong feelings for some, while others might still be processing. Both responses are valid."

The fourth circle addresses deeper systemic issues and potential changes. Questions here might include: "What barriers have you encountered in trying to build an inclusive workplace?" or "What would need to change for everyone to feel they can bring their full selves to work?" This is often where many insights emerge, but getting here requires having built trust through the earlier circles. Signs that a group is ready for this level include people building on each other's comments, showing emotional support for vulnerable shares, and starting to propose specific changes.

If the group isn't ready to move to a wider circle, that's valuable information. Maybe you hear responses becoming more guarded, see people physically pulling back, or notice participation dropping off. Rather than pushing forward, you might need to circle back: "Let's explore what makes these conversations challenging. What would help us engage more openly with each other?"

Throughout this progression, pay attention to whose voices are being heard. The widening circles shouldn't just represent deeper content but broader participation. If you notice certain people or perspectives aren't being included, create intentional openings without putting anyone on the spot: "We've heard several perspectives from leadership—I'd love to hear from people with different vantage points in the organization."

The art of this approach lies in reading the room's readiness to move outward while ensuring no one feels left behind. Some participants might be ready to dive into systemic issues immediately, while others need more time in the early circles. Your role is to find the pace that allows for both deep engagement and broad participation.

Listening emerges as the most crucial skill in facilitating these conversations, but it's a specific type of listening that makes the difference. This isn't just about staying quiet while others speak—it's about demonstrating what I call "active receptivity," a structured approach to showing genuine engagement with what's being shared.

The physical components of active receptivity start with intentional positioning. In person, this means squarely facing the speaker, maintaining comfortable but engaged eye contact, and avoiding distracting movements. In virtual settings, it means keeping your camera on when possible, positioning yourself to look directly at the camera when responding, and minimizing background distractions. Small gestures of acknowledgment—a nod, a slight lean forward, an encouraging smile—show engagement without interrupting.

Verbal affirmation requires a delicate balance. Brief acknowledging sounds or words ("mm-hmm," "yes," "I see") can encourage continued sharing, but use them sparingly to avoid breaking the speaker's flow. When someone finishes sharing, specific acknowledgment helps validate their contribution while encouraging others: "Thank you for sharing that perspective" becomes more meaningful as "Thank you for helping us understand how that policy affected your team directly."

The most powerful form of active receptivity comes through what I call "reflecting and extending." This means first echoing back the core message you heard, then asking a question that helps deepen the conversation. For instance, if someone shares an experience of feeling excluded from informal networking, you might say: "I'm hearing that these unofficial conversations have a real impact on career development. Could you help us understand what you think makes these situations happen?"

Body language provides signals about engagement levels throughout the room. Watch for what I call the "participation arc": people tend to physically lean in when they want to contribute, pull back slightly when processing difficult information, and shift position when they're disconnecting from the conversation. Learning to read these cues helps you gauge when to draw people in, when to create space for reflection, and when to shift the energy of the discussion.

Digital environments require their own approach to active receptivity. Encourage use of reaction emojis as a way to show engagement. Watch the chat for signs that people want to contribute—often someone will start typing, stop, start again, indicating they're trying to find the right words to join in. Create explicit opportunities for these voices: "I'm seeing some activity in the chat. Would anyone like to voice those thoughts?"

Managing the flow of conversation requires constant attention to group dynamics. Watch for signs that people want to contribute but might need encouragement—leaning forward, starting to speak then pulling back, or showing strong reactions to others' comments. Create natural openings with phrases like "I noticed several people nodding when Kim shared that experience. Would anyone like to build on what she said?" This technique invites participation while connecting comments to the ongoing dialogue.

The hardest moments often come when someone says something problematic or insensitive. These instances require immediate attention, but how you handle them can either shut down dialogue or create powerful learning opportunities. I teach leaders to use a three-step approach I call "Affirm, Address, and Avoid."

First, affirm the speaker's positive intent or underlying message. This step acknowledges that most problematic statements come from a place of genuine effort to engage, not malice. For instance, if someone describes a Black colleague as "very articulate," you might begin: "I can hear that you're trying to express admiration for your colleague's communication skills." This validation helps maintain psychological safety and keeps the speaker engaged in the conversation.

Next, address the problematic aspect directly but non-judgmentally. Continuing the example: "I want to share that 'articulate' has a complicated history when used to describe Black professionals, as it can imply that eloquence isn't expected from them. I know that's not what you meant, but it's important to understand why that word might land differently than intended." This step ensures the issue doesn't go unaddressed while framing it as a learning opportunity rather than a rebuke.

Finally, avoid creating a pile-on situation by deliberately shifting the conversation's direction and energy. You might say: "Let's talk about what specific qualities make someone an effective communicator in our workplace." This redirection maintains focus on the underlying positive topic while moving away from the problematic statement. It also prevents others from feeling they need to add their own corrections or criticisms of the original speaker.

This three-step approach works for various situations. If someone makes a broad generalization like "Women are naturally better at the emotional side of leadership," you might respond:

Affirm: "I appreciate you trying to recognize strengths you've observed in our women leaders."

Address: "However, when we attribute skills to natural or inherent traits of any group, we risk reinforcing stereotypes that can limit opportunities for everyone."

Avoid: "Let's discuss the specific leadership skills that contribute to team success, regardless of who demonstrates them."

The key is maintaining momentum through all three steps. Don't linger too long on any one phase. The goal is to create a brief but meaningful learning moment before moving the conversation forward constructively. Your tone should remain warm and curious throughout, signaling that this is a natural part of our learning journey together, not a departure from it.

I often explicitly tell groups: "We're all learning and growing. The measure of our success isn't avoiding all mistakes—it's how we handle them when they happen and what we learn from them." This framework helps fulfill that promise by creating clear steps for handling mistakes while maintaining the brave space we've worked to create.

Timing plays a role in managing these conversations. People need enough time to process their thoughts and feelings, but too much open-ended discussion can lead to circular conversations or emotional exhaustion. We found that 90 minutes tends to be the optimal length for these sessions—long enough for meaningful dialogue but not so long that energy and focus begin to wane. Within that time, plan for rough thirds: opening and initial sharing, deeper dialogue and exploration, and synthesis of key themes or takeaways.

Productive dialogue requires active facilitation, but the goal isn't to control the conversation. Instead, think of yourself as creating guardrails that keep the discussion focused while allowing for organic exploration of important topics. When conversations start to veer off track, gentle course corrections work better than abrupt redirections. "That's an important point that deserves its own discussion. For now, can we stay focused on . . ." helps maintain focus while acknowledging the value of tangential topics.

Throughout the conversation, pay attention to whose voices are being heard and whose might be missing. If you notice certain people or perspectives aren't being included, create intentional openings. But be careful about putting people on the spot. Instead of "Sarah, as one of our few Black managers, what do you think?" try "We haven't heard much about how this issue affects different levels of our organization. Would anyone like to speak to that?"

When strong emotions arise—and they will—resist the urge to move past them quickly or smooth them over. These moments, while uncomfortable, often contain the seeds of real understanding and change. Create space for emotion while maintaining the brave space framework: "I can hear how deeply this affects you. Thank you for being willing to share that with us. Would you like to say more about what's behind those feelings?"

The art of leading these conversations lies in balancing structure with flexibility, guidance with openness, and support with challenge. You're not there to provide answers but to facilitate discovery. You're not there to fix problems immediately but to create understanding that leads to meaningful change. Most importantly, you're there to demonstrate that difficult conversations, when handled with care and intention, can strengthen rather than divide our workplace communities.

From Dialogue to Action

How you conclude a courageous conversation is just as important as how you begin it. The final moments determine whether the dialogue leads to meaningful change or becomes what one leader called "just another meeting about diversity." The key is understanding that empathy without action can damage trust. When people share vulnerable experiences or difficult truths, they're not just looking to be heard—they're hoping for change.

The most common mistake I see organizations make is ending these conversations with vague commitments or general expressions of support. "We'll do better" or "We hear you" might feel good in the moment, but they create no accountability and often lead to frustration when nothing concrete follows. Instead, successful conclusions require a clear framework for turning dialogue into action. I teach leaders to use what I call the "Capture, Commit, and Connect" approach.

First, capture the key themes and insights that emerged during the discussion. This isn't just summarizing what was said—it's identifying the underlying patterns and opportunities for change. Think of capturing themes like creating a heat map of the conversation: what topics kept surfacing, what emotions came up repeatedly, what solutions did people gravitate toward?

Listen for three distinct types of themes. First, identify structural issues—these are challenges built into your systems and processes. You might hear people repeatedly mentioning promotion criteria, meeting schedules, or resource allocation. Second, note cultural themes—these relate to unwritten rules and behaviors, like who gets heard in meetings, how decisions really get made, or where informal networking happens. Finally, track action-oriented themes—specific changes or solutions that people propose.

Pay particular attention to intersecting themes. For example, you might notice that concerns about mentorship access overlap with observations about remote work challenges. Or feedback about communication styles might connect to concerns about performance evaluations. These intersection points often reveal the most promising areas for meaningful change.

When articulating themes back to the group, be specific but also show connections. Instead of just listing issues, frame them in terms of impact and opportunity: "I'm hearing how our current mentorship program, while well-intentioned, might be reinforcing existing disparities because informal connections determine who gets matched with senior leaders. This connects to what others shared about feeling excluded from important conversations happening in person when they work remotely. It seems like we have an opportunity to rethink how we create access to leadership and development opportunities across the board."

Numbers can help make themes concrete without reducing them to pure statistics. Note patterns like "half our small groups mentioned challenges with our current feedback process" or "this concern came up in every breakout session." This helps demonstrate that you're tracking both the content and the prevalence of various themes.

Next, commit to specific actions that address these themes. Each commitment should have a clear owner, a specific deliverable, a deadline, and a way to measure success. Instead of, "We'll work on making promotion criteria more transparent," say "By next Friday, I will share a written document outlining our current promotion criteria, and we'll schedule a follow-up session next month to review and revise these criteria as a group."

Finally, connect this conversation to your ongoing work and relationships. Schedule specific times for follow-up discussions. Establish how progress will be communicated between meetings. Create clear channels for people to raise concerns or share feedback as the work progresses. Most importantly, be explicit about how this conversation connects to future ones: "This is the first of several discussions we'll have about these issues. Next month, we'll focus specifically on revising our promotion criteria based on today's insights."

The energy of your conclusion matters enormously. You want to strike a balance between acknowledging the weight of what's been shared and creating momentum for change. Start with genuine appreciation for people's participation and vulnerability. Acknowledge that these conversations can be emotionally draining, especially for those who've shared personal experiences. Then move decisively to action, outlining the specific steps you're committing to take.

Following up effectively is crucial for maintaining trust and momentum. One manufacturing company I worked with created a simple but powerful practice: at the end of each conversation, everyone, including leadership, wrote down one specific action they would take in the next week and one they would take in the next month. These commitments weren't just filed away—they became the opening point for their next conversation, with each person reporting on their progress.

Regular, proactive communication about progress helps maintain engagement between conversations, but this requires thoughtful systems for tracking and sharing progress. Create a simple tracking document that everyone can access and understand. This isn't about bureaucracy—it's about transparency and accountability. The most effective tracking systems capture three key elements: the commitment itself, the impact it's meant to have, and the current status.

For financial commitments, like diversity-focused donations or program funding, track both the allocation and the impact. At Moody's, we developed a straightforward system: whenever funds were committed, we documented not just the amount but the expected community impact. We then checked in regularly with recipient organizations, tracking metrics like how many people were served, what programs were developed, and how funds were being used to address racial inequity. Most importantly, we shared these updates with employees who had helped select these initiatives, creating a direct line of sight between their input and real-world impact.

For internal commitments, like changes to hiring practices or mentorship programs, create what I call "impact chains." These are clear links between actions, outcomes, and organizational goals. Don't just track whether a new mentorship program launched, but monitor how many people are participating, whether it's reaching intended groups, and what participants say about their experience. Share these insights regularly, being transparent about both successes and areas needing adjustment.

The most effective tracking isn't done in isolation. We found success by incorporating progress updates into regular team meetings, adding a standing agenda item for discussing diversity commitments. This integration helps prevent these initiatives from being seen as separate from "real work" while ensuring regular accountability. When tracking reveals delays or challenges, address them openly: "We committed to revising our promotion criteria by March, but we've discovered we need more data about current promotion patterns. Here's our revised timeline, and here's how we're gathering that data."

Establish regular checkpoints that make sense for your organization's rhythm. Some commitments might need weekly monitoring, others monthly or quarterly reviews. The key is matching the tracking cadence to the nature of the commitment. Quick wins should be monitored closely to maintain momentum, while longer-term structural changes might need less frequent but more in-depth reviews.

Create feedback loops by actively soliciting input on both progress and tracking methods. Simple questions like "Are we measuring the right things?" and "Is this information helping you understand our progress?" help refine your tracking approach over time. This ongoing dialogue about how you're monitoring progress becomes part of the broader conversation about organizational change.

The most effective organizations find ways to embed these follow-up actions into their regular operations rather than treating them as separate initiatives. One leader I worked with kept a simple but powerful metric: for every hour spent in courageous conversations, how many concrete changes could she point to in the following quarter? This helped her team focus on turning dialogue into action while maintaining the human connection that made the conversations meaningful in the first place.

Remember that not every action needs to be a major institutional change. Sometimes the most powerful outcomes are the small but meaningful shifts in day-to-day interactions. One team leader shared how their group created a simple practice of starting each meeting by acknowledging someone who had helped create a more inclusive environment that week. This small ritual helped maintain momentum between larger initiatives while celebrating progress.

The key is ensuring that every conversation ends with clear next steps that honor the courage people showed in participating. When done right, the conclusion of one courageous conversation becomes the foundation for the next, creating a cycle of dialogue and action that drives real organizational change.

The Continuing Journey

As we approach the five-year mark since George Floyd's murder, some might question whether these conversations are still relevant. Haven't we moved on? Haven't organizations already made their statements, pledged their support, launched their initiatives? In a world facing new crises daily, why keep returning to these difficult dialogues?

The answer lies in understanding what made the conversations following Floyd's murder different from previous diversity discussions. For the first time in many organizations, these weren't optional conversations happening on the margins—they were central discussions involving entire workforces. They weren't just about representation statistics or unconscious bias training—they addressed fundamental questions about power, equity, and belonging in our workplaces. Most importantly, they weren't just conversations about diversity—they were conversations about how organizations live their stated values.

These conversations remain vital today precisely because they're not really about George Floyd—they're about the ongoing work of building truly inclusive organizations where every employee can thrive. The skills we've explored in this chapter—creating brave spaces, expanding dialogue through widening circles, addressing challenges constructively, and turning conversation into action—are more relevant than ever in today's workplace.

Consider how our organizational contexts have evolved since 2020. Remote and hybrid work has created new challenges around inclusion and belonging. Economic pressures have made conversations about equity and opportunity more urgent. Some organizations have retreated from their initial commitments, while others have deepened their engagement with these issues. Through it all, one truth remains constant: organizations that can have honest, productive conversations about difficult issues are better positioned to navigate change and build sustainable success.

The backlash against corporate diversity initiatives that we explored in the previous chapter makes these conversation skills even more crucial. When external pressures mount, the ability to maintain authentic dialogue about challenging issues becomes a key differentiator between organizations that can sustain their commitment to inclusion and those that retreat to superficial compliance.

What's different now isn't the need for these conversations but our understanding of how to have them effectively. We've learned that psychological safety isn't about avoiding discomfort but about creating spaces where discomfort can lead to growth. We've discovered that leadership in these moments isn't about having all the answers but about facilitating authentic dialogue. Most importantly, we've seen that real change happens not through grand statements but through sustained, structured conversations that lead to concrete actions.

The organizations that have seen lasting impact from these conversations share a common understanding: this isn't a finite project with a completion date but an ongoing journey of organizational development. They've integrated these dialogue skills into their regular operations, using them not just for discussions about diversity and inclusion but for addressing any challenging issue that requires collective engagement and action.

As we turn to examine how George Floyd's murder sparked global conversations about racial equity in organizations worldwide, remember that the skills and frameworks we've explored here aren't just tools for discussing race—they're essential capabilities for leading modern organizations through complex change. The ability to create space for difficult conversations, to engage authentically with challenging issues, and to turn dialogue into action isn't just about diversity and inclusion—it's about building organizations capable of adapting and thriving in an increasingly complex world.

The question isn't whether these conversations are still relevant—it's whether our organizations have built the muscles necessary to have them effectively. Those that have will find themselves better equipped not just to address issues of equity and inclusion, but to navigate any challenge that requires bringing diverse perspectives together in service of positive change.

8

From Commitment to Action—A Practical Guide

Throughout my career working with organizations across sectors and scales, one question comes up more than any other: "We've made commitments to diversity and inclusion—now what?" It's a question that reflects where many organizations find themselves today. They've issued statements, set goals, perhaps even created new positions or departments. But translating these commitments into meaningful change? That's where the real work begins.

The murder of George Floyd catalyzed unprecedented commitments to diversity, equity, and inclusion across corporate America. Nothing illustrates this watershed moment more clearly than the response from the Business Roundtable, America's preeminent association of chief executive officers. The Business Roundtable represents over 200 CEOs of America's leading companies, collectively supporting one in four American jobs and almost a quarter of US GDP. When these leaders speak collectively, markets listen.

On May 30, 2020, just days after George Floyd's murder, the Business Roundtable released an unprecedented statement:

We share the anger and pain felt by so many Americans at the recent killings of unarmed black men and women. Racism and brutality have no place in America.

We grieve for the families, friends and communities of George Floyd, Ahmaud Arbery and countless others. These tragedies reflect long-standing racial injustice in our country.

As the employers of more than 15 million individuals of all backgrounds, whose diversity strengthens our institutions, Business Roundtable CEOs are deeply concerned about the racial bias that continues to plague our society. At a time of great uncertainty, when communities of color are facing deep inequities, now is a time for unity and justice. We call on national, local and civic leaders to take urgent, thoughtful action to prevent future tragedies and to help our communities heal.

The significance of this statement cannot be overstated. This wasn't just another corporate press release—it was America's most powerful business leaders collectively acknowledging systemic racism and calling for change. By directly addressing racial injustice rather than speaking in vague terms about diversity, the Business Roundtable opened the floodgates for corporate America to take meaningful action. This catalyzed a wave of companies establishing comprehensive DEI strategies, creating chief diversity officer positions, and making concrete commitments to change.

Yet statements and commitments, however powerful, are just the beginning. Through decades of implementing successful diversity initiatives, I've observed that meaningful change doesn't come through isolated programs or symbolic gestures. The organizations that achieve lasting transformation are those that embed inclusive principles into every aspect of their operations. Whether you're a CEO steering a global corporation, a middle manager building team culture, an employee seeking to make a difference, or a customer choosing where to spend your dollars, everyone in the corporate ecosystem has a role to play in this transformation.

This chapter provides practical frameworks and actionable strategies for moving forward, regardless of your position or starting point. We'll explore tools for assessment, planning, and execution that are proven to help any organization progress from surface-level compliance to genuine transformation. Most importantly, we'll examine how to make these changes sustainable—not by treating diversity as a separate program, but by making it inseparable from business success itself.

I've seen firsthand how organizations struggle when they treat diversity initiatives as isolated programs rather than integral parts of their operations. A diversity office disconnected from core business units, inclusion initiatives that operate parallel to rather than within regular processes, metrics treated as separate from business performance indicators—these approaches might seem easier to implement and measure, but they ultimately limit both impact and sustainability.

The path forward requires both clarity about where we stand and vision about where we're going. Let's begin by understanding how to assess your current position and chart a course toward meaningful change. The frameworks and strategies I'll share come not from theoretical models but from real-world experience implementing these changes across organizations of all sizes and sectors. They represent lessons learned both from successes and from initiatives that fell short of their goals.

What you'll find in this chapter isn't just another set of diversity best practices. Instead, I'll provide specific tools and frameworks that have proven effective in creating lasting organizational change. We'll examine how to assess your current state accurately, build comprehensive strategies across multiple dimensions, and integrate inclusive practices into every aspect of operations. Most importantly, we'll focus on making these changes sustainable by connecting them directly to business success.

The stakes couldn't be higher. In today's global marketplace, organizations that can't effectively engage diverse talent and serve diverse markets will find themselves at a competitive disadvantage. But those that get this right—that truly embed inclusive practices into their operations—will find themselves better positioned for success in an increasingly complex and diverse world.

Let's begin this journey by understanding exactly where your organization stands and how to chart a course forward.

The DEI Maturity Model

Before rushing to implement new initiatives or replicate what other organizations are doing, it's crucial to understand exactly where your organization stands in its diversity journey. I've observed that institutional transformation follows a predictable pattern, moving through five distinct stages of maturity. Understanding these stages isn't just theoretical—they can help determine what actions will create meaningful change in your specific context.

At the first stage, organizations operate in an "unaware" state, with minimal consciousness of diversity issues. These companies often pride themselves on being "color-blind" while unknowingly perpetuating systemic barriers. They might point to basic nondiscrimination policies as evidence of fairness while failing to recognize how their practices exclude talented individuals and limit their market reach. In these organizations, discussions about diversity are often met with responses like "we just hire the best people" or "we don't see color"— statements that reveal a fundamental misunderstanding of how bias operates in systems and processes.

The "compliant" stage represents a step forward, but only a small one. Here, organizations do the minimum required to meet legal and regulatory requirements. They track basic demographic data and maintain antidiscrimination policies, but primarily to avoid liability. A company at this stage might proudly report that they've conducted their annual harassment training or updated their EEO statements, without examining whether these efforts create meaningful change. Before George Floyd's murder, most companies remained at this level, satisfied with checking boxes rather than pursuing genuine transformation.

Organizations reach the "strategic" stage when they develop intentional approaches to diversity and inclusion. This isn't just about having a plan—it's about having clear key performance indicators (KPIs) and embedding diversity goals into business objectives. At this level, you'll see companies establishing relationships with HBCUs and Latinx-serving institutions, implementing supplier diversity programs, or creating dedicated pathways for developing underrepresented talent. They're tracking metrics and setting goals, though these efforts often still operate somewhat separately from core business functions. Many companies reached this level in response to 2020's racial justice movement, implementing formal programs and making public commitments.

The shift from strategic to "integrated" marks a transformation. At this advanced stage, diversity and inclusion principles are woven into core business operations. This is where the majority of companies that engage a DEI methodology aspire to be. Rather than treating DEI as a separate function, these organizations embed inclusive practices into everything from product development to customer service. An integrated company doesn't need special initiatives to consider diverse perspectives in product design or ensure fair promotion practices—these considerations are built into their standard operating procedures. Success metrics shift from pure representation to measuring genuine inclusion and business impact.

The highest stage of maturity is "disruptive." This occurs when organizations leverage diversity and inclusion to create competitive advantages and transform their industries. These companies don't just adapt to changing demographics—they pioneer new approaches that make inclusion inseparable from innovation and growth. A disruptive organization might revolutionize their industry's hiring practices, develop groundbreaking products for previously ignored markets, or create new business models that naturally foster inclusion. Their success comes not despite their commitment to diversity but because of it.

When I work with organizations, I often find them overestimating their maturity level. A company might point to their employee resource groups or diversity training programs as evidence of integration, while their core business practices remain unchanged. The key distinction lies not in specific programs or initiatives, but in how deeply diversity considerations penetrate business operations.

Consider hiring practices as an example: a compliant organization maintains basic nondiscrimination policies, a strategic one sets diversity hiring goals, an integrated one reimagines their entire talent acquisition approach, and a disruptive one pioneers new ways of identifying and developing talent that their competitors eventually try to emulate.

Let me be clear: this progression isn't just theoretical. I see it play out repeatedly in my work. Before assessing where an organization stands, I conduct a thorough DEI audit examining everything from policies and procedures to demographics, from pay practices to promotion patterns. This comprehensive review often reveals that organizations aren't as advanced as they believe. A company might think they're "strategic" because they have a diversity officer and some programs in place, but if their core operations haven't changed, they're still essentially operating at a compliant level.

The current backlash against DEI has many organizations feeling pressure to retreat to mere compliance or even unawareness. But this framework shows why that's both practically impossible and strategically unwise. In today's global marketplace, organizations that can't effectively engage diverse talent and serve diverse markets will find themselves at a competitive disadvantage. The question isn't whether to advance through these stages, but how to do so most effectively.

Your True Position

How do you determine where your organization really stands in this progression? The key lies in comprehensive assessment across multiple dimensions. When I conduct organizational assessments, I examine several critical areas that reveal an organization's true maturity level, regardless of their stated commitments or public image.

Start with talent systems. Examine your entire talent life cycle. Where do you source candidates? What does your interview process look like? Do you have diverse interview panels? How are promotion decisions made? Look at your job descriptions. Are they written with inclusive language that focuses on competencies rather than potentially biased criteria? A common pitfall I see is organizations claiming advanced maturity while maintaining recruitment practices that inherently limit their talent pool, like requiring degrees from specific institutions when equivalent experience would serve just as well.

Next, analyze your demographic data, but go beyond simple headcount. Examine representation at different levels, pay equity across groups, promotion velocities, and turnover patterns. Pay particular attention to what I call "velocity metrics," or the rates at which different groups advance through your organization. Where do you see dropoffs in representation? I often find organizations proudly pointing to overall diversity numbers while missing concerning patterns in retention or advancement.

Examine your communication infrastructure. How do you share information? Are your channels accessible to all employees? For global organizations, do you provide materials in relevant languages? Look at your cultural celebrations and acknowledgments. Are they truly inclusive or merely performative? A telling indicator is whether your communications about diversity issues come solely from HR or diversity teams, or whether they're integrated into regular business communications.

Review your feedback mechanisms. Do you conduct regular engagement surveys? How do you track and respond to concerns about bias or unfair treatment? What's your process for handling complaints? The maturity of these systems often reveals an organization's true level of commitment. I frequently find companies claiming strategic status while lacking basic mechanisms for understanding employee experiences.

Look carefully at legal and compliance patterns. Are you seeing recurring issues or complaints around certain policies or practices? What's your track record with discrimination claims? While no organization is immune to issues, patterns in these areas often reveal systemic problems that need addressing.

Assess your market engagement. How do you understand and serve diverse customer segments? Are diverse perspectives included in product development and marketing decisions? Do you track market penetration across different communities? Many organizations claim advanced maturity while missing significant market opportunities due to limited cultural understanding.

Finally, examine your resource allocation. How do you fund diversity initiatives? Are they treated as separate programs or integrated into business unit budgets? Do you invest in developing diverse suppliers? Are resources allocated to making your workplace accessible and inclusive? Follow the money, it often tells the true story of organizational priorities.

This assessment process often reveals uncomfortable truths. Organizations that consider themselves strategic because they have diversity programs in place may discover they're still operating at a primarily compliant level. Companies proud of their public commitments might find their internal practices haven't caught up to their external messaging.

Remember, this examination isn't about judgment but about establishing a clear starting point for progress. Every organization began at the unaware stage. What matters is committing to advancement.

Understanding where you truly stand allows you to focus resources and efforts where they'll have the most impact.

Before we move on to implementation strategies, take time to honestly assess your organization across these dimensions. Are your diversity efforts truly integrated into operations, or do they exist as separate programs? Are inclusive practices built into your standard procedures, or are they add-ons? Most importantly, is your organization leveraging diversity as a competitive advantage, or merely trying to avoid problems? Understanding your true starting point is essential for charting an effective path forward.

The Four C's Framework: Building Your Implementation Strategy

Early in my career, I consulted with a global technology company that thought they had diversity figured out. They had all the programs conventional wisdom called for—employee resource groups, mentorship initiatives, diversity training, the works. Their CEO spoke passionately about inclusion in town halls. Their HR team diligently tracked representation metrics. Yet they were struggling with retention of diverse talent and facing recurring issues with product launches in international markets. When we dug deeper, we discovered their approach was fragmented: HR ran diversity programs disconnected from product development, while marketing struggled to understand diverse customers, and community engagement existed mainly as charitable giving.

This company's experience illuminated something I've seen repeatedly: the most common reason diversity initiatives fail isn't resistance or lack of commitment—it's fragmentation. Organizations implement various programs without understanding how they need to work together. I've found that sustainable change requires attention to four key dimensions: Culture, Commerce, Career, and Community. These aren't separate workstreams—they're interconnected elements that together determine whether diversity efforts succeed or fail.

The technology company's transformation illustrates why all four dimensions matter. They began by examining their culture, discovering that their "move fast and break things" mentality often marginalized voices that raised concerns about product impacts on different communities. Their desire for rapid decision-making had created an environment where thoughtful consideration of diverse perspectives was seen as an impediment rather than an asset.

This cultural insight led them to revamp their product development process. Instead of treating diversity as a compliance check at the end of development, they began including diverse perspectives from the start. Teams were restructured to ensure varied viewpoints were present in initial planning discussions. The result wasn't just better representation—it was better products. Features that might have caused problems in certain markets were identified and addressed early, saving millions in potential revisions and reputation damage.

As their products better served diverse communities, they attracted more diverse talent. As that talent advanced within the organization, they brought deeper market insights, which drove further business success. Within three years, they weren't just meeting diversity goals—they were outperforming competitors in key markets because of their more inclusive approach. Their story demonstrates why examining each dimension of the Four C's framework is essential for creating lasting change.

Let's explore each dimension in detail.

Culture: Building the Foundation

In 2019, a major advertising agency faced a crisis that perfectly illustrates why culture must be the foundation of any diversity effort. Despite having multiple review stages and a stated commitment to inclusion, they released a campaign containing imagery that many communities found deeply offensive. The incident cost them millions in pulled advertising and damaged vital client relationships. When we investigated how this could happen, we found a homogeneous creative team and a culture where junior staff—often more diverse—felt unable to raise concerns.

Their necessary transformation went far beyond the usual prescription of diversity training. They had to fundamentally restructure how teams worked together. They implemented new processes ensuring diverse perspectives at every stage of creative development, but more importantly, they had to transform their culture from one where diversity was seen as a constraint on creativity to one where diverse perspectives drive innovation.

Culture isn't just about hosting heritage month celebrations or diversity training sessions—though these have their place. It's about creating an environment where everyone can contribute fully and authentically. When I work with organizations, I look at how they run meetings, who gets heard, and what behaviors get rewarded. I examine their communication platforms, asking whether they're truly accessible to all employees. For global organizations, this means ensuring materials are available in relevant languages. For example, if you're using collaboration tools like Slack, are you creating inclusive communities where everyone can participate in discussions, or are your channels inadvertently segregated?

Cultural celebrations and acknowledgments require particularly thoughtful implementation. It's not just about sending a "Happy Holidays" email—though using inclusive language matters. It's about creating genuine opportunities for learning and connection while ensuring these celebrations are open to everyone, not just members of specific communities. The most successful organizations I've worked with transform these moments from token observances into meaningful opportunities for cross-cultural understanding and business insight.

Most importantly, culture is about fostering an environment where employees can bring their authentic selves to work. This means maintaining forums for open dialogue about social issues affecting your workforce, while being thoughtful about when and how your organization takes positions on controversial topics. The key is acknowledgment and awareness, providing space for employee voices while maintaining appropriate professional boundaries.

Commerce: Connecting Inclusion to Business Success

A regional bank I worked with learned a costly lesson about the commerce dimension of diversity. Despite having competitive products and pricing, they were struggling to grow in several urban markets. Their marketing team had invested heavily in local advertising, opened convenient branches, and trained staff in cultural sensitivity. Yet they weren't seeing the market penetration they expected. When we investigated, we discovered their "standard" lending criteria, while seemingly objective, effectively excluded many qualified borrowers from different cultural backgrounds who structured their finances differently. They were leaving millions in potential revenue on the table simply because they hadn't questioned their traditional approach to evaluating creditworthiness.

Their path forward required more than just tweaking their marketing messages. By bringing diverse perspectives into their product development process and engaging community leaders, they discovered that many potential customers were successfully managing money and building wealth, just not in ways their traditional metrics captured. They developed new ways to assess creditworthiness that better served diverse communities while maintaining strong loan performance. The result wasn't just better diversity metrics—it was better business. Within two years, they doubled their market share in previously underserved areas and discovered their new approaches worked better for all customers.

Commerce isn't just about marketing to diverse communities or creating separate product lines. It's about fundamentally understanding and serving your entire potential market. When I evaluate an organization's commerce dimension, I look at how they develop products, who's involved in key decisions, and whether they truly understand their diverse markets. Are diverse perspectives included from the earliest stages of product development, or only brought in for final review? Do your marketing messages resonate authentically across different communities, or do they rely on superficial representation?

Your supplier relationships provide another opportunity for building inclusive business practices. This isn't about just tracking diverse spending percentages—it's about developing genuine business partnerships that strengthen your entire supply chain. The most successful organizations create mentorship programs, provide development opportunities, and ensure their procurement practices don't inadvertently exclude qualified diverse businesses. These efforts don't just tick boxes—they open new sources of innovation and market insight.

Career: Creating Pathways for Development

A professional services firm I advised faced a problem that illustrates the career dimension of diversity. Despite successfully recruiting diverse entry-level talent and maintaining strong representation numbers, they couldn't understand why they struggled to retain these employees beyond middle management. Their HR team had implemented mentorship programs, created employee resource groups, and offered leadership training. Yet their diverse talent kept leaving just as they reached the cusp of senior leadership. When we investigated, we discovered their promotion criteria, while seemingly objective, favored those who matched existing leadership's communication and working styles. High-potential diverse talent often hit an invisible wall, unable to translate their proven capabilities into advancement.

Their transformation required reimagining how they evaluated and developed talent. Instead of relying on subjective assessments of "leadership presence" or "executive potential," they created clear, competency-based advancement criteria. They restructured their assignment system to ensure equitable access to career-building opportunities. Most importantly, they shifted from a mindset of "helping diverse talent adapt" to one of recognizing and valuing different leadership styles. Within two years, their promotion rates equalized across demographic groups, and retention of diverse talent increased dramatically.

Career development isn't just about hiring metrics or representation goals, though these matter. It's about creating an environment where everyone can realize their full potential. When I examine an organization's career dimension, I look at their entire talent life cycle. How are opportunities communicated? Who gets access to high-visibility projects? Are promotion criteria truly measuring capabilities, or are they unconsciously filtering for cultural fit? The most successful organizations ensure transparency in advancement paths while actively removing systemic barriers to progress.

Your performance assessment systems play a role in career development. This goes beyond annual reviews to examine how potential is identified and developed. Do your evaluation processes account for different working and communication styles? Are managers equipped to provide effective feedback across cultural differences? The organizations that excel at career development create systems that recognize and nurture talent in all its forms, not just those that match traditional models.

Most importantly, career development is about creating genuine paths to advancement, not just entry-level opportunities. This means examining every aspect of how talent is identified, developed, and promoted. Are your high-potential programs truly accessible to all? Do people see others like themselves succeeding in leadership roles? The organizations that truly transform their career dimension understand that diverse leadership isn't just about representation—it's about leveraging all available talent to drive organizational success.

Community: Extending Your Impact

A large logistics company I worked with discovered the hard way because community engagement can't be an afterthought. When they announced plans to expand their facility in a diverse urban area, they expected praise for bringing new jobs and economic development. Instead, they faced intense community opposition. Despite their corporate foundation's generous local donations and their employees' volunteer programs, residents didn't trust them. When we investigated, we found their traditional approach to community relations—focused on charitable giving and occasional volunteer events—had failed to build genuine understanding or trust with local communities. They had never meaningfully engaged with residents about their concerns over environmental impact, job accessibility, or economic opportunity.

Their transformation required completely reimagining their approach to community engagement. They created a community advisory board with real influence over local operations and environmental practices. They partnered with local schools and community colleges to develop training programs that created genuine pathways to employment. Most importantly, they shifted from seeing community relations as a public relations exercise to understanding it as a part of their business strategy. Within a year, they had not only gained community support for their expansion but built a robust local talent pipeline and strengthened their business operations through community insights.

Community engagement isn't just about charitable giving or volunteer programs, though these have their place. It's about recognizing that organizations don't exist in isolation from the communities where they operate. When I assess an organization's community dimension, I look at how deeply they understand their impact on local communities. Are they creating genuine economic opportunity? Do they understand and address community concerns? Are they building lasting partnerships that strengthen both the community and their business?

Your environmental and social impact requires particular attention in the community dimension. This means looking beyond compliance to understand how your operations affect different communities. Are impacts and benefits distributed equitably? Are you addressing historical disparities? The most successful organizations recognize that environmental and social responsibility isn't just about risk management—it's about creating sustainable value for all stakeholders.

Most importantly, community engagement is about building genuine, reciprocal relationships with the communities that support your business. This means moving beyond transactional interactions to create lasting partnerships. Are you investing in ways that build community capacity? Do you have mechanisms for hearing and responding to community voices? The organizations that excel at community engagement understand that strong communities and strong businesses support each other—you can't have one without the other.

Taking the Four C's from Theory to Practice

Understanding the framework is one thing—implementing it is another entirely. I've seen many organizations grasp the concepts intellectually but struggle with practical application. "We get it," a CEO once told me, "but where do we start?" It's a fair question. When you're facing the day-to-day reality of running a business, broad frameworks need to translate into concrete actions.

The challenge isn't just knowing what to do—it's knowing how to do it in your specific context. A global corporation's approach to talent acquisition will necessarily look different from a regional business's strategy. A tech startup's communication infrastructure will differ from a manufacturing plant's needs. Yet across industries and scales, I've found certain implementation areas consistently demand attention for successful transformation.

In the following sections, we'll dive deep into four critical implementation areas: reimagining talent practices, evolving employee resource groups, building communication infrastructure, and implementing meaningful metrics. These aren't the only areas that matter, but they represent leverage points where focused effort tends to yield outsized results.

Think of these as your primary tools for activating the Four C's framework. Each implementation area cuts across multiple dimensions of the framework. For example, how you reimagine talent practices affects not just careers but also culture and community. How you evolve your employee resource groups influences everything from commerce to culture.

Most importantly, these areas represent where theory meets reality—where abstract commitments transform into tangible change. Let's examine each in detail, focusing on practical strategies that work in real organizational contexts.

Moving from Framework to Action: Implementation Deep Dives

"This all sounds great in theory, but what does it look like in practice?"

I hear this question in almost every conversation about organizational transformation. It gets to the heart of why many diversity initiatives fail to create lasting change. Organizations often understand the need for transformation and even grasp the key principles, but struggle with the nuts and bolts of implementation.

I experienced this firsthand working with a Fortune 500 company that had made bold public commitments after 2020. They had the frameworks down. Their executive team could articulate the business case. They'd created impressive presentations about their commitment to change. But a year later, they were struggling to translate those commitments into tangible progress. Their diversity numbers hadn't moved. Employee engagement surveys showed skepticism about the company's commitment. Middle managers felt overwhelmed and uncertain about their role in the transformation.

Their experience isn't unique. In fact, it reveals a common pattern: the gap between understanding and implementation is where most organizational transformations falter. It's not enough to know what needs to change—you need concrete strategies for how to change it.

This section moves beyond frameworks to examine specific implementation strategies that work in real organizational contexts. We'll explore four critical areas where focused effort tends to yield the greatest impact: how you identify and develop talent, how you structure and leverage employee resource groups, how you build effective communication systems, and how you measure and drive progress.

Each area represents a leverage point where specific changes in practices and processes can create ripple effects throughout your organization. Most importantly, they're areas where organizations consistently struggle without clear guidance but achieve breakthrough results with the right approach.

Let's examine each area in detail, focusing on concrete strategies you can adapt to your specific context.

Reimagining Talent Practices

A law firm I advised prided itself on having "uncompromising standards." For decades, they had required candidates to be in the top 5 percent of their graduating class from one of the five most prestigious law schools. Their recruiting practices seemed objective and merit-based. Yet despite genuine efforts to increase diversity, they struggled to build a representative workforce. When we examined their approach, we discovered their supposedly objective criteria were limiting their access to exceptional talent. They were missing out on highly qualified candidates who had demonstrated their capabilities through different paths—candidates who often brought valuable perspectives and skills their traditional recruiting missed entirely.

Their transformation began with questioning basic assumptions about what predicts success. Instead of lowering standards, as some partners initially feared, they expanded their understanding of excellence. They began looking at candidates' full range of experiences and achievements, not just academic credentials. They broadened their recruitment beyond traditional feeder schools to include institutions with strong programs but different traditions. Most importantly, they developed new ways to assess the skills and qualities that determined success in their practice.

The results challenged everything they thought they knew about talent. Their new associates were just as capable as previous classes but brought broader perspectives and stronger client connection skills. Within three years, both their diversity metrics and their client satisfaction scores had improved significantly. They hadn't compromised their standards—they'd enhanced their ability to recognize excellence in all its forms.

Traditional approaches to talent management often create unintended barriers to diversity and inclusion. Standard job descriptions might use language that unconsciously signals bias. Traditional interview processes can favor candidates who match existing cultural norms rather than those who could best do the job. Even well-intentioned development programs can perpetuate disparities if they're not thoughtfully designed.

Reimagining talent practices requires examining your entire talent life cycle. Where do you source candidates? How do you evaluate potential? What determines who advances? Most importantly, are your processes measuring what matters for success in the role, or are they unconsciously filtering for familiar patterns?

Job descriptions provide a starting point. Beyond removing obviously biased language, examine what you're really requiring. Are degree requirements necessary, or could equivalent experience serve? Are you listing nice-to-have qualities as must-haves? The most effective organizations focus on core competencies rather than arbitrary credentials.

Interview processes deserve particular attention. Diverse interview panels help, but only if they have real input into decisions. Structured interviews with clear evaluation criteria reduce the impact of individual bias. Most importantly, ensuring interviewers understand how to recognize different ways candidates might demonstrate capabilities opens doors to talent that might otherwise be overlooked.

Development and promotion practices often harbor hidden barriers. Are high-visibility assignments distributed equitably? Do your definitions of leadership potential unconsciously favor certain styles over others? The most successful organizations create transparent advancement criteria while ensuring everyone has access to the experiences needed to progress.

Pay particular attention to how potential is identified and developed. Many organizations miss promising talent simply because it doesn't match traditional models of success. Creating multiple paths for advancement and recognizing different ways of demonstrating capability help ensure you're leveraging all available talent.

Most importantly, remember that reimagining talent practices isn't about lowering standards—it's about raising your ability to recognize and develop excellence in all its forms. Organizations that get this right don't just improve their diversity metrics. They enhance their overall talent capabilities, accessing deeper pools of capability that their previous approaches missed.

The key is maintaining rigor while removing artificial barriers. Clear competency requirements, structured evaluation processes, and transparent development paths increase standards by ensuring decisions are based on capabilities rather than comfort. When organizations truly reimagine their talent practices, they don't just become more diverse—they become more effective at identifying and developing the talent they need to succeed.

Evolving Employee Resource Groups

A retail chain I worked with had all the standard employee resource groups: women's network, Black employees' network, LGBTQ+ alliance, veterans' group, and others. They held cultural celebrations, organized volunteer events, and provided social support for their members. Yet when we examined their impact, we found these groups operating almost entirely separate from the business. Despite having direct access to market insights and talent networks, they were seen primarily as social clubs. Their activities, while meaningful for members, weren't influencing key business decisions or driving organizational change.

Their transformation began with reimagining what these groups could be. Instead of just planning events, each group partnered with specific business units to provide market insights and innovation ideas. Their Asian Employee Network helped identify opportunities in emerging markets. Their Parents Network provided feedback on product development. Their Veterans Network strengthened community partnerships and recruitment efforts. Most importantly, they shifted from being closed affinity groups to becoming business resource groups open to all employees interested in their mission.

The results demonstrated why employee resource groups need to evolve beyond their traditional role. The groups' market insights led to successful product launches. Their talent networks helped attract diverse candidates. Their cross-cultural programming improved collaboration across the organization. They had transformed from support networks into strategic assets.

Traditional approaches to employee resource groups often limit their potential impact. Many organizations still treat them primarily as cultural celebration committees or support groups. While these functions matter, they represent just a fraction of what these groups can contribute. The most successful organizations recognize these groups as business resources, providing market insights, developing talent, and driving innovation.

Strategic alignment proves essential for this evolution. Each group needs clear connections to business objectives, with concrete ways to contribute to organizational success. This isn't about burdening employee volunteers with business responsibilities—it's about creating meaningful opportunities for impact while developing leadership capabilities.

Resource allocation plays a role in this transformation. Token budgets and volunteer leadership signal that groups aren't taken seriously. The most effective organizations provide dedicated staff support, meaningful operating budgets, and executive sponsorship. They treat these groups as strategic investments rather than employee clubs.

Leadership development through these groups deserves particular attention. Leading a business resource group provides valuable experience managing cross-functional projects, influencing without authority, and driving organizational change. The most successful organizations create structured opportunities for group leaders to present to executive committees, manage substantial budgets, and lead strategic initiatives.

Cross-functional participation proves essential for maximum impact. While maintaining authenticity requires having community members in leadership roles, including allies and advocates broadens impact and accelerates change. The key is balancing inclusion with representation—ensuring groups remain authentic voices for their communities while engaging broader organizational support.

Most importantly, evolving these groups means treating them as genuine business partners rather than symbolic initiatives. This requires clear accountability in both directions—groups commit to delivering business value while the organization commits to providing necessary support and acting on their insights.

The organizations that get this right don't just improve their diversity metrics. They create powerful engines for innovation, talent development, and market insight. Their employee resource groups become key drivers of business success, demonstrating why inclusion isn't just about doing good—it's about doing better business.

Building Effective Communication Infrastructure

Good intentions aren't enough when it comes to communication. A global technology company I advised had invested heavily in collaboration tools, maintained an active internal social media presence, and regularly shared leadership updates. Yet their employee engagement surveys revealed deep disconnects. Remote workers felt out of the loop. Employees in different regions received inconsistent messages. Their heavy reliance on text-based platforms created barriers for employees with disabilities. Most concerningly, many employees felt unsafe raising concerns about inclusion issues.

Their transformation required fundamentally rethinking how information flowed through the organization. They created a multilayered communication structure that included regular town halls where employees could raise concerns directly with leadership, anonymous feedback channels for sensitive issues, and digital platforms accessible to employees across shifts and locations. Most importantly, they established clear protocols for addressing concerns, ensuring every issue raised received appropriate follow-up.

The results showed why communication infrastructure is crucial for genuine inclusion. Employee engagement scores improved significantly. Issues that might have previously festered were identified and addressed early. Most importantly, they built trust by demonstrating that raising concerns led to actual change.

Traditional approaches to organizational communication often create unintended barriers to inclusion. All-hands meetings scheduled at times that work for headquarters might exclude global teams. Digital platforms that work well for office staff might be impractical for frontline workers. Even well-intentioned diversity communications can backfire if they're not thoughtfully implemented.

Effective communication infrastructure requires systematic attention to both information sharing and feedback gathering. How do different employees receive important information? What channels exist for raising concerns? Most importantly, how do you ensure communication flows in all directions, not just top-down?

Engagement surveys serve as a tool when properly designed and implemented. Rather than annual check-ins, successful organizations implement regular pulse surveys that track specific aspects of inclusion. Do employees feel heard in meetings? Can they bring their authentic selves to work? Do they have access to development opportunities? And do they trust that their feedback will lead to action?

Crisis communication demands particular attention in diverse organizations. Whether responding to social issues affecting your workforce or addressing internal challenges, organizations need clear protocols for acknowledging concerns while maintaining appropriate professional boundaries. The key is creating structured opportunities for dialogue while ensuring consistent messaging.

Cultural celebrations and acknowledgments require thoughtful communication strategies. It's not just about sending the right messages—it's about creating genuine opportunities for learning and connection. The most successful organizations transform these moments from token observances into meaningful opportunities for cross-cultural understanding.

Digital platforms require careful consideration of accessibility and inclusion. Are your communication tools accessible to employees with disabilities? Do they work effectively across different languages and cultural contexts? Most importantly, do they create inclusive communities or inadvertently reinforce silos?

Regular leadership communication plays a vital role in sustaining inclusion efforts. The most effective organizations establish consistent cadence for sharing progress on diversity initiatives, acknowledging challenges, and highlighting successes. These aren't just top-down broadcasts—they include structured opportunities for dialogue and feedback.

Most importantly, communication infrastructure must support genuine dialogue rather than just information dissemination. This means creating multiple channels while maintaining consistent messaging, ensuring every voice can be heard while providing clear paths for action on feedback received.

Implementing Meaningful Metrics

A financial services firm I worked with tracked representation percentages religiously, celebrated improvements in their hiring statistics, and proudly reported their progress in annual diversity reports. Yet despite improving numbers at entry levels, they weren't seeing lasting change. Diverse talent wasn't advancing. Market penetration in diverse communities remained flat. Employee engagement scores showed persistent gaps. Their metrics were measuring activity, but not impact.

Their transformation began with reimagining what success looked like. Instead of just tracking headcount, they developed a comprehensive measurement framework that included pay equity analysis controlling for relevant factors, promotion velocity comparisons across demographic groups, and engagement scores broken down by team and identity. They connected diversity metrics to business outcomes— market share in diverse communities, innovation metrics, client satisfaction across different groups.

The results revealed why meaningful measurement matters. They discovered that while their hiring was diverse, their promotion practices favored certain backgrounds. Their market share data revealed untapped opportunities in communities they thought they were serving well. Their new metrics helped them identify and address systemic barriers they hadn't previously recognized.

Traditional approaches to diversity metrics often focus on what's easy to measure rather than what matters. Simple representation numbers, while important, don't tell you whether people feel included, have opportunities to advance, or can contribute their best work. Without meaningful metrics, organizations risk celebrating superficial progress while missing deeper problems.

Effective measurement requires examining multiple dimensions of inclusion. Beyond basic demographic data, how quickly do different groups advance? Where do you see drop-offs in representation? And importantly, how do inclusion metrics connect to business performance? The most successful organizations create dashboards that show both leading and lagging indicators of change.

Promotion and development metrics require particular attention. It's not enough to know how many diverse candidates you hire—you need to understand their experience once they're in the organization. Are they getting access to career-critical assignments? Are they advancing at similar rates? Do they have access to influential networks and mentors? These patterns often reveal systemic barriers that pure representation numbers miss.

Market impact metrics provide another measurement area. How well do you serve diverse markets? Are your products and services meeting different community needs? Are you capturing the business opportunity that diversity presents? Organizations that excel at measurement connect inclusion metrics directly to market performance.

Employee experience metrics deserve systematic attention too. Regular pulse surveys can track whether people feel heard in meetings, have access to opportunities, and can bring their authentic selves to work. The key is measuring not just sentiment but also concrete indicators of inclusion—who gets heard in meetings, who receives challenging assignments, and whose ideas get implemented.

Supplier diversity measurement goes beyond spend goals to examine real impact. Are you building lasting partnerships with diverse suppliers? Are these relationships driving innovation and market insight? Are you creating sustainable economic impact in the communities you serve?

Transparency plays a vital role in effective measurement as well. While some organizations keep diversity data closely guarded, the most successful ones share metrics openly with employees. This transparency builds trust while creating shared accountability for improvement. When everyone can see the metrics, everyone becomes invested in moving them.

Most importantly, metrics must drive action, not just reporting. When measurement reveals problems, organizations need clear processes for developing and implementing solutions. The most effective organizations create regular review cycles where metrics inform strategy adjustment and resource allocation.

The organizations that get this right don't just track numbers—they create measurement systems that drive genuine transformation. Their metrics become powerful tools for identifying opportunities, removing barriers, and accelerating progress toward true inclusion.

Making It All Work

As we've explored these implementation areas, a truth emerges: successful transformation isn't about executing isolated initiatives—it's about creating reinforcing cycles of change. Each area we've examined connects to and strengthens the others. When you reimagine talent practices, you create new opportunities for employee resource groups to drive value. As communication infrastructure improves, your metrics become more meaningful and actionable. When metrics reveal opportunities, your talent practices evolve to capture them.

This interconnection reflects why the Four C's framework remains so powerful. Your talent practices shape both Culture and Career dimensions. Employee resource groups influence Commerce and Community. Communication infrastructure strengthens Culture while supporting all other dimensions. Metrics help you understand and improve performance across every dimension.

Transformation is like renovating a house while living in it. You can't stop daily operations while you implement changes, but you also can't keep operating exactly as before. The key is making strategic improvements that create momentum for further change. Maybe you start by reimagining how you evaluate talent, which leads naturally to evolving how resource groups develop leadership capabilities. Or perhaps you begin with improving communication infrastructure, which helps you gather better metrics and identify where to focus talent initiatives.

The organizations that succeed in this transformation share certain characteristics. They maintain focus on business impact while doing the hard work of cultural change. They create clear accountability while providing people the support to meet new expectations. Most importantly, they recognize that this work is never truly "done"—it becomes an integral part of how the organization operates and evolves.

The current backlash against diversity initiatives has many organizations feeling pressure to retreat to simpler approaches or abandon certain efforts entirely. But the organizations that understand these implementation areas as fundamental business capabilities recognize that retreat isn't an option. In today's complex business environment, the ability to identify and develop talent from all backgrounds, gather insights from diverse perspectives, communicate effectively across differences, and measure what matters isn't optional—it's essential for success.

As you move forward with your own transformation efforts, remember that you don't have to tackle everything at once. Start where you have the most energy and opportunity in your organization. Use early successes to build momentum for broader change. Most importantly, keep focusing on the connections between these areas, using improvements in one area to drive progress in others.

Integration vs. Isolation: Making Inclusion Inseparable from Operations

The most common mistake organizations make with diversity initiatives isn't resistance or lack of commitment—it's isolation. The contrast between isolation and integration manifests in various ways across organizations. Consider how differently two technology companies approached increasing diversity in their engineering teams. The first created a separate diversity recruiting team and established special hiring programs for underrepresented groups. While well intentioned, this approach marked diverse candidates as "special hires," creating stigma and resistance from existing teams. The second company instead transformed their entire recruitment process, establishing new assessment criteria that better predicted actual job performance, expanding their recruitment sources, and training all hiring managers in inclusive practices.

Similar contrasts appear in product development. A consumer goods company initially created a separate team focused on products for diverse markets. This isolated approach led to limited success and some notable missteps, as the "diversity products" team lacked deep integration with core business functions. When they shifted to embedding diverse perspectives within all product development teams while providing these tools and training for understanding different market segments, their innovation capabilities improved across all product lines.

Leadership development demands particular attention in this transformation. Rather than treating inclusive leadership as a special skill, organizations must embed it into all leadership development programs. This means reimagining how leaders are selected, developed, and evaluated. What behaviors get rewarded? How do leaders ensure all team members contribute in meetings? How do they allocate challenging assignments? How do they handle disagreement and conflict across cultural differences?

Business planning represents another area for systematic change. Organizations must move beyond having separate diversity initiatives to making inclusion part of every unit's strategy and goals. This requires transforming how planning happens at every level. Are diverse perspectives included in initial strategy development? How are resources allocated? Most importantly, how is inclusion integrated into implementation and measurement?

Systems and technology infrastructure must also evolve to support integration. Organizations need to examine how their core systems either enable or hinder inclusion. Does your project management system make it easy or hard for managers to assign work equitably? Does your knowledge management system privilege certain communication styles over others? The most successful organizations ensure their systems naturally enable inclusive practices rather than requiring special effort to work around them.

Resource allocation often reveals how deeply organizations have integrated inclusion into their operations. Instead of maintaining separate diversity budgets, every business unit must factor inclusion into their regular resource planning. This means considering accessibility, cultural competency, and diverse needs in every investment decision. These aren't special diversity expenses but standard business requirements.

The transition from isolation to integration isn't easy. It requires organizations to reimagine fundamental processes rather than simply adding diversity components to existing structures. Yet organizations often resist integration because it seems more challenging than running separate diversity programs. While the isolated approach might appear simpler initially, it ultimately proves more costly and less effective. When diversity initiatives operate separately from core business functions, they're more vulnerable to budget cuts, face greater resistance, and struggle to create lasting change.

When inclusion becomes inseparable from operations, organizations stop asking whether they can afford to invest in diversity and start recognizing they cannot afford not to.

Building Tomorrow's Organizations Today

The tools and frameworks outlined in this chapter provide a roadmap for implementing meaningful change, but they represent just the beginning of organizational transformation. As we've seen, successful diversity and inclusion efforts require more than isolated programs or initiatives—they demand fundamental changes in how organizations operate, make decisions, and define success.

The current political backlash against diversity initiatives has forced many organizations to adjust their language and approach. Some have rebranded their efforts, moving diversity work under broader umbrellas like "talent" or "inclusion." Others have quietly scaled back visible programs while maintaining their core commitment to change. Yet the fundamental forces driving this transformation—changing demographics, evolving market demands, the need for innovation and adaptation—aren't diminishing. If anything, they're accelerating.

Consider the broader context in which organizations now operate. By 2045, the United States will be a majority-minority nation. Gen Z, the most diverse generation in history, is entering the workforce with different expectations about inclusion and purpose. Globally, economic power continues to shift, requiring organizations to understand and serve increasingly diverse markets. Technology is transforming how we work, creating both challenges and opportunities for inclusion.

Artificial intelligence offers a perfect example of why inclusion can't be optional. AI systems trained on biased data perpetuate and amplify those biases. Organizations that lack diverse perspectives in their technology development risk creating products that fail in key markets or face costly remediation. Yet those that get it right—that build inclusive practices into their AI development from the start—gain powerful tools for expanding opportunity and enhancing decision-making.

The most successful organizations aren't retreating from their diversity commitments—they're evolving how they implement them. They're moving beyond defensive postures about why diversity matters to proactive strategies for leveraging diverse perspectives to drive innovation and growth. They're shifting from treating inclusion as a separate consideration to making it integral to every business decision.

This evolution suggests we're entering a new phase in how organizations approach diversity, equity, and inclusion. The question is no longer whether to embrace these principles, but how to implement them most effectively in an increasingly complex environment. Organizations that master the implementation strategies we've explored—reimagining talent practices, evolving employee resource groups, building effective communication infrastructure, and implementing meaningful metrics—while truly integrating inclusion into their operations will be best positioned to thrive.

9

The Inevitable Future of Inclusion

As we've traced the evolution of diversity, equity, and inclusion from its catalytic moment in Minneapolis through cycles of progress and resistance, one truth has become increasingly clear: while individual organizations might retreat from their outward DEI commitments, the fundamental forces driving workplace transformation aren't diminishing—they're accelerating.

The backlash against DEI we explored in previous chapters isn't a sign of failure but rather evidence of success. When companies feel compelled to maintain their diversity efforts even while rebranding them, when they invest in new training programs even while avoiding certain terminology, when they integrate inclusive practices into core operations even while dismantling dedicated DEI departments, you know the changes are real and lasting.

But to understand where we're heading, we need to look beyond current headlines about corporate retreats or political attacks. Three powerful forces are converging to shape the future of work: demographic shifts that will fundamentally alter the American workforce, technological advances that are transforming how we identify and develop talent, and political-economic pressures that are forcing organizations to reimagine their relationship with diverse communities.

These forces aren't operating in isolation—they're interconnected and mutually reinforcing. Demographic changes are driving political transformation. Technology is enabling new approaches to inclusion. Economic pressures are demanding innovative solutions. Understanding how these forces interact is crucial for any organization hoping to thrive in the decades ahead.

This chapter examines these converging forces and their implications for the future of business. We'll explore not just what's changing, but why these changes are inevitable, and how forward-thinking organizations can position themselves to succeed in an increasingly diverse and complex marketplace. The question isn't whether these transformations will occur, but who will lead them and who will be left behind.

Demographic Destiny

When JPMorgan Chase CEO Jamie Dimon addressed shareholders in early 2024, he didn't mince words about America's changing demographics: "This isn't a political statement—it's mathematics." He is right, as the numbers tell an undeniable story: by 2045, the United States will become a "minority-majority" nation, with non-Hispanic whites comprising less than 50 percent of the population.[1] Among racial minorities, Census projections show the most dramatic growth in multiracial populations, Asians, and Hispanics, with projected 2018–2060 growth rates of 176, 93, and 86 percent, respectively.[2]

But this transformation isn't waiting for some distant future—it's already reshaping American business in profound and irreversible ways. The most immediate shift is happening in our workforce. By 2025, Generation Z—the most ethnically diverse generation in American history—will comprise 27 percent of the workforce.[3] This generation brings radically different expectations about work itself: one in four workers aged 18–34 has never worked in a traditional office, having joined the workforce during or after the COVID-19 pandemic. They're seeking not just employment, but purpose—38 percent report taking time for workout classes during the workday, and 42 percent say their employers actively encourage flexible scheduling.[4]

Unlike previous generations, these workers bring not just demographic diversity but fundamentally different expectations about inclusion, purpose, and workplace culture. A 2023 Deloitte survey found that 77 percent of Gen Z employees would refuse to work for companies they perceived as insufficiently committed to diversity and inclusion, regardless of salary offerings.[5] Perhaps more tellingly, 84 percent prioritize workplace community, with an overwhelming 95 percent saying office social events boost engagement—a stark contrast to previous generations' preferences.[6]

The Latinx population growth represents perhaps the most significant demographic shift. Census projections indicate that by 2040, Latinx people will constitute approximately 28 percent of the US population, up from 19 percent in 2020.[7] The drivers of this growth are complex: immigration contributes to one-third of Hispanic population growth, with natural increase—the excess of births over deaths—accounting for the remainder.[8] This isn't just about numbers—it represents a fundamental transformation in consumer markets, talent pools, and eventually, leadership composition.

But focusing solely on ethnic and racial demographics misses other shifts. Women now earn 58 percent of bachelor's degrees and 60 percent of master's degrees in the United States.[9] Yet as of 2024, women still held only 7.4 percent of Fortune 500 CEO positions—an all-time high.[10] This growing disconnect between educational achievement and leadership representation creates what management experts term a "talent tension" that organizations can no longer ignore. The pipeline of qualified female leaders isn't just full—it's overflowing, and companies that fail to tap this talent pool risk falling behind competitors who do.

The implications of these shifts extend far beyond HR metrics or marketing strategies. They're reshaping every aspect of how organizations operate, from product development to supply chain management. Organizations are discovering that they cannot effectively serve increasingly diverse markets without diverse leadership. As Apple CEO Tim Cook noted, "If you believe, as we believe, that diversity leads to better products, and we're all about making products that enrich people's lives, then you obviously put a ton of energy behind diversity the same way you would put a ton of energy behind anything else that is truly important."[11]

The generational aspect of this transformation proves particularly significant. A 2024 Pew Research study revealed that 82 percent of

Gen Z workers believe workplace diversity directly impacts innovation and performance.[12] The study found stark generational contrasts: while 68 percent of workers under 30 say focusing on workplace diversity is fundamentally good for business, this drops to 46 percent among workers aged 50–64. Even more revealing, about three-quarters of Gen Z employees report regularly discussing issues of race and equity with colleagues—not because of corporate initiatives, but because they view these conversations as fundamental to workplace effectiveness.[13]

The impact on corporate governance has been equally profound. Research shows that boards with greater demographic diversity demonstrate markedly higher engagement with long-term strategy and environmental, social, and governance issues.[14] These boards are more likely to engage in strategic discussions about the company's future and demonstrate higher levels of engagement with critical governance issues. A Spencer Stuart study found that effective boards are increasingly moving beyond simple diversity metrics to focus on creating genuine inclusion, with leading companies implementing comprehensive succession planning that explicitly considers diverse perspectives and experiences.[15]

The demographic realities help explain both the intensity of current DEI backlash and its ultimate futility. Organizations aligned with the historical power bases view these demographic changes in cataclysmic terms of Armageddon. But those attempting to resist these changes aren't just fighting social trends—they're fighting market forces. The math is simple but compelling: Census projections show that by 2060, just 36 percent of Americans under age 18 will be non-Hispanic White, with Hispanics accounting for 32 percent. Meanwhile, these demographic shifts will occur unevenly across age groups—by 2060, the elderly population will remain majority white, creating unprecedented generational diversity dynamics.[16]

Most importantly, these demographic shifts require organizations to evolve from viewing diversity as a challenge to manage into seeing it as a competitive advantage to leverage. The Pew Research data shows this shift is already occurring: 56 percent of employed US adults say focusing on increasing diversity, equity, and inclusion at work is a good thing, with support rising to 68 percent among workers under 30.[17] Success requires moving beyond simple representation metrics to building genuine cultural competency throughout the organization. It demands rethinking everything from product development to talent acquisition to leadership development through the lens of an increasingly diverse marketplace.

The organizations that thrive in the coming decades won't be those with the most sophisticated diversity programs—they'll be those that have made diverse perspectives and inclusive practices so fundamental to their operations that they no longer need special programs or initiatives. As the Pew Research data demonstrates, younger generations already view diversity not as an optional initiative but as a fundamental business imperative: they're 28 percentage points more likely than Baby Boomers to see workplace diversity as directly impacting innovation and performance.[18] For forward-thinking organizations, the question isn't whether to embrace these demographic changes but how to position themselves to benefit from them.

The AI Revolution in DEI

When Joy Buolamwini discovered in 2015 that facial recognition software couldn't detect her dark-skinned face but could recognize a white plastic mask, she exposed a fundamental truth about artificial intelligence: AI systems don't just solve problems—they reflect and potentially amplify the biases of their creators. Nearly a decade later, as AI transforms every aspect of business operations, this lesson remains crucial for understanding both the promise and peril of AI in advancing diversity, equity, and inclusion.

The integration of AI into DEI practices represents perhaps the most significant technological shift since the introduction of applicant tracking systems in the 1990s.[19] But unlike those early systems, which simply digitized existing processes, AI is fundamentally reimagining how organizations approach inclusion. The transformation spans every aspect of the employee life cycle, from recruitment through retirement, creating both unprecedented opportunities and novel challenges.

The most immediate impact of AI on DEI efforts appears in talent acquisition. Traditional recruitment practices often reinforced existing biases through reliance on personal networks, subjective evaluations, and pattern matching based on past hires. AI-powered platforms are disrupting this model in several ways. Consider how IBM transformed its hiring practices using AI. Rather than simply screening resumes for keywords, their system analyzes skills and potential, regardless of how candidates acquired them. Within 18 months of implementation, IBM increased its diversity hiring by 35 percent while reducing time-to-hire by 23 percent.[20]

However, early experiments with AI recruitment also revealed potential pitfalls. Amazon's notorious 2013 attempt to build an AI hiring tool demonstrated how algorithms can amplify existing biases when trained on historical data reflecting past discrimination. The company discovered their system was penalizing resumes containing the word "women's" (as in "women's chess club captain") because historical hiring data showed a preference for male candidates. Despite attempts to modify the system to neutralize gender bias, Amazon ultimately lost confidence in its ability to ensure gender neutrality and abandoned the project.[21]

The challenge of algorithmic bias remains significant. A 2024 University of Washington study found stark racial and gender biases in how AI systems ranked resumes across more than 3 million comparisons between resumes and job descriptions. The research revealed complex patterns of intersectional bias: the systems favored white-associated names 85 percent of the time versus Black-associated names 9 percent of the time, and male-associated names 52 percent of the time versus female-associated names 11 percent of the time. Perhaps most troublingly, the systems never preferred Black male names over white male names in any comparison. The study also found unique intersectional effects—while showing the smallest disparity between white female and white male names, the systems preferred Black female names 67 percent of the time versus 15 percent of the time for Black male names.[22]

Despite these challenges, companies are finding ways to leverage AI effectively for DEI. According to recent data, 80 percent of companies using AI-driven recruitment tools report an improvement in diversity hiring outcomes. The technology has shown particular promise in reducing time-to-hire by 40 percent while increasing the diversity of candidate pools by 35 percent. Microsoft's recent innovations in this space are particularly noteworthy—their 2024 DEI-specific

AI model uses sentiment analysis to gauge candidate experience throughout the hiring process, helping identify potential pain points that might unintentionally alienate applicants from underrepresented groups.[23]

Healthcare organizations are demonstrating particularly impressive results with AI-driven inclusion efforts. Stanford Health Care's AI-powered chatbot transformed their recruitment process, driving 35,000 unique visits and generating over 11,000 candidate leads in just six months. More importantly, the system dramatically reduced barriers to access—candidates can now complete applications at their convenience from mobile devices, and support tickets in the recruiter queue dropped from 50 per week to just one or two. The system also enables proactive identification of common application obstacles, allowing the organization to address potential barriers before they impact candidates.[24]

Meanwhile, Thermo Fisher Scientific is using AI to revolutionize internal mobility, exceeding their goal of filling 40 percent of open roles with internal talent by achieving a 46 percent internal hiring rate. Their approach combines an AI-powered talent marketplace with automated campaigns and peer-to-peer networking, all built on a foundational AI model using an ontology of roles and skills to rapidly create career progressions. The system continuously learns and updates as employees move within the organization and as new talent joins, creating a dynamic platform for internal advancement.[25]

The future of AI in DEI isn't about replacing human judgment but augmenting it. Leading organizations are demonstrating how this balanced approach can transform talent acquisition while maintaining human oversight. Mastercard's experience provides a compelling example: their implementation of AI-driven recruitment marketing and automated scheduling has led to dramatic improvements, including growing their talent community from less than 100,000 profiles to over 1 million in just one year. Their success extends beyond mere numbers—they've achieved an 11 percent higher application conversion rate compared to industry averages and generated 141,000 more leads than typical for their sector. Perhaps most impressively, 88 percent of interviews are now scheduled within 24 hours of the request, reducing scheduling time by more than 85 percent.[26]

The Political and Economic Transformation

The backlash against DEI in 2024 revealed something deeper than partisan politics—it exposed fundamental tensions about power, economics, and the future of American society. By 2040, the electorate will look dramatically different than it does today. The Brookings Institution studies show that Gen Z will become the first majority nonwhite generation in American history by 2026. This transformation runs deeper than simple demographics—a survey by the Public Religion Research Institute found that while more than half of Republicans believe the United States should be "a strictly Christian nation," nearly as many Gen Zers and millennials say they have no religious affiliation at all. As the research notes, "Diversity is a baseline" for these younger voters, who demonstrate markedly different attitudes toward inclusion than previous generations.[27]

The economic implications are equally profound. Research from the Federal Reserve Bank of San Francisco indicates that racial and gender gaps in labor force participation cost the US economy approximately $2.6 trillion annually in lost GDP. This isn't just about employment numbers—the study found that differences in educational attainment make the largest contributions to racial gaps, while differences in employment and hours drive gender gaps. Even when controlling for education levels, Black workers are more likely than their white counterparts to work in jobs that don't require their level of education, meaning their talent is systematically underutilized.[28]

The Fed's analysis suggests these costs will likely increase given population trends. Their projections show that without significant progress in closing these gaps, disparities in labor market outcomes could become a major restraining factor on US growth over the next 20 years. The researchers note that "the effects are cumulative, limiting innovation, invention, and entrepreneurship which set the foundation for growth today and growth in the future."[29]

Healthcare and social services provide a telling example of this intersection between demographics, economics, and inclusion. As America's population ages, the demand for healthcare workers continues to surge. The Bureau of Labor Statistics projects that healthcare occupations will add approximately 1.9 million new jobs between 2023 and 2033. Healthcare practitioners and technical occupations command a median annual wage of $80,820, substantially above the median for all occupations of $48,060. However, healthcare support occupations—which often have more diverse workforces—earned a median of just $36,140.[30]

The regulatory landscape is evolving rapidly in response to these pressures. California's pay transparency law requires companies with 15 or more employees to include pay scales in all job postings and maintain detailed compensation records. The law mandates that employers keep pay records for each employee throughout their employment plus three years after separation, with significant fines for noncompliance.[31]

Similar legislation across multiple states has created what employment lawyers call a "compliance patchwork." Pay transparency laws have been enacted in California, Colorado, Connecticut, Hawaii, Illinois, Maryland, Nevada, New York, Rhode Island, Washington, and Washington, DC, along with numerous local jurisdictions. Many of these laws create private rights of action, meaning applicants can bring claims against employers for noncompliance. The challenge is particularly acute for organizations employing remote workforces or recruiting nationally, as they may be subject to transparency laws beyond their physical locations.[32]

The global dimension adds further complexity. The European Union's Corporate Sustainability Reporting Directive, effective in 2024, requires organizations to provide detailed descriptions of workforce policies, information on worker engagement, and specific metric data relating to diversity, wages, compensation, health, and safety. The directive represents one of the most significant shifts ever in corporate reporting requirements, demanding comprehensive disclosure about workforce policies, engagement with workers' representatives, and specific metrics on diversity, compensation, and workplace incidents.[33]

Perhaps most significantly, voting rights have emerged as a battleground in this transformation. Research from the Brennan Center for Justice shows that new voting restrictions disproportionately impact communities of color. Studies have documented consistently longer wait times for voters of color on Election Day, greater difficulties with vote-by-mail options, and disproportionate impacts from polling place consolidation. The impact is particularly severe for Native American voters, who face extensive barriers to ballot access.[34]

Corporate America's response to these challenges has evolved significantly. When Delta Airlines CEO Ed Bastian condemned Georgia's voting restrictions in 2021, he explicitly acknowledged the racial implications, stating that "after having time to fully understand all that is in the bill, coupled with discussions with leaders and employees in the Black community, it's evident that the bill includes provisions that will make it harder for many underrepresented voters, particularly Black voters, to exercise their constitutional right to elect their representatives."[35]

By 2024, corporate leaders increasingly recognized that staying silent on voting rights carried its own risks. According to Fast Company's analysis, "protecting voting rights, civil rights, and the peaceful transfer of power is both the right thing to do and smart strategy." The report notes that while companies don't need to weigh in on every issue, they should determine their red lines when it comes to core questions about democracy.[36]

Looking ahead, the intersection of political and economic forces suggests that inclusion will become increasingly inseparable from business success. The Federal Reserve's research is unequivocal—closing racial gaps in key areas of economic participation could generate significant additional income for saving, investing, and consumption, leading to substantial increases in aggregate output. Their analysis suggests that eliminating disparities in labor market opportunities and outcomes will be critical to producing faster growth and maintaining global competitiveness.[37] Organizations that understand this reality and position themselves accordingly will be better equipped to thrive in an increasingly diverse marketplace.

The Integration Imperative

In late 2024, when Microsoft disbanded its dedicated DEI team, many observers interpreted it as a retreat from diversity commitments. However, in reality Microsoft did not abandon inclusion efforts; it integrated them more deeply into various departments, aiming to provide a more holistic approach while maintaining their commitment to socio-cultural diversity, equal opportunity, and inclusivity.[38]

The integration imperative emerges from a simple but powerful insight: lasting change doesn't come from separate initiatives but from transforming how organizations fundamentally operate. Consider how Mastercard approached this challenge. Rather than maintaining diversity as a separate function, they rebuilt key aspects of their talent acquisition process. One innovative example is their implementation of an AI-based game used to vet candidates that doesn't record demographic data, instead advancing candidates based solely on their ability to complete specific tasks. Their use of Microsoft Teams provides insight into employee work patterns, including time allocation and meeting participation, while their automated scheduler has created an 87 percent productivity improvement in interview scheduling.[39]

Technology companies face unique challenges in this integration, particularly around artificial intelligence and product development. Microsoft's experience with AI bias led them to develop a comprehensive framework for identifying and addressing bias across five key categories. Their research shows that dataset bias occurs when training data doesn't represent customer diversity—similar to a young child defining the world purely on the small amount they can see. Association bias emerges when systems reinforce cultural stereotypes, like AI assuming all pilots are male and flight attendants are female. Automation bias appears when automated decisions override social considerations, comparable to a beautification filter that imposes European beauty standards on all faces. Interaction bias develops when humans deliberately manipulate AI systems, like teaching chatbots to use offensive language, while confirmation bias manifests in oversimplified personalization, similar to repeatedly recommending dinosaur toys to a child who received one as a gift.

Microsoft's approach emphasizes that these biases aren't binary "good vs. evil" issues, but rather exist on a spectrum where bias can appear in subtle, everyday experiences. They've learned that AI needs oversight to address not just major pitfalls but also seemingly mundane microaggressions that build up over time to cause feelings of exclusion. Their framework stresses the importance of empowering users to continually train AI systems, arguing that gaining diverse customer insights early in a safe training environment can prevent unintentional outcomes. Microsoft's research shows that teams with diverse outlooks can identify these biases more easily, making inclusive development teams essential for creating unbiased AI systems.[40]

The integration imperative demands new approaches to measurement and accountability. Salesforce demonstrates this evolution through their data-driven approach to inclusion. Their equality dashboard powered by Tableau allows HR leaders to see real-time data about representation, hires, attrition, and promotions by both race and gender. They've learned that managing diversity requires the same meticulous, data-driven approach used for other business metrics. Their Equality Advisory Board meets quarterly to review detailed metrics, including the distribution of headcount by demographic, promotion rates, and attrition patterns.

This data-driven approach extends to their self-identification program, which allows employees to voluntarily identify across multiple dimensions including gender, nationality, race and ethnicity, sexual orientation, disability, and military status. The company uses this data confidentially—not even managers have visibility into individual responses—to better understand their communities and address gaps in representation. In one instance, this data helped them identify and fix an issue where military reserve employees' benefits were being disrupted during deployment. Importantly, they emphasize intersectionality in their analysis, recognizing that "each community has very unique, distinct challenges compared to others—and no community is a monolith."[41]

Even procurement practices are being transformed through this integrated approach. Walmart discovered that access to working capital was the biggest challenge for diverse and minority-owned suppliers. In response, they launched an expanded early payment program in partnership with C2FO, offering qualified diverse or minority-owned suppliers faster payments at their lowest rates. This initiative builds on their Supplier Inclusion Program, which in the previous year had sourced more than $13.1 billion in goods and services from diverse suppliers. The program includes plans to partner with leading global and minority-owned banks to provide additional funding capabilities.[42]

Apple's experience demonstrates how integrated inclusive practices can drive innovation that benefits all users. Features originally designed for accessibility have become mainstream functionalities that enhance the experience for all users. Their Sound Recognition feature can detect specific sounds like doorbells or running water, while Back Tap allows users to trigger custom actions by tapping the back of their device. Their Headphone Accommodations feature uses sophisticated audio adjustments that can be customized through a series of listening tests, demonstrating how accessibility features can evolve into universal enhancements.[43]

Looking ahead, the integration imperative will only grow stronger. Netflix's approach to content development illustrates this evolution—rather than treating diversity as a separate initiative, they've made personalization and diverse content central to their strategy. Their approach combines sophisticated data analytics with strategic partnerships and social media engagement. By analyzing vast amounts of data on viewer behavior, preferences, and engagement, Netflix makes informed decisions about content acquisition and production. They've built their recommendation engine to consider not just what content performs well overall, but how it resonates across different communities and viewing contexts.

The company actively leverages social media platforms to build connections with diverse audience segments, creating shareable content that generates organic growth and community engagement. Their investment in original content production has been particularly strategic, allowing them to create programming that fills gaps in traditional media offerings while appealing across demographic boundaries. This integrated approach to diversity has proven crucial for global expansion—Netflix's localization strategy tailors content to different cultural preferences while maintaining a commitment to showcasing diverse perspectives that can connect with audiences worldwide.[44]

This integration represents a fundamental shift in how organizations approach inclusion—moving from isolated programs to transformed operations that embed inclusive practices into every aspect of work. Success requires not just strategic planning but also innovative approaches to leadership development and real-world implementation. As research from McKinsey & Company demonstrates, companies in the top quartile for ethnic and cultural diversity on executive teams are 33 percent more likely to have industry-leading profitability.[45]

Looking Ahead: Key Trends and Predictions

When considering the future of diversity, equity, and inclusion, we must look beyond current political debates and corporate retreats to understand the fundamental forces reshaping how organizations operate. The evidence presented throughout this chapter points to several key trends that are likely to accelerate in coming years.

First, the integration of diversity considerations into core business processes will likely intensify. This trend suggests a future where diversity isn't a separate function but an integral part of how organizations operate, from product development through customer service.

Artificial intelligence will likely play an increasingly central role in this transformation, but not in the ways many expect. As we've seen from Microsoft's research into AI bias, success requires careful attention to multiple forms of potential bias—from dataset limitations to algorithmic assumptions.[46] The future isn't about turning decisions over to algorithms but about using technology thoughtfully to expand human capability while maintaining human wisdom in decisions.

The transformation of measurement and accountability practices pioneered by companies like Salesforce points to another likely trend. Their approach of using real-time dashboards to track representation, hires, attrition, and promotions—while considering intersectionality—suggests future organizations will need increasingly sophisticated ways to measure inclusion's impact.[47]

Accessibility appears poised to move from being a special accommodation to a fundamental design principle. Apple's experience demonstrates how features originally designed for accessibility can become mainstream enhancements that benefit all users.[48] This suggests a future where universal design principles become standard practice rather than special initiatives.

Content development and market strategy will likely continue evolving toward more integrated approaches to diversity. Netflix's success with using sophisticated data analytics to understand diverse audience preferences while maintaining broad appeal demonstrates the potential of this approach.[49]

Even procurement and supply chain practices seem likely to transform. Walmart's early payment program for diverse suppliers suggests a future where organizations must think creatively about removing structural barriers to participation.[50]

The demographic realities driving these changes appear clear. As labor shortages persist and markets become increasingly diverse, organizations that don't develop genuine capability in understanding and serving different communities will likely find themselves at a competitive disadvantage.

Looking ahead, the question isn't whether these changes will occur but who will be ready for them. The research and examples presented throughout this chapter suggest that excellence and inclusion strengthen each other. The future appears to belong not to those who view diversity as a challenge to be managed but to those who understand it as a driver of innovation, growth, and sustainable success.

10

The Choice Ahead

IN DECEMBER 2024, as many companies quietly retreated from their diversity commitments, Costco took a remarkable stand. Facing pressure from conservative activists to abandon its diversity initiatives, the retail giant didn't just defend its programs—it challenged the very premise that inclusion was optional for business success. "Among other things, a diverse group of employees helps bring originality and creativity to our merchandise offerings, promoting the 'treasure hunt' that our customers value," the company stated in its proxy statement. "We believe (and member feedback shows) that many of our members like to see themselves reflected in the people in our warehouses with whom they interact."[1]

Costco's stance wasn't just corporate posturing—it reflected a deeper truth about the transformation sparked by George Floyd's murder: while individual companies might modify their language or rebrand their initiatives, the fundamental changes in how organizations operate cannot simply be undone. The gains extend far beyond racial equity. From expanded parental benefits to innovative programs for neurodivergent employees, from transformed supplier relationships to revolutionized product development processes, these aren't just diversity programs anymore—they've become integral to how successful organizations operate.

181

The journey from those first urgent conference calls in May 2020 to today's evolving business landscape reveals profound lessons about institutional change. We've witnessed unprecedented commitments—over $340 billion pledged toward racial equity initiatives. We've seen dramatic improvements in board diversity, with the percentage of Fortune 1000 companies lacking racial or ethnic diversity plummeting from 38 percent to 10 percent. Most importantly, we've watched organizations move from viewing diversity as a separate initiative to recognizing it as fundamental to business success.

And we've seen backlash. Companies have retreated from public commitments under political pressure. Diversity roles have been eliminated or rebranded. Training programs have been scaled back. But these surface-level fluctuations mask a deeper transformation. Even as some organizations publicly distance themselves from diversity terminology, they're quietly embedding inclusive practices more deeply into their operations. The most successful companies have discovered that genuine inclusion isn't about programs or initiatives—it's about fundamentally transforming how they operate.

The market forces driving this transformation have proven more powerful than any political backlash. By 2040, Latinx people will constitute the largest ethnic group in America. Generation Z—the most diverse generation in history—already comprises a quarter of the workforce. Women earn 58 percent of bachelor's degrees and 60 percent of master's degrees. These aren't political statements—they're demographic realities that organizations must navigate to remain competitive.

The business case for inclusion has moved beyond abstract arguments to concrete market imperatives. McKinsey's research shows organizations with the highest racial, ethnic, and gender diversity are 39 percent more likely to deliver above-average profits. But more telling than these statistics are the specific market advantages inclusive organizations achieve. Companies that effectively serve diverse communities and develop diverse talent consistently outperform their peers across every meaningful metric.

This transformation manifests differently across industries but follows consistent patterns. Target didn't just increase representation—they fundamentally reimagined how stores serve urban communities. Microsoft moved beyond fixing biased algorithms to embedding inclusive practices into their entire approach to artificial intelligence development. WarnerMedia transformed not just who tells stories but how stories get developed and distributed. JPMorgan Chase evolved from settling discrimination lawsuits to revolutionizing community banking.

The most successful organizations recognize that integration isn't a destination but a journey of continuous improvement. They build feedback loops that help them identify areas for enhancement, adapt to changing needs, and maintain momentum even when faced with setbacks or resistance. They understand that excellence and inclusion strengthen each other—the practices that make organizations more inclusive often make them simply better at what they do.

This new reality demands evolved capabilities from leaders at every level. Traditional management skills—setting clear goals, monitoring metrics, driving accountability—remain important but insufficient. Today's leaders must develop what we call "inclusive intelligence"—the ability to leverage diverse perspectives for better decisions while creating environments where everyone can contribute fully. This isn't just about managing diversity—it's about harnessing the power of difference to drive innovation and growth.

We're Not Going Back

As we look ahead, several capabilities emerge as essential for thriving in an increasingly diverse world. First is what we call "adaptive inclusion"—the ability to evolve practices quickly as needs and opportunities change. This isn't about rigid programs but about building flexible systems that can respond to evolving demographics, market demands, and stakeholder expectations.

Technology will play an increasingly crucial role in this evolution. Artificial intelligence is already transforming how organizations identify talent, develop leaders, and serve diverse markets. But as we've learned from early experiments with AI, technology must augment rather than replace human judgment. The most successful organizations will be those that leverage technology to enhance inclusion while maintaining human wisdom in decisions.

Building resilient inclusion strategies requires systematic attention to four key areas: Culture, Commerce, Career, and Community. Culture isn't just about celebration or awareness—it's about creating environments where different perspectives genuinely influence decisions. Commerce means understanding how inclusion drives business success, from product development to market expansion. Career focuses on ensuring everyone has genuine opportunities for growth and advancement. Community recognizes that organizations don't exist in isolation but must contribute to broader societal progress.

The cost of failing to adapt grows steeper every year. Organizations that retreat from inclusion initiatives in response to political pressure may score short-term points with certain constituencies, but they're positioning themselves poorly for long-term success. The market itself enforces these realities, punishing companies that can't effectively serve diverse communities or develop diverse talent.

Throughout my career, I've witnessed countless organizations grapple with diversity and inclusion. I've seen well-intentioned initiatives fail and unexpected successes emerge from genuine commitment to change. What's different now isn't just the urgency of the moment or the clarity of the business imperative—it's the depth of transformation that has already occurred.

Companies have the right to refine, rebrand, customize, and redesign their approaches to inclusion. Some may retreat from certain language or modify how they describe their efforts. But the fundamental changes in how organizations operate—changes catalyzed by that tragic moment in Minneapolis—have become inseparable from business excellence itself. The gains made in parental benefits, neurodiversity programs, supplier diversity, and countless other areas represent not just social progress but essential business evolution.

This isn't just about business success—it's about building organizations that help create the society we want to live in. When we make our workplaces more inclusive, we don't just improve business outcomes—we create opportunities for people to contribute their full potential to meaningful work. We don't just serve diverse markets—we help build communities where everyone can thrive.

The transformation ahead won't be easy. We'll face resistance, experience setbacks, and make mistakes along the way. But the direction is clear and the imperative compelling. As history has repeatedly shown, meaningful social transformation, once achieved, proves remarkably resilient. The organizations that thrive won't be those that resist change but those that embrace it, building the capabilities needed to succeed in an increasingly diverse and complex world.

The question isn't whether these changes will persist—they've become too fundamental to how successful organizations operate. The real question is who will lead the next evolution in how businesses harness the power of difference to drive innovation and growth. The opportunity—and the responsibility—lies with each of us to create organizations where excellence and inclusion strengthen each other, where different perspectives drive innovation, and where everyone has the chance to contribute their best work to meaningful goals.

The future is coming. And thanks to the transformation sparked by George Floyd's murder, it will be more inclusive than ever before. The choice now is not whether to embrace this change, but how to lead it.

Notes

Introduction

1. McKinsey & Company, "Diversity Wins: How Inclusion Matters," McKinsey & Company, 2020, https://www.mckinsey.com/featured-insights/diversity-and-inclusion/diversity-wins-how-inclusion-matters.
2. Bourke, Juliet, "The Diversity and Inclusion Revolution: Eight Powerful Truths," Deloitte Insights, January 22, 2018, https://www2.deloitte.com/us/en/insights/deloitte-review/issue-22/diversity-and-inclusion-at-work-eight-powerful-truths.html.
3. Albanesius, Chloe, "iPad Loses Market Share, But Still Crushes Tablet Rivals," PCMag, January 31, 2013, https://www.pcmag.com/news/ipad-loses-market-share-but-still-crushes-tablet-rivals.
4. Keizer, Gregg, "Microsoft Writes off Nearly $1B to Account for Surface RT Bomb," ComputerWorld, July 19, 2013, https://www.computerworld.com/article/1409993/microsoft-writes-off-nearly-1b-to-account-for-surface-rt-bomb.html.
5. Zheng, Hongwei, Weihua Li, and Dashun Wang, "Expertise Diversity of Teams Predicts Originality and Long-Term Impact in Science and Technology," arXiv preprint, October 10, 2022, https://arxiv.org/abs/2210.04422.
6. Schwarz, Robert, "Corporate Racial Equality Investments—One Year Later," Harvard Law School Forum on Corporate Governance, August 30, 2021, https://corpgov.law.harvard.edu/2021/08/30/corporate-racial-equality-investments-one-year-later/.

7. Klawans, Justin, "Companies That Have Rolled Back DEI Initiatives," The Week, December 3, 2024, https://theweek.com/business/companies-dei-rollback.

8. Dumas, Breck, "Diversity, Equity and Inclusion Programs Took a Hit in 2023," Fox Business, December 29, 2023, https://www.foxbusiness.com/politics/diversity-equity-inclusion-programs-took-hit-2023.

9. Hood, Julia, and Rebecca Knight, "6 Ways DEI Programs Are Evolving as Companies Reorganize, Home in on Employee Skills, and Leverage the Power of AI," Business Insider, November 26, 2024, https://www.businessinsider.com/dei-evolves-as-the-culture-changes-and-ai-takes-hold-2024-11.

10. Masterson, Victoria, "These Countries Are the Best at Attracting, Developing and Retaining Talent," World Economic Forum, November 16, 2023, https://www.weforum.org/stories/2023/11/most-talent-competitive-countries-2023.

11. Knight, Rebecca, "As Some Companies Scale Back on DEI, Others Double Down on Their Efforts," Business Insider, October 23, 2024, https://www.businessinsider.com/companies-data-driven-strategies-tools-refine-dei-belonging-efforts-decisions-2024-10.

12. Hood, Julia, and Rebecca Knight, "6 Ways DEI Programs Are Evolving as Companies Reorganize, Home in on Employee Skills, and Leverage the Power of AI," Business Insider, November 26, 2024, https://www.businessinsider.com/dei-evolves-as-the-culture-changes-and-ai-takes-hold-2024-11.

Chapter 1

1. Associated Press, "George Floyd Had Started New Life in Minnesota," Patch, May 28, 2020.

2. Extreme Weather Watch, "Minneapolis May 25 Weather Records," accessed December 28, 2024.

3. Associated Press, "George Floyd Had Started New Life in Minnesota," Patch, May 28, 2020.

4. CBS News, "For George Floyd, a Complicated Life and a Notorious Death," June 10, 2020.

5. Associated Press, "George Floyd Had Started New Life in Minnesota," Patch, May 28, 2020.

6. Christianity Daily, "George Floyd Was Christian Involved in Bible Ministry Work," June 1, 2020.

7. Vox, "George Floyd and the Cascade of Crises in Black America," June 1, 2020.
8. Texas State Historical Association, "Floyd, George Perry, Jr. (1973–2020)," May 10, 2023.
9. CBS News, "For George Floyd, a Complicated Life and a Notorious Death," June 10, 2020.
10. BBC News, "George Floyd, the Man Whose Death Sparked US Unrest," May 31, 2020.
11. SBS News, "George Floyd, from 'I Want to Touch the World' to 'I Can't Breathe,'" June 10, 2020.
12. Bored Panda, "After All These Years, George Floyd's 2nd-Grade Teacher Kept His Essay on How He Wanted to Become a Supreme Court Justice," June 8, 2020.
13. Associated Press, "George Floyd Had Started New Life in Minnesota," Patch, May 28, 2020.
14. Christianity Daily, "George Floyd Was Christian Involved in Bible Ministry Work," June 1, 2020.
15. MPR News, "Friends, Family of Man Who Died in MPD Custody Remember 'Big Floyd,'" May 26, 2020.
16. Associated Press, "George Floyd Had Started New Life in Minnesota," Patch, May 28, 2020.
17. Vox, "George Floyd and the Cascade of Crises in Black America," June 1, 2020.
18. Georgetown University Free Speech Project, "Protests Erupt Across the World in Response to Police Killing of George Floyd," June 28, 2020.
19. GPB News, "Cashier Says He Offered to Pay After Realizing Floyd's $20 Bill Was Fake," March 31, 2021.
20. The Hill, "Transcript of George Floyd Death Shows He Said He Was Dying, Officers Said He Was Fine Because He Could Speak," July 8, 2020.
21. Star Tribune, "Descended from Cops, Thomas Lane Saw His Minneapolis Police Career Last 4 Days," August 29, 2020.
22. MPR News, "George Floyd Killing: Police Bodycam Video Details Fatal Arrest," July 15, 2020.
23. CBS News, "Teen Who Recorded George Floyd's Death Speaks Out: 'It Made Me Realize How Dangerous It Is to Be Black in America,'" May 26, 2021.
24. BBC News, "George Floyd Death: Chauvin 'Trained to Stay Away from Neck,'" April 6, 2021.
25. Georgetown University Free Speech Project.
26. WTSP, "Read George Floyd's Full Autopsy Report," June 3, 2020.

27. National Museum of African American History and Culture, "How George Floyd's Death Became a Catalyst for Change."
28. Associated Press, "Timeline of Events Since George Floyd's Arrest and Murder," January 20, 2022.
29. Al Jazeera, "A Timeline of the George Floyd and Anti-Police Brutality Protests," June 11, 2020.
30. Blake, Sam, "Why the George Floyd Protests Feel Different—Lots and Lots of Mobile Video," dot.LA, June 12, 2020.
31. Szabo, Liz, "Rubber Bullets Are Supposed to Be 'Less Than Lethal,' But They Can Still Kill or Maim," PBS NewsHour, June 3, 2020.
32. Anderson, Monica, et al., "#BlackLivesMatter Surges on Twitter After George Floyd's Death," Pew Research Center, June 10, 2020.
33. Ang, Prisca, "Instagram Goes Dark for #blackouttuesday to Raise Awareness about Racism," The Straits Times, June 3, 2020.
34. BBC News, "George Floyd: Huge Protests Against Racism Held Across US," June 7, 2020.
35. BBC News, "George Floyd Death: Thousands Join UK Protests," May 31, 2020.
36. France 24, "Clashes Break Out at Paris's Banned George Floyd-Inspired Protest," June 3, 2020.
37. Nguyen, Kevin, "Enormous Crowds March in Sydney Black Lives Matter Protest After Last-Ditch Win in Court of Appeal," ABC News, June 6, 2020.
38. Francois, Myriam, "Adama Traoré: How George Floyd's Death Energised French Protests," BBC News, May 19, 2021.
39. Bliszczyk, Aleksandra, "Indigenous Groups in Australia Overwhelmed with Support Due to Black Lives Matter Rallies," SBS News, June 11, 2020.
40. Kirby, Jen, "'Black Lives Matter' Has Become a Global Rallying Cry Against Racism and Police Brutality," Vox, June 12, 2020.
41. Neeson, Johanna, "26 Powerful George Floyd Murals Seen Around the World," Reader's Digest, December 9, 2022.
42. Mazziotta, Julie, "CrossFit CEO's Racist Tweet Prompts Many Gyms—and Reebok—to Cut Ties with the Brand," People, June 8, 2020.
43. Sherman, Natalie, "George Floyd: Why Are Companies Speaking Up This Time?" BBC News, June 6, 2020.
44. Tilo, Dexter, "Did the Aftermath of George Floyd's Murder Lead to Positive Change in the Workplace?" Human Capital America, June 20, 2023.
45. Toraif, Noor et al., "From Colorblind to Systemic Racism: Emergence of a Rhetorical Shift in Higher Education Discourse," PLOS ONE, August 3, 2023.

46. Schwarz, Robert, "Corporate Racial Equality Investments—One Year Later," Harvard Law School Forum on Corporate Governance, August 30, 2021.

47. Ogbogu, Stephanie, "PepsiCo CEO Pledges Over $400 Million to Empower Black Employees & Their Communities," AfroTech, June 16, 2020.

48. NCRC, "PNC Bank, NCRC Announce $88 Billion Community Investment Commitment," April 27, 2021.

49. Mitchell, Aaron, and Shannon Alwyn, "Building Economic Opportunity for Black Communities," Netflix, June 30, 2020.

50. Google, "2023 Diversity Annual Report"; McIntyre, Lindsay-Rae, "2022 Diversity & Inclusion Report: Driving Progress Through Greater Accountability and Transparency," Microsoft Blog, October 27, 2022.

51. M&T Bank, "M&T Bank Expands Financial Access, Removes Language Barriers with 100 New Multicultural Banking Centers," PR Newswire, January 13, 2022.

52. Thorbecke, Catherine, "Starbucks to Tie Executive Compensation to Meeting Its Diversity Goals," ABC News, October 15, 2020.

53. Tilo, Dexter, "Did the Aftermath of George Floyd's Murder Lead to Positive Change in the Workplace?" Human Capital America, June 20, 2023.

54. Alonso Perez-Chao, Fernando, and Elisabeth Pipic, "These Companies Are Successfully Scaling Up Diversity, Equity and Inclusion (DEI) Initiatives Across the Globe," World Economic Forum, January 8, 2024.

55. Sony Music, "Sony Music Group Appoints Tiffany R. Warren Executive Vice President, Chief Diversity and Inclusion Officer," October 14, 2020.

56. Sault, Samantha, "Davos Agenda: What You Need to Know About the Future of Work," World Economic Forum, January 24, 2021.

57. Markovitz, Gayle, "The Legacy of George Floyd: Here's How Business Can Address Inequality and Promote Justice," World Economic Forum, June 5, 2020.

58. Statista Research Department, "Number of People Shot to Death by the Police in the United States from 2017 to 2024*, by Race," Statista, December 9, 2024.

59. History.com Editors. "The Hashtag #BlackLivesMatter First Appears, Sparking a Movement." History.com. Last modified July 13, 2020. https://www.history.com/this-day-in-history/blacklivesmatter-hashtag-first-appears-facebook-sparking-a-movement.

60. Bankoff, Caroline, "Medical Examiner Says That NYPD Chokehold Killed Eric Garner," New York Magazine, August 1, 2014.

61. History.com Editors, "Michael Brown Is Killed by a Police Officer in Ferguson, Missouri," HISTORY, August 8, 2024.

62. History.com Editors, "12-Year-Old Tamir Rice Shot and Killed by Police," HISTORY, November 23, 2024.

63. Gunter, Joel, "Baltimore Police Death: How Did Freddie Gray Die?" BBC News, May 1, 2015.

64. BBC News, "Breonna Taylor: What Happened on the Night of Her Death?" BBC News, October 8, 2020.

65. BBC News, "Ahmaud Arbery: What You Need to Know About the Case," BBC News, November 22, 2021.

66. Armstrong, Megan, Eathyn Edwards, and Duwain Pinder, "Corporate Commitments to Racial Justice: An Update," McKinsey & Company, February 21, 2023.

67. Vera, Amir and Daniel Wolfe, "Seeking Justice: A Timeline Since the Death of George Floyd," CNN, March 2021.

68. Deliso, Meredith, "Darnella Frazier, Who Recorded Video of George Floyd's Death, Recognized by Pulitzer Board," ABC News, June 11, 2021.

69. McCarthy, Bill, "What the First Police Statement About George Floyd Got Wrong," PolitiFact, April 22, 2021.

70. O'Donoghue, Gary, "George Floyd: Expert Witness Criticises Use of Force During Arrest," BBC News, April 7, 2021.

71. U.S. Bureau of Labor Statistics, "The Employment Situation—April 2020," News Release, May 8, 2020.

72. U.S. Bureau of Labor Statistics, "Payroll Employment Down 20.5 Million in April 2020."

73. U.S. Bureau of Labor Statistics, "The Employment Situation—April 2020."

74. Centers for Disease Control and Prevention, "Risk for COVID-19 Infection, Hospitalization, and Death by Race/Ethnicity," CDC, April 23, 2021.

75. Nielsen, "COVID-19: Tracking the Impact on Media Consumption," Nielsen, March 2020.

76. Sherman, Natalie, "George Floyd: Why Are Companies Speaking Up This Time?" BBC News, June 6, 2020.

77. Massie, Graeme, "Elon Musk Slammed for Saying DEI Is 'Another Word for Racism,'" The Independent, January 4, 2024.

78. Impelli, Matthew, "Trump Ramps Up His War on 'Woke,'" Newsweek, March 2, 2023.

79. Hurley, Bevan, "Trump has declared war on DEI. What will change?" The Times, January 29, 2025, https://www.thetimes.com/us/news-today/article/dei-programs-funding-companies-government-s0t5356jd.

80. Bickerton, James, "Walmart to Toyota: Major Companies Rolling Back DEI Policies," Newsweek, November 26, 2024.
81. Ellis, Nicquel Terry, and Catherine Thorbecke, "DEI Efforts Are Under Siege. Here's What Experts Say Is at Stake," CNN, January 7, 2024.
82. Herzlich, Taylor, "Jack Daniel's Maker Scraps DEI Policies After Threat of 'Anti-Woke' Boycott," New York Post, August 22, 2024.

Chapter 2

1. Portocarrero and Carter, "Diversity Initiatives in the US Workplace."
2. Portocarrero and Carter, "Diversity Initiatives in the US Workplace."
3. Encyclopedia.com, "Philadelphia Plan."
4. Encyclopedia.com, "Philadelphia Plan."
5. Investopedia, "Equal Pay Act of 1963."
6. History.com, "Watts Riots."
7. JSTOR Daily, "Did the 1965 W Riots Change Anything?"
8. Detroit Historical Society, "Uprising of 1967."
9. History.com, "1967 Detroit Riots."
10. Friedman, "Black Caucus Groups at Xerox Corp. (A)."
11. Friedman, "Black Caucus Groups at Xerox Corp."
12. Friedman, "Black Caucus Groups at Xerox Corp. (A)."
13. Friedman, "Black Caucus Groups at Xerox Corp. (A)."
14. Portocarrero and Carter, "Diversity Initiatives in the US Workplace."
15. Encyclopedia.com, "Philadelphia Plan."
16. Woodward, "Borrowed Agency."
17. Encyclopedia.com, "Philadelphia Plan."
18. IBM, "Our History."
19. Feitz, "Creating a Multicultural Soul."
20. FindLaw, "Griggs v. Duke Power Co."
21. Britannica, "Griggs v. Duke Power Co."
22. BlackPast.org, "The Philadelphia Plan (1967–1970)."
23. Encyclopedia.com, "Philadelphia Plan."
24. BlackPast.org, "The Philadelphia Plan (1967–1970)."
25. U.S. Department of Labor, "About OFCCP: History."
26. Dobbin and Kalev, "The Origins and Effects of Corporate Diversity Programs."
27. U.S. Department of Labor, "About OFCCP: History."
28. Miller and Schmutte, "The Dynamics of Referral Hiring and Racial Inequality."
29. Wilson and Rodgers, "Black-White Wage Gaps Expand."

30. Morrison, "Diversity Initiatives in the US Workplace."
31. Glickel, "A History of Recruitment."
32. FindLaw, "Steelworkers v. Weber."
33. FindLaw, "Steelworkers v. Weber."
34. FindLaw, "Johnson v. Transportation Agency."
35. Department of Labor, "The Glass Ceiling Initiative."
36. Department of Labor, "The Glass Ceiling Initiative."
37. DiPasquale and Glaeser, "The L.A. Riot and the Economics of Urban Unrest."
38. Holstead, "Post-1992 Los Angeles Riot Neighborhood Redevelopment."
39. Bernstein Litowitz Berger & Grossmann LLP, "Roberts v. Texaco, Inc."
40. Newsweek Staff, "Texaco's Troubles."
41. Time, "Texaco Will Pay Historic Settlement."
42. Velazquez, "The Americans with Disabilities Act and Its Strong Impact."
43. Casey, "Employee Resource Groups."
44. Thomas, "IBM Finds Profit in Diversity."
45. Thomas, "IBM Finds Profit in Diversity."
46. Quillian et al., "Meta-analysis of Field Experiments."
47. Hellerstein et al., "Changes in Workplace Segregation."
48. Hunt, Vivian, and Celia Huber. "Corporate Diversity: If You Don't Measure It, It Won't Get Done." McKinsey & Company, 2024.
49. Hunt, Vivian, and Celia Huber.
50. Ascend, "The Diversity-Equity Gap in the Fortune 500: Too Few Racial Minority Executives," February 2023.
51. University of New Hampshire, "Research Finds DEI Initiatives During Certain Presidencies Can Affect Bottom Line," September 28, 2023.
52. Ojha, Shankar, "HR Software Evolution: A Comprehensive Journey from Manual Processes to Fully Automated Systems in Modern Human Resources," QHRM Blog, August 2, 2024.
53. Vedantam, Shankar, "Most Diversity Training Ineffective, Study Finds," The Washington Post, January 20, 2008.
54. Naughton, Eileen, "Our Focus on Pay Equity," Google Blog, April 11, 2017.
55. Huet, Ellen, "Salesforce Begins Paving a Long Road to Equal Pay," Forbes, August 19, 2015.
56. Saez de Tejada Cuenca, Anna, "U.S. and Europe Lead Global Efforts to Diversify Suppliers," IESE Insight, October 30, 2024.
57. Ojha, Shankar, "HR Software Evolution: A Comprehensive Journey from Manual Processes to Fully Automated Systems in Modern Human Resources," QHRM Blog, August 2, 2024.

58. Paula Alexander Becker, "The Future of Affirmative Action After Grutter v. Bollinger," Journal of Business and Economics Research 2, no. 10 (October 2004): 67–80.
59. Fairchild, Angie, and Olga Hawn, "Gender Inequality and Company Actions: How Do Wall Street and Main Street React?" Kenan Insight, November 16, 2023.
60. Kerber, Ross, and Simon Jessop, "American Companies Facing Pressure to Reveal Data on Diversity of Employees," Insurance Journal, July 6, 2020.
61. Wilson, Valerie, and William M. Rodgers III, "Black-White Wage Gaps Expand with Rising Wage Inequality," Economic Policy Institute, September 20, 2016.
62. Golden, Hellen, "History of DEI: The Evolution of Diversity Training Programs," NDNU, January 1, 2024.
63. GI Group Holding. "How a D&I (Diversity and Inclusion) Culture Can Create Meaningful Impact for Employees," December 29, 2024.
64. GI Group Holding.
65. Billings, Mary Brooke, April Klein, and Yanting Crystal Shi, "Investors' Response to the #MeToo Movement: Does Corporate Culture Matter?" Review of Accounting Studies 27 (2022): 897–937.
66. Boyle, David, and Amanda Cucchiara, "Social Movements and HR: The Impact of #MeToo," CAHRS White Paper, December 2018.

Chapter 3

1. Armstrong, Megan, Eathyn Edwards, and Duwain Pinder, "Corporate Commitments to Racial Justice: An Update," McKinsey & Company, February 21, 2023.
2. Armstrong, Edwards, and Pinder, "Corporate Commitments."
3. Armstrong, Edwards, and Pinder, "Corporate Commitments."
4. Armstrong, Edwards, and Pinder, "Corporate Commitments."
5. Mishra, Subodh, "Racial and Ethnic Diversity on U.S. Corporate Boards—Progress Since 2020," Harvard Law School Forum on Corporate Governance, July 21, 2022.
6. Mishra, "Racial and Ethnic Diversity."
7. De la Parra, Daniela, "Exposure to Race Issues: Firm Responses and Market Reactions After George Floyd's Murder," Kenan Insight, June 13, 2024.
8. Markovitz, Gayle, "The Legacy of George Floyd: Here's How Business Can Address Inequality and Promote Justice," World Economic Forum, June 5, 2020.

9. Wise, Chelsea. "Black Beyond Measure—Lessons on Celebrating Black History Month," The Spark Mill, February 14, 2020.

10. Estrada, Sheryl, "Diversity as a 'Business Imperative': A Q&A with Target's D&I Chief," HR Dive, April 14, 2021.

11. Heilweil, Rebecca, "Target's History of Working with Police Is Not a Good Look Right Now," Vox, June 5, 2020.

12. Heilweil, Rebecca, "Target's History of Working with Police Is Not a Good Look Right Now."

13. Norfleet, Nicole, "Target CEO Says Company Taking Steps to Be 'True Leader' in Diversity, Inclusion," Star Tribune, May 22, 2021.

14. Estrada, Sheryl, "Diversity as a 'Business Imperative': A Q&A with Target's D&I Chief."

15. Norfleet, Nicole, "Target CEO Says Company Taking Steps to Be 'True Leader' in Diversity, Inclusion."

16. Estrada, Sheryl, "Diversity as a 'Business Imperative': A Q&A with Target's D&I Chief."

17. Casiano, Louis. "Target Reopening Looted, Ransacked Minneapolis Store," Fox Business, November 12, 2020.

18. Casiano, Louis, "Target Reopening Looted, Ransacked Minneapolis Store."

19. Target Corporation, "Target Provides Update on Commitment to Spend $2 Billion with Black-Owned Businesses," Target Corporation, May 10, 2022, https://corporate.target.com/press/release/2022/05/target-provides-update-on-commitment-to-spend-2-bi#:~:text=MINNEAPOLIS%20%2C%20May%2010%2C%202022%20%2F,by%20the%20end%20of%202025.

20. Buolamwini, Joy, "How I Accidentally Became a Fierce Critic of AI," The Boston Globe, October 26, 2023.

21. Buolamwini, Joy, "How I Accidentally Became a Fierce Critic of AI," The Boston Globe, October 26, 2023.

22. Buolamwini, Joy, "How I Accidentally Became a Fierce Critic of AI," The Boston Globe, October 26, 2023.

23. Hardesty, Larry, "Study Finds Gender and Skin-Type Bias in Commercial Artificial-Intelligence Systems," MIT News Office, February 11, 2018.

24. Simonite, Tom, "Photo Algorithms ID White Men Fine—Black Women, Not So Much," Wired, February 6, 2018.

25. Microsoft, "About Microsoft," Accessed December 19, 2024.

26. Rivero, Nicolás, "The Influential Project That Sparked the End of IBM's Facial Recognition Program," Quartz, June 10, 2020.

27. Simonite, Tom, "Photo Algorithms ID White Men Fine—Black Women, Not So Much," Wired, February 6, 2018.

28. Humphries, Fred, "Our Annual Report: 'Racial Equity Initiative: Strengthening Our Communities,'" Microsoft (blog), June 9, 2021.

29. BBC News, "George Floyd: Microsoft Bars Facial Recognition Sales to Police," June 11, 2020.

30. Crampton, Natasha, "The Building Blocks of Microsoft's Responsible AI Program," Microsoft on the Issues (blog), January 19, 2021.

31. Bird, Sarah, "Responsible AI Investments and Safeguards for Facial Recognition," Microsoft Azure Blog, June 21, 2022.

32. Wolf, Jessica, "2020 Hollywood Diversity Report: A Different Story Behind the Scenes," UCLA Newsroom, February 6, 2020.

33. McNary, Dave, "WarnerMedia CEO John Stankey on Diversity: 'We've Got More Work to Do,'" Yahoo Entertainment, September 26, 2019.

34. Press, Joy, "Hollywood's DEI Programs Have Begun to D-I-E," Vanity Fair, December 18, 2024.

35. WarnerMedia, "WarnerMedia Celebrates 20 Years of Supplier Diversity," Business Wire, March 30, 2022.

36. Abrams, Bryan, "Chatting with WarnerMedia's Senior Vice President of Equity & Inclusion Karen Horne," Motion Picture Association, March 29, 2022.

37. Winslow, George, "WarnerMedia Issues Diversity Report Showing Progress and Challenges," TV Technology, October 14, 2021.

38. Yost, Billy, "WarnerMedia Drives Changes for All to See," Hispanic Executive, March 7, 2022.

39. Dunn, Jonathan et al., "Black Representation in Film and TV: The Challenges and Impact of Increasing Diversity," McKinsey & Company, March 2021.

40. Dunn, Jonathan, et al.

41. Abrams, Bryan, "Chatting with WarnerMedia's Senior Vice President of Equity and Inclusion Karen Horne," Motion Picture Association, March 29, 2022.

42. Winslow, George, "WarnerMedia Issues Diversity Report Showing Progress and Challenges," TV Technology, October 14, 2021.

43. Press, Joy, "Hollywood's DEI Programs Have Begun to D-I-E," Vanity Fair, December 18, 2024.

44. Milano, Ashley, "JPMorgan Chase Settles Mortgage Discrimination Lawsuit for $55 M," Top Class Actions, January 24, 2017.

45. Brown, Sherrod, and Robert Menendez, "Brown, Menendez Lead Letter Asking JPMorgan Chase to Remember Its Own History," US Senate Committee on Banking, Housing, and Urban Affairs, December 20, 2019.
46. Federal Reserve Board, "Insured US-Chartered Commercial Banks That Have Consolidated Assets of $300 Million or More," Federal Reserve Board Releases, September 30, 2024.
47. JPMorgan Chase, "2022 Racial Equity Commitment Audit Report," November 22, 2022.
48. Schmidt, Ann, "JPMorgan's Jamie Dimon Reacts to Floyd Protests," Fox Business, May 30, 2020.
49. McKinney, Jeffrey, "JPMorgan Chase Makes $30 Billion Commitment to Help Close the Racial Wealth Gap," Black Enterprise, October 9, 2020.
50. McKinney, Jeffrey, "JPMorgan Chase Makes $30 Billion Commitment to Help Close the Racial Wealth Gap."
51. McKinney, Jeffrey, "JPMorgan Chase Makes $30 Billion Commitment to Help Close the Racial Wealth Gap."
52. JPMorgan Chase, "Growing More than Just Business," JPMorgan Chase Newsroom, April 25, 2023.
53. JPMorgan Chase, "Growing More than Just Business."
54. Dimon, Jamie. Annual Report 2022. Chairman and Chief Executive Officer, JPMorgan Chase, April 4, 2023.
55. Dimon, Jamie. Annual Report 2022.
56. Romano, Aja, "Google Has Fired the Engineer Whose Anti-Diversity Memo Reflects a Divided Tech Culture," Vox, August 8, 2017.
57. Romano, Aja, "Google Has Fired the Engineer Whose Anti-Diversity Memo Reflects a Divided Tech Culture,"
58. Sydell, Laura, "Google CEO Cuts Vacation Short to Deal with Crisis over Diversity Memo," NPR, August 8, 2017.
59. Sydell, Laura, "Google CEO Cuts Vacation Short to Deal with Crisis over Diversity Memo."
60. Brown, Danielle and Melonie Parker, Google Diversity Annual Report 2019.
61. Brown, Danielle and Melonie Parker, Google Diversity Annual Report 2019.
62. Pichai, Sundar, "Our Commitments to Racial Equity," Google Blog, June 17, 2020.
63. Copeland, Rob, "Google Sets Hiring Goal to Advance Black Executives," Kanarys, June 26, 2020.
64. Pichai, Sundar, "Our Commitments to Racial Equity."

65. Ighodaro, Omose, "How Google Is Sticking to—and Soaring Past—Its DEI Goals," BBC Worklife, February 15, 2024.

66. Google, "Raise Awareness About Unconscious Bias," Re:Work.

67. Fairygodboss, "How the Head of Retention at Google Infuses Empathy into Her Leadership Style," https://fairygodboss.com/career-topics/how-the-head-of-retention-at-google-infuses-empathy-into-her-leadership-style.

68. Brown, Danielle and Melonie Parker, Google Diversity Annual Report 2019.

69. Parker, Melonie, "Focused on Progress: Our 2022 Diversity Annual Report," Google Blog, May 19, 2022.

70. Ighodaro, Omose, "How Google Is Sticking to—and Soaring Past—Its DEI Goals."

71. Brown, Danielle and Melonie Parker, Google Diversity Annual Report 2019.

72. Pichai, "Our Commitments to Racial Equity," Google Blog.

73. Brown, Danielle and Melonie Parker, Google Diversity Annual Report 2019.

74. Parker, Melonie, "Focused on Progress: Our 2022 Diversity Annual Report."

75. Ighodaro, Omose, "How Google Is Sticking to—and Soaring Past—Its DEI Goals."

76. Ighodaro, Omose, "How Google Is Sticking to—and Soaring Past—Its DEI Goals."

77. Brown, Danielle and Melonie Parker, Google Diversity Annual Report 2019.

78. Brown, Danielle and Melonie Parker, Google Diversity Annual Report 2019.

79. Ighodaro, Omose, "How Google Is Sticking to—and Soaring Past—Its DEI Goals."

Chapter 4

1. Lang, Cady, "What the Artists Behind George Floyd Murals Around the World Want Us to Remember," Time, 2022.

2. Lang, Cady, "What the Artists Behind George Floyd Murals Around the World Want Us to Remember."

3. Watson, Katy, "Brazil's Racial Reckoning: 'Black Lives Matter Here, Too,'" BBC News, 2020.

4. Watson, Katy, "Brazil's Racial Reckoning: 'Black Lives Matter Here, Too,'" BBC News, 2020.
5. King, Esther, "Europe Seeks Own Response to Black Lives Matter," Politico, 2020.
6. King, Esther, "Europe Seeks Own Response to Black Lives Matter."
7. King, Esther, "Europe Seeks Own Response to Black Lives Matter."
8. King, Esther, "Europe Seeks Own Response to Black Lives Matter."
9. Abdel-Magied, Yassmin, "Why the Protests in the U.S. Are an Awakening for Non-Black People Around the World," Time, 2020.
10. Challenger, Gray & Christmas, Inc., "85% of Companies Discussed George Floyd & The Protests," 2020.
11. Gardner, "Caste Remains Off-Limits in Corporate India's Drive for Diversity," Financial Times, 2024.
12. Gardner, Hannah, "Caste Remains Off-Limits in Corporate India's Drive for Diversity."
13. Gardner, Hannah, "Caste Remains Off-Limits in Corporate India's Drive for Diversity."
14. Out Leadership, "Out Leadership-Sponsored Study Released by the Center for Talent Innovation in Davos," 2016.
15. Maersk, "LGBTQIA+ Inclusion at Maersk," 2024.
16. Out Leadership, "Out Leadership-Sponsored Study Released by the Center for Talent Innovation in Davos."
17. Out Leadership, "Out Leadership-Sponsored Study Released by the Center for Talent Innovation in Davos."
18. Moore and Woods, "Influencing Our Ecosystem to Promote Racial Justice," Cisco, 2022.
19. Unilever, "Unilever Commits to Help Build a More Inclusive Society," 2021.
20. Unilever, "Unilever Commits to Help Build a More Inclusive Society."
21. HSBC, "HSBC Shares UK Employee Ethnic Representation Data," 2020.
22. HSBC, "HSBC Shares UK Employee Ethnic Representation Data."
23. Sherman, Louise, "Celebrating Black History Month at HSBC," 2021.
24. Gardner, Hannah, "Caste Remains Off-Limits in Corporate India's Drive for Diversity."
25. Gardner, Hannah, "Caste Remains Off-Limits in Corporate India's Drive for Diversity."
26. HSBC, "HSBC Shares UK Employee Ethnic Representation Data."
27. Unilever, "Unilever Commits to Help Build a More Inclusive Society."
28. Schifrin, Nick, and Layla Quran, "Outrage over George Floyd Catalyzes Movements for Racial Justice Abroad," PBS NewsHour, 2020.

29. BBC, "50:50 The Equality Project Award Entry," 2024.
30. BBC, "The BBC's Pioneering 50:50 Project Expanded to Include Ethnicity and Disability," 2020.
31. BBC, "The BBC's Pioneering 50:50 Project Expanded to Include Ethnicity and Disability."
32. Reinstein, Julia, "Cate Blanchett, Ava DuVernay, Kristen Stewart, and Salma Hayek Just Protested in Cannes," BuzzFeed News, 2018.
33. Perez Alfaro, Clara et al., "A Path for Greater Diversity in Film Festivals," Arts Management and Technology Laboratory, 2021.
34. AfroCannes, "What Is AfroCannes," 2024.
35. Mgbolu, Charles, "Cannes 2024: African Films Make Bold Statements," TRT Afrika, 2024.
36. Al Jazeera, "'Hypocrites': Bollywood Actors Slammed over George Floyd Stand," 2020.
37. Sheth, Sudev, et al., "Bollywood, Skin Color and Sexism," Harvard Business School, 2021.
38. King, Esther, "Europe Seeks Own Response to Black Lives Matter," Politico, 2020.
39. King, Esther, "Europe Seeks Own Response to Black Lives Matter."
40. King, Esther, "Europe Seeks Own Response to Black Lives Matter."
41. King, Esther, "Europe Seeks Own Response to Black Lives Matter."
42. King, Esther, "Europe Seeks Own Response to Black Lives Matter."
43. King, Esther, "Europe Seeks Own Response to Black Lives Matter."
44. King, Esther, "Europe Seeks Own Response to Black Lives Matter."
45. Participedia, "Black Lives Matter (BLM) and Repercussions in Brazil," 2024.
46. Participedia, "Black Lives Matter (BLM) and Repercussions in Brazil."
47. Gutierrez, Barbara, "Protests in Brazil Highlight Racism and Police Brutality," University of Miami News, 2020.
48. Deutsche Welle, "Floyd Killing Spurs Fresh Protests Across Europe," 2020.
49. Deutsche Welle, "Germany to Launch Racism Study Among Police," 2020.
50. European Roma Rights Centre, "Roma Rights Activists Take Police Killing of Stanislav Tomáš to European Court," 2023.
51. Truu, Maani, "George Floyd: How a Nine Minute Video Reignited a Decades-Old Civil Rights Movement in Australia," SBS News, 2021.
52. Mao, Frances, "George Floyd Death: Australians Defy Virus in Mass Anti-Racism Rallies," BBC News, 2020.
53. Mao, Frances, "George Floyd Death: Australians Defy Virus in Mass Anti-Racism Rallies."

54. France 24, "After the Death of George Floyd, Africa Mobilises Against Police Violence," 2020.
55. France 24, "After the Death of George Floyd, Africa Mobilises Against Police Violence."
56. France 24, "After the Death of George Floyd, Africa Mobilises Against Police Violence."
57. France 24, "After the Death of George Floyd, Africa Mobilises Against Police Violence."
58. Participedia, "Black Lives Matter (BLM) and Repercussions in Brazil," 2024.
59. France 24, "After the Death of George Floyd, Africa Mobilises Against Police Violence."

Chapter 5

1. Kessler, Will, "Businesses Ditch 'Diversity' Initiatives in Droves Amid Economic Uncertainty," The Daily Caller, November 27, 2023.
2. Colvin, Caroline, "DEI Job Postings Are Down. Why Do These Roles Lack Longevity?" HR Dive, August 14, 2024.
3. Alcalde, M. Cristina, "Assault on DEI: Critics Use Simplistic Terms to Attack the Programs," Seattle Post-Intelligencer, December 18, 2024.
4. Bennett, Geoff, and Courtney Norris, "How Some Companies Are Scaling Back DEI Initiatives after Conservative Backlash," PBS NewsHour, August 27, 2024.
5. Barrett, Annalisa, "*African American Representation on Fortune 1000 Boards: 2022 Edition,*" KPMG Board Leadership Center, 2023.
6. Kessler, Will, "Businesses Ditch 'Diversity' Initiatives in Droves Amid Economic Uncertainty," The Daily Caller, November 27, 2023.
7. 600 US 181(2023).
8. Kessler, Will, "Businesses Ditch 'Diversity' Initiatives in Droves Amid Economic Uncertainty," The Daily Caller, November 27, 2023.
9. Bennett, Geoff, and Courtney Norris, "How Some Companies Are Scaling Back DEI Initiatives after Conservative Backlash," PBS NewsHour, August 27, 2024.
10. Colvin, Caroline, "DEI Job Postings Are Down. Why Do These Roles Lack Longevity?" HR Dive, August 14, 2024.
11. Shepherd, Tiah, "GOP Rep. Burchett Calls Harris a 'DEI Hire,'" The Hill, July 22, 2024.
12. Shepherd, Tiah, "GOP Rep. Burchett Calls Harris a 'DEI Hire,'" The Hill, July 22, 2024.

13. Irwin, Lauren, "Another Republican Labels Harris 'DEI Hire,'" The Hill, July 24, 2024.
14. Alfonseca, Kiara, "Kamala Harris Faces Racial 'DEI' Attacks Amid Campaign for the 2024 Presidency," ABC News, July 23, 2024.
15. Alfonseca, Kiara, "Kamala Harris Faces Racial 'DEI' Attacks Amid Campaign for the 2024 Presidency," ABC News, July 23, 2024.
16. Schott, Bryan, "Baltimore Bridge Collapse Caused by DEI Efforts, Utah Rep. Phil Lyman Says," The Salt Lake Tribune, March 26, 2024.
17. Bunn, Curtis, "Utah Lawmaker Blames 'Diversity' for Baltimore Bridge Collapse," Yahoo News, March 28, 2024.
18. Schott, Bryan, "Baltimore Bridge Collapse Caused by DEI Efforts, Utah Rep. Phil Lyman Says," The Salt Lake Tribune, March 26, 2024.
19. Walker, Corey, "Don't Blame DEI for Baltimore Bridge Collapse," Washington Examiner, March 28, 2024.
20. Robertson, Nick, "Moore Denounces DEI Blame for Bridge Collapse: 'I Have No Time for Foolishness,'" The Hill, March 31, 2024.
21. Robertson, Nick, "Moore Denounces DEI Blame for Bridge Collapse: 'I Have No Time for Foolishness,'" The Hill, March 31, 2024.
22. U.S. Senate, "Senator Vance & Rep. Cloud Introduce Legislation to Eliminate All DEI Programs from the Federal Government," press release, June 12, 2024.
23. Kamar, Lucile, "Debunking 5 Misconceptions Around Diversity and Inclusion," All Things Insights, February 29, 2024.
24. Walker, Corey, "Don't Blame DEI for Baltimore Bridge Collapse," Washington Examiner, March 28, 2024.
25. Pop Culture Dictionary, "Cancel Culture," July 31, 2020.
26. Clark, Meredith D., "DRAG THEM: A Brief Etymology of So-Called 'Cancel Culture,'" Communication and the Public 5, no. 3–4 (2020): 88–92.
27. Cook, Shannon, "How Millennials & Gen Z Are Pushing Brands on Diversity and Inclusion," BusinessBecause, March 3, 2021.
28. Cook, Shannon, "How Millennials & Gen Z Are Pushing Brands on Diversity and Inclusion," BusinessBecause, March 3, 2021.
29. Nesvig, Kara K., and Sara Delgado, "Munroe Bergdorf Joins L'Oréal Paris as Consultant After Calling Out the Brand," Teen Vogue, June 9, 2020.
30. Planting, Sasha, "Clicks Stores Trashed Over Racist Ad," Daily Maverick, September 8, 2020.
31. BBC, The Talk: Sharon Osbourne Leaves US Show After Racism Row," BBC News, March 27, 2021.
32. BBC, Piers Morgan Leaves ITV's Good Morning Britain After Row Over Meghan Remarks," BBC News, March 10, 2021.

33. Brill, Gabrielle, "Cancel Culture: Inciting Corporate Social Accountability," University of Richmond Law Review, January 25, 2021.

34. Impelli, Matthew, "Is Starbucks Banning Pride Decorations? What We Know," Newsweek, June 13, 2023.

35. Otten, Tori, "Starbucks Denies Union Allegations of a Ban on Pride Decorations," The New Republic, June 13, 2023.

36. Winsor, Morgan, and Kelly McCarthy, "Men Arrested at Starbucks Were There for Business Meeting Hoping to Change 'Our Lives,'" ABC News, April 19, 2018.

37. CBS News, "Black Men Arrested at Philadelphia Starbucks Say They Feared for Their Lives," April 19, 2018.

38. Fitzpatrick, Alex, "Starbucks Is Closing Thousands of Stores for Racial Bias Training. Here's How Much Money It Could Lose," TIME, April 17, 2018.

39. Cerullo, Megan, "Gucci Turban Costing $790 Sparks Outrage Among Sikhs," CBS News, May 16, 2019.

40. D'Innocenzio, Anne, "Target to Reduce Number of Stores Carrying Pride-Themed Merchandise," AP News, May 11, 2024.

41. Scarcella, Mike, "Target Must Face Shareholder Lawsuit over Pride Backlash," Yahoo Finance, December 4, 2024.

42. Flood, Brian, and Suzanne O'Halloran, "Target Market Cap Losses Hit $15.7 Billion, Shares Approach 52-Week Low Amid Woke Backlash," FOX Business, June 12, 2023.

43. Bickerton, James, "Bud Light Stock Suffers Huge Tumble as Company Loses $4 Billion in One Week," Newsweek, June 1, 2023.

44. Cooper, Alex, "Dylan Mulvaney Breaks Silence After Transphobic Backlash Over Bud Light Partnership," Advocate, April 27, 2023.

45. Wiggins, Christopher, "Anheuser-Busch Execs on Leave After Right-Wing Fuss Over Dylan Mulvaney Collaboration," Advocate, April 24, 2023.

46. Keenan, Sara, "Major Media Companies Lose 4 Black Diversity Leaders—A Step Backwards?" People of Color in Tech, July 3, 2023.

47. Parisi, Kristen, "The Next DE&I Component to Rebrand: Employee Resource Groups," HR Brew, August 27, 2024.

48. HR News Canada, "Goodbye DEI, Hello I&D: SHRM Adopts New Acronym for Diversity." HR News Canada, July 9, 2024.

49. Mohan, Pavithra, "SHRM, a Leading HR Organization, Is No Longer Focusing on 'Equity' in Its DEI Approach," Fast Company, July 12, 2024.

50. Ferguson, Jackie, "Here's How a Chief Belonging Officer Can Revive DEI Efforts," Reworked, January 12, 2024.

51. Keenan, Sara, "Companies Are Ditching the E in DEI to Avoid Legal Risks," People of Color in Tech, October 29, 2024.
52. Butcher, Jonathan, "Restoring Equality in Employment: Sinking the DEI Ship," The Heritage Foundation, November 27, 2024.
53. Wang, Alexandr, "Meritocracy at Scale," Scale AI, June 13, 2024.
54. Davis, Dominic-Madori, and Kyle Wiggers, "Silicon Valley Leaders Are Once Again Declaring 'DEI' Bad and 'Meritocracy' Good—But They're Wrong," TechCrunch, June 23, 2024.
55. Davis, Dominic-Madori, and Kyle Wiggers, "Silicon Valley Leaders Are Once Again Declaring 'DEI' Bad and 'Meritocracy' Good—But They're Wrong," TechCrunch, June 23, 2024.
56. Davis, Dominic-Madori, and Kyle Wiggers, "Silicon Valley Leaders Are Once Again Declaring 'DEI' Bad and 'Meritocracy' Good—But They're Wrong," TechCrunch, June 23, 2024.
57. Parisi, Kristen, "The Next DE&I Component to Rebrand: Employee Resource Groups," HR Brew, August 27, 2024.
58. Butcher, Jonathan, "Restoring Equality in Employment: Sinking the DEI Ship," The Heritage Foundation, November 27, 2024.
59. Ferguson, Jackie, "Here's How a Chief Belonging Officer Can Revive DEI Efforts," Reworked, January 12, 2024.
60. Davis, Dominic-Madori, and Kyle Wiggers, "Silicon Valley Leaders Are Once Again Declaring 'DEI' Bad and 'Meritocracy' Good—But They're Wrong," TechCrunch, June 23, 2024.
61. Davis, Dominic-Madori, and Kyle Wiggers, "Silicon Valley Leaders Are Once Again Declaring 'DEI' Bad and 'Meritocracy' Good—But They're Wrong," TechCrunch, June 23, 2024.
62. Butcher, Jonathan, "Restoring Equality in Employment: Sinking the DEI Ship," The Heritage Foundation, November 27, 2024.
63. Keenan, Sara, "Companies Are Ditching the E in DEI to Avoid Legal Risks," People of Color in Tech, October 29, 2024.

Chapter 6

1. Howland, Daphne, "No, Not All Companies Are Abandoning Diversity, Equity, and Inclusion. Here's Why," Retail Dive, September 23, 2024.
2. Congressional Black Caucus, "What Good Looks Like: A Corporate Accountability Report on Diversity, Equity, and Inclusion," September 2024.
3. Kessler, Will, "Businesses Ditch 'Diversity' Initiatives in Droves Amid Economic Uncertainty," The Daily Caller, November 27, 2023.

4. Blake, Suzanne, "America Slashes Inclusivity Spending," Newsweek, November 27, 2023.

5. Blake, Suzanne, "America Slashes Inclusivity Spending," Newsweek, November 27, 2023.

6. Unzipped Staff, "Elizabeth A. Morrison Named New Chief Diversity, Inclusion & Belonging Officer," Levi Strauss & Co., November 17, 2020.

7. Unzipped Staff, "Quick Questions With Our New Chief DE&I and Talent Officer," Levi Strauss & Co., August 25, 2024.

8. Telford, Taylor, and Julian Mark, "DEI Is Getting a New Name. Can It Dump the Political Baggage?" The Washington Post, May 5, 2024.

9. Telford, Taylor, and Julian Mark, "DEI Is Getting a New Name. Can It Dump the Political Baggage?" The Washington Post, May 5, 2024.

10. Telford, Taylor, and Julian Mark, "DEI Is Getting a New Name. Can It Dump the Political Baggage?" The Washington Post, May 5, 2024.

11. Howland, Daphne, "No, Not All Companies Are Abandoning Diversity, Equity, and Inclusion. Here's Why," Retail Dive, September 23, 2024.

12. Hood, Julia, and Rebecca Knight, "6 Ways DEI Programs Are Evolving," Business Insider, November 26, 2024.

13. Carnahan, Becca, "6 Best Practices for Creating an Inclusive and Equitable Interview Process," Harvard Business School Recruiting, May 25, 2023.

14. Hood, Julia, and Rebecca Knight, "6 Ways DEI Programs Are Evolving," Business Insider, November 26, 2024.

15. Ousterout, Jamie, "The Latest DEI Trends & Predictions for 2024," The Diversity Movement, 2024.

16. 2023 Supplier Diversity Benchmarking Report, Supplier.io, 2023.

17. Telford, Taylor, and Julian Mark, "DEI Is Getting a New Name. Can It Dump the Political Baggage?" The Washington Post, May 5, 2024.

18. Ousterout, Jamie, "The Latest DEI Trends & Predictions for 2024," The Diversity Movement, 2024.

19. Murray, Sarah, "Rescuing Diversity from the DEI Backlash," Financial Times, June 20, 2024.

20. Moran, Catherine Douglas, "5 Ways Target Is Pushing Customer-Driven Innovations," Grocery Dive, January 19, 2023.

21. Moran, Catherine Douglas, "5 Ways Target Is Pushing Customer-Driven Innovations."

22. "Target Commits $100 Million Through 2025 for Black Communities." Philanthropy News Digest, October 13, 2021.

23. Moran, Catherine Douglas, "5 Ways Target Is Pushing Customer-Driven Innovations."

24. Clarence-Smith, Louisa, "Microsoft Lays Off Diversity and Inclusion Team," The Times, July 18, 2024.

25. Lay-Flurrie, Jenny, "Disability Data: Improving Representation to Drive AI Innovation," Microsoft On the Issues (blog), October 17, 2024.

26. Lay-Flurrie, Jenny, "Disability Data: Improving Representation to Drive AI Innovation."

27. Press, Joy, "Hollywood's DEI Programs Have Begun to D-I-E," Vanity Fair, December 18, 2024.

28. Press, Joy, "Hollywood's DEI Programs Have Begun to D-I-E."

29. Press, Joy, "Hollywood's DEI Programs Have Begun to D-I-E."

30. Luminate, "2024 Entertainment Diversity Report."

31. Abrams, Bryan, "Chatting With WarnerMedia's Senior Vice President of Equity & Inclusion Karen Horne," Motion Picture Association, March 29, 2022.

32. Yost, Billy, "WarnerMedia Drives Changes for All to See," Hispanic Executive, March 7, 2022.

33. Press, Joy, "Hollywood's DEI Programs Have Begun to D-I-E."

34. Dunn, Jonathan et al., "Black Representation in Film and TV: The Challenges and Impact of Increasing Diversity," McKinsey & Company, March 2021.

35. Luminate, "2024 Entertainment Diversity Report."

36. Godoy, Jody, and Disha Raychaudhuri, "Some Companies Alter Diversity Policies after Conservatives' Lawsuit Threat," Reuters, December 18, 2023.

37. JPMorgan Chase, "2022 Racial Equity Commitment Audit Report," November 22, 2022.

38. "Growing More than Just Business," JPMorgan Chase Newsroom, April 25, 2023.

39. Dimon, Jamie, Annual Report 2022.

40. Dimon, Jamie, Annual Report 2022.

41. JPMorgan Chase, "2022 Racial Equity Commitment Audit Report."

42. Dimon, Jamie, Annual Report 2022.

43. Lattice, "All Hands: IBM's Obed Louissaint on the Importance of Skills-Based Hiring," July 7, 2022.

44. Perez-Chao, F. A., and E. Pipic, "These Companies Are Successfully Scaling Up Diversity, Equity and Inclusion (DEI) Initiatives Across the Globe," World Economic Forum, January 8, 2024.

45. Saha, Rubel et al., "Impact of Diversity and Inclusion on Firm Performance," Journal of Risk and Financial Management, August 8, 2024.

46. MIT Sloan Management Review, "Should Companies Refrain from Making Political Statements?" May 31, 2023.

Chapter 9

1. Frey, William H, "The US Will Become 'Minority White' in 2045, Census Projects," Brookings, March 14, 2018.
2. Vespa, Jonathan, David M. Armstrong, and Lauren Medina, "*Demographic Turning Points for the United States: Population Projections for 2020 to 2060*" (Washington, DC: U.S. Census Bureau, February 2020).
3. Syeda, Sahlah, "Study Predicts 3 Ways Gen Z Will Continue to Change the Workplace in 2025," YourTango, December 13, 2024.
4. Syeda, 2024, "Study Predicts 3 Ways Gen Z Will Continue to Change the Workplace in 2025."
5. Jeffery-Morrison, Michaela, "Attracting and Retaining Gen-Z Through Diversity and Inclusion," Forbes, June 9, 2023.
6. Syeda, "Study Predicts 3 Ways Gen Z Will Continue to Change the Workplace in 2025."
7. Vespa et al., "Demographic Turning Points for the United States: Population Projections for 2020 to 2060."
8. Vespa et al., "Demographic Turning Points for the United States: Population Projections for 2020 to 2060."
9. National Center for Education Statistics, "Degrees Conferred by Race/Ethnicity and Sex," Accessed December 23, 2024.
10. Hinchliffe, Emma, "The Number of Female CEOs in the Fortune 500 Hits an All-Time Record," Fortune, May 18, 2020.
11. White, Jonno, "Top 450 Leadership Quotes on Diversity and Inclusion," Consult Clarity, March 13, 2023.
12. Minkin, Rachel, "Diversity, Equity and Inclusion in the Workplace," Pew Research Center, May 17, 2023.
13. Minkin, "Diversity, Equity and Inclusion in the Workplace."
14. Anderson, George, and Julie Hembrock Daum, "Board Composition: The Road to Strategic Refreshment and Succession," Spencer Stuart, March 2021.
15. Anderson and Daum, "Board Composition: The Road to Strategic Refreshment and Succession."
16. Vespa et al., "Demographic Turning Points for the United States: Population Projections for 2020 to 2060."
17. Minkin, "Diversity, Equity and Inclusion in the Workplace."
18. Minkin, "Diversity, Equity and Inclusion in the Workplace."
19. Apple, Amari, "AI Transforms Diversity and Inclusion in Modern Workplaces," Rolling Out, December 3, 2024.

20. Williams, Trey, "IBM's HR Team Saved 12,000 Hours in 18 Months after Using A.I. to Automate 280 Tasks," Yahoo Finance, June 26, 2023.

21. Winick, Erin, "Amazon Ditched AI Recruitment Software Because It Was Biased Against Women," MIT Technology Review, October 10, 2018.

22. Milne, Stefan, "AI Tools Show Biases in Ranking Job Applicants' Names According to Perceived Race and Gender," University of Washington News, October 31, 2024.

23. Jani, Namee, "Generative AI and the Future of Recruitment: Insights from Microsoft's Push for AI-Powered Diversity Hiring," Datafloq, October 25, 2024.

24. Blehar, "7 Companies Successfully Using AI in Their Recruiting Strategies."

25. Blehar, "7 Companies Successfully Using AI in Their Recruiting Strategies."

26. Blehar, Maggie, "7 Companies Successfully Using AI in Their Recruiting Strategies," Phenom, May 2, 2024.

27. Smith, Carl, "How Much Could Younger Voters Affect Future Election Outcomes?" Governing, April 10, 2023.

28. Buckman, Shelby R., Laura Y. Choi, Mary C. Daly, and Lily M. Seitelman, "The Economic Gains from Equity," Federal Reserve Bank of San Francisco, April 2021.

29. Buckman et al., "The Economic Gains from Equity."

30. U.S. Bureau of Labor Statistics, "Healthcare Occupations," Accessed December 24, 2024.

31. Yadidsion, Danny, "Understanding California's Pay Transparency Laws: What Employers Need to Know in 2024," Labor Law PC.

32. Graham, Nicole Lazarz, Esq., "Navigating the Patchwork of Pay Transparency Laws," Journal of Accountancy, May 1, 2024.

33. Bracken, John et al., "The EU Corporate Sustainability Reporting Directive | Employment Law Implications," The Employer Report, November 19, 2024.

34. Brennan Center for Justice, "The Impact of Voter Suppression on Communities of Color," January 10, 2022.

35. Garner, Marcus K., "Delta CEO Blasts Georgia Election Law, Calls It 'Unacceptable,'" Patch, March 31, 2021.

36. Schwerin, Dan, "CEOs Can't Hide from This Election," Fast Company, April 9, 2024.

37. Buckman et al., "The Economic Gains from Equity."

38. Carter, Mason, "Microsoft Disbands Diversity Team Amid Criticism," Baseline Magazine, July 23, 2024.

39. McGlauflin, Paige, and Paolo Confino, "How Mastercard Is Using A.I. to Streamline Its Recruiting Process," Yahoo Finance, June 28, 2023.

40. Chou, Joyce, Roger Ibars, and Oscar Murillo, "In Pursuit of Inclusive AI," Microsoft.

41. Gonçalves, Isabel, "4 Ways Data Drives Diversity in the Workplace," Salesforce Blog, December 9, 2021.

42. McCall, Scott, and Megan Crozier, "Accelerating Our Commitment to Diverse and Minority Suppliers," Walmart Corporate Newsroom, April 28, 2021.

43. Dove, Jackie, "Major iOS 14 Accessibility Features Benefit Everyone," Digital Trends, April 25, 2023.

44. McLaughlin, Justin, "Netflix Marketing Strategy: Streaming Success," Brand Credential, December 8, 2023.

45. Robinson, Joseph, "How Are Companies Adapting Their Leadership Development Programs to Foster Greater Diversity and Inclusion?" Flevy Insights.

46. Chou, Joyce, Roger Ibars, and Oscar Murillo, "In Pursuit of Inclusive AI," Microsoft.

47. Gonçalves, Isabel, "4 Ways Data Drives Diversity in the Workplace," Salesforce Blog, December 9, 2021.

48. Dove, Jackie, "Major iOS 14 Accessibility Features Benefit Everyone," Digital Trends, April 25, 2023.

49. McLaughlin, Justin, "Netflix Marketing Strategy: Streaming Success," Brand Credential, December 8, 2023.

50. McCall, Scott, and Megan Crozier, "Accelerating Our Commitment to Diverse and Minority Suppliers," Walmart Corporate Newsroom, April 28, 2021.

Chapter 10

1. Meyersohn, Nathaniel, "Costco Is Pushing Back—Hard—against the Anti-DEI Movement," CNN. Last modified December 27, 2024, https://edition.cnn.com/2024/12/27/business/costco-dei/index.html.

Bibliography

Abdel-Magied, Yassmin. "Why the Protests in the U.S. Are an Awakening for Non-Black People Around the World." Time, June 5, 2020. https://time.com/5848914/global-protests-racism-police.

Abrams, Bryan. "Chatting With WarnerMedia's Senior Vice President of Equity and Inclusion Karen Horne." Motion Picture Association, March 29, 2022. https://www.motionpictures.org/2022/03/chatting-with-warnermedias-senior-vice-president-of-equity-inclusion-programs-karen-horne.

Academy of Motion Picture Arts and Sciences. "Academy Establishes Representation and Inclusion Standards for Oscars® Eligibility." Oscars.org, September 8, 2020. https://www.oscars.org/news/academy-establishes-representation-and-inclusion-standards-oscarsr-eligibility

ACT-SO Chattanooga. n.d. "Famous Alumni." Accessed December 15, 2024. https://www.actsochattanooga.org/famous-alumni.

Afrocannes. "What Is AfroCannes." Accessed December 21, 2024. https://www.afrocannes.com/about.

Aghadjanian, Nina. "Nike's 'Don't Do It' Anti-Racism Ad Receives Mixed Reviews." AList Daily, June 1, 2020. https://www.alistdaily.com/lifestyle/nike-dont-do-it-anti-racism-ad-draws-mixed-reviews/.

Ahmaud Arbery: What You Need to Know About the Case. BBC News, November 22, 2021. https://www.bbc.com/news/world-us-canada-52623151.

Al Jazeera. "'Hypocrites': Bollywood Actors Slammed over George Floyd Stand." June 8, 2020. https://www.aljazeera.com/features/2020/6/8/hypocrites-bollywood-actors-slammed-over-george-floyd-stand.

Al Jazeera. "A Timeline of the George Floyd and Anti-Police Brutality Protests." Al Jazeera, June 11, 2020.

Albanesius, Chloe. "iPad Loses Market Share, But Still Crushes Tablet Rivals." PCMag, January 31, 2013. https://www.pcmag.com/news/ipad-loses-market-share-but-still-crushes-tablet-rivals.

Alcalde, M. Cristina. "Assault on DEI: Critics Use Simplistic Terms to Attack the Programs, But They Are Key to Uprooting Workplace Bias." Seattle Post-Intelligencer, December 18, 2024. https://www.seattlepi.com/news/article/assault-on-dei-critics-use-simplistic-terms-to-19987858.php.

Alfonseca, Kiara. "Kamala Harris Faces Racial 'DEI' Attacks Amid Campaign for the 2024 Presidency." ABC News, July 23, 2024. https://abcnews.go.com/Politics/kamala-harris-faces-racial-dei-attacks-amid-campaign/story?id=112196464.

Alonso Perez-Chao, Fernando, and Elisabeth Pipic. 2024. "These Companies Are Successfully Scaling Up Diversity, Equity and Inclusion (DEI) Initiatives Across the Globe." World Economic Forum. January 8, 2024. https://www.weforum.org/stories/2024/01/organizations-impactful-corporate-dei-initiatives.

Anderson, George, and Julie Hembrock Daum. "Board Composition: The Road to Strategic Refreshment and Succession." Spencer Stuart, March 2021. https://www.spencerstuart.com/research-and-insight/the-road-to-strategic-board-succession.

Anderson, Monica, Michael Barthel, Andrew Perrin, and Emily A. Vogels. "#BlackLivesMatter Surges on Twitter After George Floyd's Death." Pew Research Center, June 10, 2020. https://www.pewresearch.org/short-reads/2020/06/10/blacklivesmatter-surges-on-twitter-after-george-floyds-death/.

Ang, Prisca. "Instagram Goes Dark for #blackouttuesday to Raise Awareness about Racism." The Straits Times, June 3, 2020. https://www.straitstimes.com/lifestyle/instagram-goes-dark-for-blackouttuesday-to-raise-awareness-about-racism.

Apple, Amari. "AI Transforms Diversity and Inclusion in Modern Workplaces." Rolling Out, December 3, 2024. https://rollingout.com/2024/12/03/ai-transforms-dei-mordern-workplaces.

Armstrong, Megan, Eathyn Edwards, and Duwain Pinder. "Corporate Commitments to Racial Justice: An Update." McKinsey & Company, February 21, 2023. https://www.mckinsey.com/bem/our-insights/corporate-commitments-to-racial-justice-an-update.

Ascend. The Diversity-Equity Gap in the Fortune 500: Too Few Racial Minority Executives. February 2023. https://static1.squarespace.com/static/621f898a98dc785cd663ab7b/t/6660abf3dfa3a04b506736dc/1717611514540/TheDiversityEquityGap_Paper_6.5.24.pdf.

Associated Press. "George Floyd Had Started New Life in Minnesota." Patch, May 28, 2020. Accessed December 28, 2024. https://patch.com/minnesota/southwestminneapolis/george-floyd-had-started-new-life-minnesota.

Associated Press. "Timeline of Events Since George Floyd's Arrest and Murder." Last modified January 20, 2022. Accessed December 28, 2024. https://apnews.com/article/george-floyd-death-timeline-2f9abbe6497c2fa4adaebb92ae179dc6.

Averstad, Pontus, David Baboolall, David Quigley, Alejandro Beltrán, Eitan Lefkowitz, Alexandra Nee, and Gary Pinshaw. "The State of Diversity in Global Private Markets: 2022." McKinsey & Company, November 1, 2022. https://www.mckinsey.com/industries/private-capital/our-insights/the-state-of-diversity-in-global-private-markets-2022.

Bankoff, Caroline. "Medical Examiner Says That NYPD Chokehold Killed Eric Garner." New York Magazine, August 1, 2014. https://nymag.com/intelligencer/2014/08/medical-examiner-says-chokehold-killed-garner.html.

Barker, Shane. "Google's Diversity Schemes: Navigating Challenges and Maintaining Commitment in 2025." Expert Beacon, last updated October 10, 2024. https://expertbeacon.com/googles-diversity-schemes-navigating-challenges-and-maintaining-commitment-in-2024.

Barrett, Annalisa. African American Representation on Fortune 1000 Boards: 2022 Edition. KPMG Board Leadership Center. Accessed December 22, 2024. https://kpmg.com/kpmg-us/content/dam/kpmg/boardleadership/pdf/2023/african-american-representation-fortune-1000-boards-2022-edition.pdf.

BBC News. "George Floyd Death: Thousands Join UK Protests." BBC News, May 31, 2020. https://www.bbc.com/news/uk-england-london-52868465.

BBC News. "George Floyd: Huge Protests Against Racism Held Across US." BBC News, June 7, 2020. https://www.bbc.com/news/world-us-canada-52951093.

BBC News. "George Floyd: Microsoft Bars Facial Recognition Sales to Police." BBC News, June 11, 2020. https://www.bbc.com/news/business-53015468.

BBC News. "Who is Sundar Pichai and What Does Alphabet Do?" BBC News, December 4, 2019. https://www.bbc.com/news/technology-50656803.

BBC. "50:50 The Equality Project Award Entry." Accessed December 21, 2024. https://www.bbc.com/5050/awards-entry.

BBC. "The BBC's Pioneering 50:50 Project Expanded to Include Ethnicity and Disability." Published October 22, 2020. https://www.bbc.co.uk/mediacentre/latestnews/2020/5050-project-expended-to-include-ethnicity-and-disability.

Becker, Paula Alexander. "The Future of Affirmative Action After Grutter v. Bollinger." Journal of Business & Economics Research 2, no. 10 (October 2004): 67–80. https://web.archive.org/web/20101122025154id_/http://cluteinstitute-onlinejournals.com/PDFs/2004103.pdf.

Bennett, Geoff, and Courtney Norris. "How Some Companies Are Scaling Back DEI Initiatives after Conservative Backlash." PBS News Hour, August 27, 2024. https://www.pbs.org/newshour/show/how-some-companies-are-scaling-back-dei-initiatives-after-conservative-backlash.

Benstead, Sean. "Europe's Romani Population Can't Breathe." Jacobin, July 18, 2021. https://jacobin.com/2021/07/europe-roma-czech-republic-stanislav-tomas-police-killing-world-romani-congress-movement.

Bernstein Litowitz Berger & Grossmann LLP. "Roberts v. Texaco, Inc. (Texaco Discrimination Litigation)." Bernstein Litowitz Berger & Grossmann LLP. Accessed December 28, 2024. https://www.blbglaw.com/cases-investigations/roberts-v-texaco-inc.

Bibliography: Bispo, Alexandre Araujo. "The Afro Project Emerges in a Context of Historical Violence." Contemporary and América Latina (C& América Latina), October 12, 2020. https://amlatina.contemporaryand.com/editorial/the-afro-project-emerges-in-a-context-of-historical-violence.

Bickerton, James. "Bud Light Stock Suffers Huge Tumble as Company Loses $4 Billion in One Week." Newsweek, June 1, 2023. https://www.newsweek.com/bud-light-stock-suffers-huge-tumble-company-loses-4-billion-one-week-1803836.

Bickerton, James. "Walmart to Toyota: Major Companies Rolling Back DEI Policies." Newsweek, November 26, 2024. https://www.newsweek.com/walmart-toyota-all-major-companies-rolling-back-dei-policies-1991849.

Billings, Mary Brooke, April Klein, and Yanting Crystal Shi. "Investors' Response to the #MeToo Movement: Does Corporate Culture Matter?" Review of Accounting Studies 27 (2022): 897–937. Published July 18, 2022. https://link.springer.com/article/10.1007/s11142-022-09695-z.

Birch, Kate. "How Salesforce Is Creating a More Diverse, Inclusive Culture." Business Chief, January 28, 2022. https://businesschief.com/leadership-and-strategy/how-salesforce-is-creating-a-more-diverse-inclusive-culture.

Bird, Sarah. "Responsible AI Investments and Safeguards for Facial Recognition." Microsoft Azure Blog, June 21, 2022. https://azure.microsoft

.com/en-us/blog/responsible-ai-investments-and-safeguards-for-facial-recognition.

Blake, Sam. "Why the George Floyd Protests Feel Different—Lots and Lots of Mobile Video." dot.LA, June 12, 2020. https://dot.la/george-floyd-video-2646171522.html.

Blake, Suzanne. "America Slashes Inclusivity Spending." Newsweek, November 27, 2023. https://www.newsweek.com/american-companies-cutting-down-inclusivity-initiatives-dei-1847300.

Blehar, Maggie. "7 Companies Successfully Using AI in Their Recruiting Strategies." Phenom, May 2, 2024. https://www.phenom.com/blog/examples-companies-using-ai-recruiting-platform.

Bliszczyk, Aleksandra. 2020. "Indigenous Groups in Australia Overwhelmed with Support Due to Black Lives Matter Rallies." SBS News, June 11, 2020. https://www.sbs.com.au/news/article/indigenous-groups-in-australia-overwhelmed-with-support-due-to-black-lives-matter-rallies/cvur8ajhs.

Bond, P. "After Coca-Cola Backlash, LinkedIn Removes Diversity Lesson Telling Employees to 'Be Less White.'" Newsweek, February 23, 2021. https://www.newsweek.com/linkedin-removes-diversity-lesson-less-white-1571205.

Boucher, Ashley. "Mother of George Floyd's Daughter Speaks Out After His Death: 'He Will Never Walk Her Down the Aisle.'" People, June 2, 2020. Accessed December 28, 2024. https://people.com/crime/mother-of-george-floyd-daughter-speaks-out-death.

Bourke, Juliet. 2018. "The Diversity and Inclusion Revolution: Eight Powerful Truths." Deloitte Insights, January 22, 2018. https://www2.deloitte.com/us/en/insights/deloitte-review/issue-22/diversity-and-inclusion-at-work-eight-powerful-truths.html.

Boyle, David, and Amanda Cucchiara. "Social Movements and HR: The Impact of #MeToo." CAHRS White Paper, December 2018. https://www.shrm.org/content/dam/en/shrm/executive-network/Social%20Movements%20and%20HR-%20The%20Impact%20of%20MeToo.pdf.

Boynton, Jennifer. "More Than Words: A Discussion with Shari Slate, Cisco's Chief Inclusion and Collaboration Officer." February 1, 2021. https://blogs.cisco.com/csr/more-than-words-a-qa-with-shari-slate-vice-president-inclusive-future-strategy.

Bracken, John, Jonathan Tuck, Carl Richards, Rachel Wilson, and Tiziana de Virgilio. "The EU Corporate Sustainability Reporting Directive | Employment Law Implications." The Employer Report, November 19, 2024. https://www.theemployerreport.com/2024/11/the-eu-corporate-sustainability-reporting-directive-employment-law-implications.

Brennan Center for Justice. "The Impact of Voter Suppression on Communities of Color." Fact Sheet, January 10, 2022. https://www.brennancenter.org/our-work/research-reports/impact-voter-suppression-communities-color.

"Breonna Taylor: What Happened on the Night of Her Death?" BBC News, October 8, 2020. https://www.bbc.com/news/world-us-canada-54210448.

Brill, Gabrielle. "Cancel Culture: Inciting Corporate Social Accountability." University of Richmond Law Review, January 25, 2021. https://lawreview.richmond.edu/2021/01/25/cancel-culture-inciting-corporate-social-accountability.

Brown, Danielle, and Melonie Parker. Google Diversity Annual Report 2019. Google, 2019. https://services.google.com/fh/files/misc/google_2019_diversity_annual_report.pdf.

Brown, Sean. "Corporate Diversity: If You Don't Measure It, It Won't Get Done." McKinsey & Company, Podcast, March 6, 2020. https://www.mckinsey.com/capabilities/strategy-and-corporate-finance/our-insights/corporate-diversity-if-you-dont-measure-it-it-wont-get-done.

Brown, Sherrod, and Robert Menendez. "Brown, Menendez Lead Letter Asking JPMorgan Chase to Remember Its Own History When Responding to 'Abhorrent' Racial Discrimination." US Senate Committee on Banking, Housing, and Urban Affairs, December 20, 2019. https://www.banking.senate.gov/newsroom/minority/brown-menendez-lead-letter-asking-jpmorgan-chase-to-remember-its-own-history-when-responding-to-abhorrent-racial-discrimination.

Buckman, Shelby R., Laura Y. Choi, Mary C. Daly, and Lily M. Seitelman. "The Economic Gains from Equity." Federal Reserve Bank of San Francisco, April 2021. https://www.frbsf.org/wp-content/uploads/wp2021-11.pdf.

Bunn, Curtis. "Utah Lawmaker Blames 'Diversity' for Baltimore Bridge Collapse." Yahoo News, March 28, 2024. https://www.yahoo.com/news/utah-lawmaker-blames-diversity-baltimore-222746563.html.

Buolamwini, Joy. "How I Accidentally Became a Fierce Critic of AI." The Boston Globe, October 26, 2023. https://www.bostonglobe.com/2023/10/26/opinion/unmasking-ai-joy-buolamwini-facial-recognition/.

Burt, Sharelle. 2023. "Thanks to Black Employees, HBCUs See Increase in Corporate Donations." Black Enterprise. June 1, 2023. https://www.blackenterprise.com/hbcus-seeing-increase-in-corporate-donations-thanks-to-black-employees.

Butcher, Jonathan. "Restoring Equality in Employment: Sinking the DEI Ship." The Heritage Foundation, November 27, 2024. https://www.heritage

.org/progressivism/report/restoring-equality-employment-sinking-the-dei-ship.

Campbell, Lloyd E. "Corporate Boards Are Making Progress on Diversity, But There's More to Do." Spencer Stuart, December 2021. https://www.spencerstuart.com/research-and-insight/corporate-boards-are-making-progress-on-diversity-but-theres-more-to-do.

Carnahan, Becca. "6 Best Practices for Creating an Inclusive and Equitable Interview Process." Harvard Business School Recruiting Insights and Advice Blog, May 25, 2023. https://www.hbs.edu/recruiting/insights-and-advice/blog/post/6-best-practices-to-creating-inclusive-and-equitable-interview-processes.

Carter, Mason. "Microsoft Disbands Diversity Team Amid Criticism." Baseline Magazine, July 23, 2024. https://www.baselinemag.com/news/microsoft-disbands-diversity-team-amid-criticism.

Carville, Olivia. "Google 'Walkout for Real Change' Sees Thousands Leave Work Globally to Protest Sexual Misconduct Handling." Bloomberg, November 2, 2018. https://www.gadgets360.com/others/news/google-walkout-for-real-change-sees-thousands-leave-work-globally-to-protest-sexual-misconduct-handl-1941651.

Casey, Judith C. "Employee Resource Groups: A Strategic Business Resource for Today's Workplace." Boston College Center for Work & Family, November 2021. https://archive.hshsl.umaryland.edu/handle/10713/17334.

CBS Minnesota. "For George Floyd, A Complicated Life and a Notorious Death." CBS News, June 10, 2020. Accessed December 28, 2024. https://www.cbsnews.com/minnesota/news/for-george-floyd-a-complicated-life-and-a-notorious-death.

CBS News. "Black Men Arrested at Philadelphia Starbucks Say They Feared for Their Lives." CBS News, updated on 19 April 2018. https://www.cbsnews.com/news/starbucks-arrest-rashon-nelson-donte-robinson-feared-for-their-lives.

Centers for Disease Control and Prevention. "Risk for COVID-19 Infection, Hospitalization, and Death by Race/Ethnicity." CDC, April 23, 2021.

Cerullo, Megan. "Gucci Turban Costing $790 Sparks Outrage Among Sikhs." CBS News, May 16, 2019. https://www.cbsnews.com/news/gucci-turban-sparks-outrage-in-sikh-community.

CFA Institute. "The Importance of Teams." Future Professional. Accessed December 15, 2024. https://futureprofessional.cfainstitute.org/changing-roles/the-importance-of-teams.

Challenger, Gray & Christmas, Inc. "85% of Companies Discussed George Floyd and the Protests; Will This Moment Lead to Equitable Hiring?" June 23, 2020. https://www.challengergray.com/blog/85-companies-discussed-george-floyd-protests-will-moment-lead-equitable-hiring.

Chappell, Bill. "Cashier Says He Offered to Pay After Realizing Floyd's $20 Bill Was Fake." GPB News, March 31, 2021. Accessed December 28, 2024. https://www.gpb.org/news/live-updates-trial-over-george-floyds-killing/2021/03/31/cashier-says-he-offered-pay-after.

Chou, Joyce, Roger Ibars, and Oscar Murillo. "In Pursuit of Inclusive AI." Microsoft. Accessed December 24, 2024. https://inclusive.microsoft.design/tools-and-activities/InPursuitofInclusiveAI.pdf.

Christianity Daily. "George Floyd Was Christian Involved in Bible Ministry Work." Christianity Daily, June 1, 2020. Accessed December 28, 2024. https://www.christianitydaily.com/news/george-floyd-was-christian-involved-in-bible-ministry-work.html.

Chrysopoulos, Philip. "What Does 'I Can't Breathe' Mean to AfroGreeks?" Greek Reporter, July 28, 2020. https://greekreporter.com/2020/07/28/what-does-i-cant-breathe-mean-to-afrogreeks.

Clarence-Smith, Louisa. "Microsoft Lays off Diversity and Inclusion Team." The Times, July 18, 2024. https://www.thetimes.com/business-money/article/microsoft-lays-off-diversity-and-inclusion-team-zppg6h32s.

Clark, Meredith D. "DRAG THEM: A Brief Etymology of So-Called 'Cancel Culture.'" Communication and the Public 5, no. 3–4 (2020): 88–92. https://journals.sagepub.com/doi/pdf/10.1177/2057047320961562.

Clark, Meredith. "Levi's Addresses Backlash After Using AI Models to 'Increase Diversity' in Online Shopping." The Independent, March 29, 2023. https://www.independent.co.uk/life-style/fashion/levis-ai-models-diversity-backlash-b2310280.html.

Cohen, Li. "Teen Who Recorded George Floyd's Death Speaks Out: 'It Made Me Realize How Dangerous It Is to Be Black in America.'" CBS News, May 26, 2021. Accessed December 28, 2024. https://www.cbsnews.com/news/darnella-frazier-george-floyd-black-america.

Collins, Jon. "Friends, Family of Man Who Died in MPD Custody Remember 'Big Floyd.'" MPR News, May 26, 2020. Accessed December 28, 2024. https://www.mprnews.org/story/2020/05/26/friends-family-of-man-who-died-in-mpd-custody-remember-big-floyd.

Collins, Jon. "George Floyd Killing: Police Bodycam Video Details Fatal Arrest." MPR News, July 15, 2020. Accessed December 28, 2024. https://www.mprnews.org/story/2020/07/15/george-floyd-killing-police-bodycam-video-details-fatal-arrest.

Collinson, Jenny, and Lengwe Sinkala. 2024. "A Global Perspective: Why Diversity Matters in Human Factors Engineering (HFE)." ClariMed, November 13, 2024. https://clarimed.com/resources/blog/global-perspective-why-diversity-matters-in-human-factors-engineering.

Colvin, Caroline. "DEI Job Postings Are Down. Why Do These Roles Lack Longevity?" HR Dive, August 14, 2024. https://www.hrdive.com/news/dei-job-postings-are-down-why-do-these-roles-lack-longevity/724241.

Congressional Black Caucus. "Letter Regarding Corporate Accountability in Diversity, Equity, and Inclusion". December 15, 2023. https://cbc.house.gov/uploadedfiles/congressional_black_caucus_letter_re_corporate_accountability.pdf.

Congressional Black Caucus. "What Good Looks Like: A Corporate Accountability Report on Diversity, Equity, and Inclusion." September 2024. Accessed December 22, 2024. https://cmcp.org/wp-content/uploads/2024/09/congressional_black_caucus_corporate_accountability_report.pdf.

Cook, Shannon. "How Millennials and Gen Z Are Pushing Brands on Diversity and Inclusion." BusinessBecause, March 3, 2021. https://www.businessbecause.com/news/insights/7504/millennial-gen-z-diversity-and-inclusion.

Cooper, Alex. "Dylan Mulvaney Breaks Silence After Transphobic Backlash Over Bud Light Partnership." Advocate. April 27, 2023. https://www.advocate.com/people/dylan-mulvaney-bud-light-backlash.

Copeland, Rob. "Google Sets Hiring Goal to Advance Black Executives." Kanarys, June 26, 2020. https://app.kanarys.com/article/google-sets-hiring-goal-to-advance-black-executives.

Cox, Taylor Jr., and Carol Smolinski. Managing Diversity and Glass Ceiling Initiatives as National Economic Imperatives. Ann Arbor, MI: The University of Michigan, January 31, 1994. https://ecommons.cornell.edu/server/api/core/bitstreams/b459513d-e810-4cdd-81d3-e8376565927a/content.

Crampton, Natasha. "The Building Blocks of Microsoft's Responsible AI Program." Microsoft On the Issues (blog), January 19, 2021. https://blogs.microsoft.com/on-the-issues/2021/01/19/microsoft-responsible-ai-program/.

Daigle, Craig, "Review: The 1970s: The Great Transformation in American Foreign Relations." Reviews in American History 46, no. 1 (March 2018): 168–176. https://www.jstor.org/stable/48558695.

Davis, Dominic-Madori, and Kyle Wiggers. "Silicon Valley Leaders Are Once Again Declaring 'DEI' Bad and 'Meritocracy' Good—But They're Wrong." TechCrunch, June 23, 2024. https://techcrunch.com/

2024/06/23/silicon-valley-leaders-are-once-again-declaring-dei-bad-and-meritocracy-good-but-theyre-wrong.

De la Parra, Daniela. "Exposure to Race Issues: Firm Responses and Market Reactions After George Floyd's Murder." Kenan Insight, June 13, 2024. https://kenaninstitute.unc.edu/kenan-insight/exposure-to-race-issues-firm-responses-and-market-reactions-after-george-floyds-murder.

Deliso, Meredith. "Darnella Frazier, Who Recorded Video of George Floyd's Death, Recognized by Pulitzer Board." ABC News, June 11, 2021. https://abcnews.go.com/US/darnella-frazier-recognized-pulitzer-prizes-george-floyd-video/story?id=78225202.

Deng, Boer. "George Floyd, the Man Whose Death Sparked US Unrest." BBC News, May 31, 2020. Accessed December 28, 2024. https://www.bbc.com/news/world-us-canada-52871936.

Department of Labor. The Glass Ceiling Initiative: A Report. Washington, DC: Department of Labor, 1991. https://files.eric.ed.gov/fulltext/ED340653.pdf.

Detroit Historical Society. "Uprising of 1967." Encyclopedia of Detroit. https://detroithistorical.org/learn/encyclopedia-of-detroit/uprising-1967.

Dimock, Michael. "How America Changed During Barack Obama's Presidency." Pew Research Center, January 10, 2017. https://www.pewresearch.org/social-trends/2017/01/10/how-america-changed-during-barack-obamas-presidency.

Dimon, Jamie, and Eric J. Pan. "Jamie Dimon in Conversation with Eric J. Pan." 2021 ICI General Membership Meeting, May 5, 2021. https://www.ici.org/video/21_gmm_dimonejp.

Dimon, Jamie. Annual Report 2022. Chairman and Chief Executive Officer, JPMorgan Chase, April 4, 2023. https://reports.jpmorganchase.com/investor-relations/2022/ar-ceo-letters.htm.

D'Innocenzio, Anne. "Target to Reduce Number of Stores Carrying Pride-Themed Merchandise After Last Year's Backlash," AP News, updated May 11, 2024. https://apnews.com/article/target-lgbtq-pride-667ab2f654 5645f5f86ca76394e531d6.

Dionysia Johnson-Massie, Holly M. Robbins, Grady B. Murdock, and Cindy-Ann L. Thomas. "Ricci v. DeStefano: Talk About a Rock and a Hard Place: Employers Required to Pick Between Disparate Treatment and Disparate Impact Claims." Littler Mendelson P.C., July 10, 2009. https://www.littler.com/publication-press/publication/ricci-v-destefano-talk-about-rock-and-hard-place-employers-required.

DiPasquale, Denise, and Edward L. Glaeser. "The L.A. Riot and the Economics of Urban Unrest." NBER Working Paper Series, no. 5456 (February 1996). https://www.nber.org/system/files/working_papers/w5456/w5456.pdf.

Dobbin, Frank and Alexandra Kalev, "The Origins and Effects of Corporate Diversity Programs." In *Oxford Handbook of Diversity and Work*, ed. Quinetta Roberson (New York: Oxford University Press, 2013), 253–281.

Dove, Jackie. "Major iOS 14 Accessibility Features Benefit Everyone." Digital Trends, April 25, 2023. https://www.digitaltrends.com/mobile/major-ios-14-accessibility-features-benefit-everyone.

Dumas, Breck. "Diversity, Equity and Inclusion Programs Took a Hit in 2023." Fox Business. December 29, 2023. https://www.foxbusiness.com/politics/diversity-equity-inclusion-programs-took-hit-2023.

Dunn, Jonathan, Sheldon Lyn, Nony Onyeador, and Ammanuel Zegeye. "Black Representation in Film and TV: The Challenges and Impact of Increasing Diversity." McKinsey & Company, March 2021. https://responsiblemediaforum.org/downloadDocumentFile?document=394.

East Carolina University. "ECU Statements on George Floyd and Events in Minneapolis and Greenville." Statement from ECU Interim Chancellor Ron Mitchelson, ECU News Services, June 1, 2020. https://news.ecu.edu/2020/05/31/ecu-george-floyd-minneapolis.

Easterly, Edward. "Diversity Recruiting: How Does Fisher Impact Affirmative Action in Employment?" National Association of Colleges and Employers (NACE), August 1, 2016. https://www.naceweb.org/public-policy-and-legal/legal-issues/61214807-3175-4295-b723-2ca79bc272b1.

Edwards, D. Leveraging Data and AI to Advance Diversity, Equity, and Inclusion. Board.org., December 12, 2023. https://board.org/dei/resources/leveraging-data-and-ai-to-advance-diversity-equity-and-inclusion.

Edy, Jill A. "Watts Riots of 1965." Britannica. Last updated November 27, 2024. https://www.britannica.com/event/Watts-Riots-of-1965.

Eggert, Nalina. "Was Google Wrong to Fire James Damore after Memo Controversy?" BBC News, August 8, 2017. https://www.bbc.com/news/world-40865261.

Elias, Amanuel. "The Many Forms of Contemporary Racism." CRIS Consortium, January 14, 2021. https://www.crisconsortium.org/blog/the-many-forms-of-contemporary-racism.

Ellis, Nicquel Terry, and Catherine Thorbecke. "DEI Efforts Are Under Siege. Here's What Experts Say Is at Stake." CNN, January 7, 2024. https://ktvz.com/news/national-world/cnn-national/2024/01/07/dei-efforts-are-under-siege-heres-what-experts-say-is-at-stake.

Encyclopaedia Britannica. "Bakke Decision." Britannica. https://www.britannica.com/event/Bakke-decision.

Encyclopaedia Britannica. "Causes and Effects of the American Civil Rights Movement." Encyclopaedia Britannica. Accessed December 18, 2024. https://www.britannica.com/summary/Causes-and-Effects-of-the-American-Civil-Rights-Movement.

Encyclopaedia Britannica. "Griggs v. Duke Power Co." Britannica. https://www.britannica.com/event/Griggs-v-Duke-Power-Co.

Encyclopedia.com. "Philadelphia Plan." Encyclopedia.com. https://www.encyclopedia.com/history/encyclopedias-almanacs-transcripts-and-maps/philadelphia-plan.

Estrada, Sheryl. "Diversity as a 'Business Imperative': A Q&A with Target's D&I Chief," HR Dive, April 14, 2021. https://www.hrdive.com/news/diversity-as-a-business-imperative-a-qa-with-targets-di-chief/598389.

Extreme Weather Watch. "Minneapolis May 25 Weather Records." Accessed December 28, 2024. https://www.extremeweatherwatch.com/cities/minneapolis/day/may-25.

Facas, Eric. "We Can't Let Boycotts Be Dismissed as Cancel Culture, They're Democracy at Its Finest." Media Cause, July 24, 2020. https://mediacause.com/corporate-cancel-culture-is-democracy-at-its-finest.

Fairchild, Angie, and Olga Hawn. "Gender Inequality and Company Actions: How Do Wall Street and Main Street React?" Kenan Insight, November 16, 2023. https://kenaninstitute.unc.edu/kenan-insight/gender-inequality-social-movement-and-company-actions-how-do-wall-street-and-main-street-react.

Fairygodboss. "How the Head of Retention at Google Infuses Empathy into Her Leadership Style." Fairygodboss, updated August 1, 2024. https://fairygodboss.com/career-topics/how-the-head-of-retention-at-google-infuses-empathy-into-her-leadership-style.

Federal Reserve Board. "Insured U.S.-Chartered Commercial Banks That Have Consolidated Assets of $300 Million or More, Ranked by Consolidated Assets as of September 30, 2024." Federal Reserve Board Releases. Accessed December 19, 2024. https://www.federalreserve.gov/releases/lbr/current.

Feitz, Lindsey. "Creating a Multicultural Soul: Avon, Corporate Social Responsibility, and Race in the 1970s." In The Business of Black Power, ed. Laura Warren Hill and Julia Rabig. (Published online by Cambridge University Press, February 14, 2023). https://www.cambridge.org/core/books/abs/business-of-black-power/creating-a-multicultural-soul-avon-corporate-social-responsibility-and-race-in-the-1970s/24FE5 42A63E3EB6185C97ACF05A21F3D.

Feloni, Richard. "These Are the Corporate Responses to the George Floyd Protests That Stand Out." Just Capital, June 30, 2020. https://just capital.com/news/notable-corporate-responses-to-the-george-floyd-protests. Accessed December 16, 2024.

Ferguson, Jackie. "Here's How a Chief Belonging Officer Can Revive DEI Efforts." Reworked, January 12, 2024. https://www.reworked.co/leadership/heres-how-a-chief-belonging-officer-can-revive-dei-efforts.

Fernandez, Manny, and Audra D.S. Burch. "George Floyd, from 'I Want to Touch the World' to 'I Can't Breathe.'" The New York Times, June 10, 2020. Accessed December 28, 2024. https://www.sbs.com.au/news/article/george-floyd-from-i-want-to-touch-the-world-to-i-cant-breathe/qmwpj2lx4.

FindLaw. "Griggs v. Duke Power Co., 401 U.S. 424 (1971)." Written with the help of AI, legally reviewed by Balrina Ahluwalia, Esq. https://caselaw.findlaw.com/court/us-supreme-court/401/424.html.

FindLaw. "Johnson v. Transportation Agency, 480 U.S. 616 (1987)." https://caselaw.findlaw.com/court/us-supreme-court/480/616.html.

FindLaw. "Steelworkers v. Weber, 443 U.S. 193 (1979)." https://caselaw.findlaw.com/court/us-supreme-court/443/193.html.

"Fisher v. University of Texas." Oyez. Accessed December 29, 2024. https://www.oyez.org/cases/2015/14-981.

Fitzpatrick, Alex. "Starbucks Is Closing Thousands of Stores for Racial Bias Training. Here's How Much Money It Could Lose." Time, April 17, 2018. https://time.com/5243608/starbucks-closing-racial-bias.

Flood, Brian, and Suzanne O'Halloran. "Target Market Cap Losses Hit $15.7 Billion, Shares Approach 52-Week Low Amid Woke Backlash." Fox Business, June 12, 2023. https://www.foxbusiness.com/media/target-market-cap-losses-hit-15-7-billion-share-near-52-week-low-amid-woke-backlash.

"Floyd Killing Spurs Fresh Protests Across Europe." Deutsche Welle, June 6, 2020. https://www.dw.com/en/george-floyd-killing-spurs-fresh-protests-across-europe/a-53706536.

Fontinelle, Amy. "Equal Pay Act of 1963: Overview, Benefits, and Criticisms." Investopedia. Updated July 22, 2024. https://www.investopedia.com/equal-pay-act-1963-5207271.

France 24. "Clashes Break Out at Paris's Banned George Floyd-Inspired Protest." France 24, June 3, 2020. https://www.france24.com/en/20200603-

clashes-at-paris-s-george-floyd-inspired-protest-despite-covid-19-gathering-ban.

Francois, Myriam. "Adama Traoré: How George Floyd's Death Energised French Protests." BBC News, May 19, 2021. https://www.bbc.com/news/world-us-canada-57176500.

Frey, William H. "The US Will Become 'Minority White' in 2045, Census Projects." Brookings, March 14, 2018. https://www.brookings.edu/articles/the-us-will-become-minority-white-in-2045-census-projects.

Fried, Joseph P. "Howard Golden, Who Led, and Defended, Brooklyn, Dies at 98." The New York Times, January 24, 2024. https://www.nytimes.com/2024/01/24/nyregion/howard-golden-dead.html.

Friedman, Raymond A. "Black Caucus Groups at Xerox Corp. (A)." Harvard Business School Case 491-047, January 1991. (Revised November 1994.)

Gardner, Hannah. 2024. "Caste Remains Off-Limits in Corporate India's Drive for Diversity." Financial Times, November 13, 2024. https://www.ft.com/content/b0a7eb5e-2f03-4855-81ea-3d8fd07e4b26.

Garner, Marcus K. "Delta CEO Blasts Georgia Election Law, Calls It 'Unacceptable.'" Patch, March 31, 2021. https://patch.com/georgia/atlanta/delta-ceo-blasts-georgia-election-law-calls-it-unacceptible.

O'Donoghue Gary. "George Floyd: Expert Witness Criticises Use of Force During Arrest." BBC News, April 7, 2021. https://www.bbc.com/news/world-us-canada-56669914.

"George Floyd Death: Chauvin 'Trained to Stay Away from Neck.'" BBC News, April 6, 2021. Accessed December 28, 2024. https://www.bbc.com/news/world-us-canada-56653065.

"Germany to Launch Racism Study Among Police." Deutsche Welle, June 11, 2020. https://www.dw.com/en/germany-to-launch-study-probing-racism-among-police/a-53779238.

Gersen, Jeannie Suk. "Can a College Class Still Be Diverse?" The New Yorker, September 21, 2024. https://www.newyorker.com/news/the-lede/can-a-college-class-still-be-diverse.

Gershon, Livia. "Did the 1965 Watts Riots Change Anything?" JSTOR Daily, July 13, 2016. https://daily.jstor.org/did-the-1965-watts-riots-change-anything.

Gillette, Howard, Jr. "Philadelphia Plan." The Encyclopedia of Greater Philadelphia, 2013. https://philadelphiaencyclopedia.org/essays/philadelphia-plan-2.

Glaze, Derryl. "Microsoft Takes a Bold Step Towards Diversity: Setting Diversity Goals in Performance Reviews." Culture DEI, December 21, 2023. https://www.culture-dei.com/microsoft-takes-a-bold-step-towards-diversity-setting-diversity-goals-in-performance-reviews.

Glickel, Henry. "A History of Recruitment—Era 2: The 1980s to 1990." EMinfo, September 13, 2023. https://www.eminfo.com/articles-a-history-of-recruitment--era-2-the-1980s-to-1990-1013.php.

Godoy, Jody, and Disha Raychaudhuri. "Some Companies Alter Diversity Policies after Conservatives' Lawsuit Threat." Reuters, December 18, 2023. https://www.reuters.com/business/some-companies-alter-diversity-policies-after-conservatives-lawsuit-threat-2023-12-18/.

Golden, Hellen. "History of DEI: The Evolution of Diversity Training Programs." NDNU, January 1, 2024. https://www.ndnu.edu/history-of-dei-the-evolution-of-diversity-training-programs.

Golland, David Hamilton. "The Philadelphia Plan (1967–1970)." BlackPast, May 26, 2014. https://www.blackpast.org/african-american-history/philadelphia-plan-1967.

Gonçalves, Isabel. "4 Ways Data Drives Diversity in the Workplace." Salesforce Blog, December 9, 2021. https://www.salesforce.com/blog/diversity-in-the-workplace.

Goodman, Nanette, Fatma Altunkol Wise, Fitore Hyseni, Lauren Gilbert, and Peter Blanck. "Disability Inclusion in Corporate Supplier Diversity Initiatives." Journal of Occupational Rehabilitation 34 (2024): 373–386. https://link.springer.com/article/10.1007/s10926-024-10190-2.

Google. "Raise Awareness About Unconscious Bias." Re:Work. Accessed December 26, 2024. https://rework.withgoogle.com/en/guides/unbiasing-raise-awareness.

Google. "2023 Diversity Annual Report." Google Belonging. Accessed December 15, 2024. https://about.google/belonging/diversity-annual-report/2023.

Graham, Nicole Lazarz. "Navigating the Patchwork of Pay Transparency Laws." Journal of Accountancy, May 1, 2024. https://www.journalofaccountancy.com/issues/2024/may/navigating-the-patchwork-of-pay-transparency-laws.html.

"Growing More than Just Business." Originally published on Politico. JPMorgan Chase Newsroom, April 25, 2023. https://www.jpmorganchase.com/newsroom/stories/growing-more-than-just-business.

Gruman, Galen. "What's Really Behind Silicon Valley's Apparent Racism." InfoWorld, August 2, 2016. https://www.infoworld.com/article/2246897/whats-really-behind-silicon-valleys-apparent-racism.html.

Gunter, Joel. "Baltimore Police Death: How Did Freddie Gray Die?" BBC News, May 1, 2015. https://www.bbc.com/news/world-us-canada-32546204.

Gupta, Nandita. "Developing with Accessibility in Mind at Microsoft." Engineering at Microsoft, May 16, 2024. https://devblogs.microsoft

.com/engineering-at-microsoft/developing-with-accessibility-in-mind-at-microsoft.

Gutierrez, Barbara. "Protests in Brazil Highlight Racism and Police Brutality." University of Miami News, June 22, 2020. https://news.miami.edu/stories/2020/06/protests-in-brazil-highlight-racism-and-police-brutality.html.

"H&M Probes Alleged Myanmar Factory Abuses as Pressure Intensifies." Al Jazeera, August 16, 2023. https://www.aljazeera.com/economy/2023/8/16/hm-probes-alleged-myanmar-factory-abuses-as-pressure-intensifies.

"H&M Says It Will 'Phase Out' Sourcing from Myanmar." The Straits Times, updated November 15, 2024, https://www.straitstimes.com/world/europe/hm-says-it-will-phase-out-sourcing-from-myanmar.

Hardesty, Larry. "Study Finds Gender and Skin-Type Bias in Commercial Artificial-Intelligence Systems." MIT News Office, February 11, 2018. https://news.mit.edu/2018/study-finds-gender-skin-type-bias-artificial-intelligence-systems-0212.

Hayes, Kelly Taylor. "As Donations Surge, Nonprofits Bail Out George Floyd Protesters Across America." Fox5 NY, June 2, 2020. https://www.fox5ny.com/news/as-donations-surge-nonprofits-bail-out-george-floyd-protesters-across-america.

Heilweil, Rebecca. "Target's History of Working with Police Is Not a Good Look Right Now," Vox, updated June 5, 2020, https://www.vox.com/recode/2020/6/1/21277192/target-looting-police-george-floyd-protests.

Hellerstein, Judith, David Neumark, and Melissa McInerney. "Changes in Workplace Segregation in the United States Between 1990 and 2000: Evidence from Matched Employer-Employee Data." NBER Working Paper Series, no. 13080 (May 2007). National Bureau of Economic Research. http://www.nber.org/papers/w13080.

Herzlich, Taylor. "Jack Daniel's Maker Scraps DEI Policies after Threat of 'Anti-Woke' Boycott." New York Post, August 22, 2024. https://nypost.com/2024/08/22/business/jack-daniels-maker-scraps-dei-policies-after-threat-of-boycott.

Hinchliffe, Emma. "The Number of Female CEOs in the Fortune 500 Hits an All-Time Record." Fortune, May 18, 2020. https://fortune.com/2020/05/18/women-ceos-fortune-500-2020.

History.com Editors. "12-Year-Old Tamir Rice Shot and Killed by Police." History, November 23, 2024. https://www.history.com/this-day-in-history/tamir-rice-killed-by-police. Accessed December 16, 2024.

History.com Editors. "1967 Detroit Riots." History, updated March 23, 2021, originally published September 27, 2017. https://www.history.com/topics/1960s/1967-detroit-riots.

History.com Editors. "Michael Brown Is Killed by a Police Officer in Ferguson, Missouri." History, updated August 8, 2024, originally published August 6, 2020. https://www.history.com/this-day-in-history/michael-brown-killed-by-police-ferguson-mo. Accessed December 16, 2024.

History.com Editors. "The Hashtag #BlackLivesMatter First Appears, Sparking a Movement." History.com, updated July 12, 2021, originally published July 10, 2020. https://www.history.com/this-day-in-history/blacklivesmatter-hashtag-first-appears-facebook-sparking-a-movement.

History.com Editors. "Watts Rebellion." History, updated June 24, 2020, originally published September 28, 2017. https://www.history.com/topics/1960s/watts-riots.

Holstead, Joseph. "Post-1992 Los Angeles Riot Neighborhood Redevelopment." OLR Research Report 2002-R-0002, January 15, 2002. https://www.cga.ct.gov/2002/rpt/2002-R-0002.htm.

Hood, David. "Companies Quietly Ramp Up DEI Efforts Amid Political Turmoil." Bloomberg Law, June 3, 2024. https://news.bloomberglaw.com/esg/companies-quietly-ramp-up-dei-efforts-amid-political-turmoil.

Hood, Julia, and Rebecca Knight. "6 Ways DEI Programs Are Evolving as Companies Reorganize, Home in on Employee Skills, and Leverage the Power of AI." Business Insider, November 26, 2024. Accessed December 22, 2024. https://www.businessinsider.com/dei-evolves-as-the-culture-changes-and-ai-takes-hold-2024-11.

Houeix, Romain. "After the Death of George Floyd, Africa Mobilises Against Police Violence." France 24, June 13, 2020. https://www.france24.com/en/20200613-after-the-death-of-george-floyd-africa-mobilises-against-police-violence.

"How a D&I (Diversity and Inclusion) Culture Can Create Meaningful Impact for Employees." GI Group Holding. Accessed December 29, 2024. https://www.gigroupholding.com/insights/diversity-inclusion-meaningful-impact-employees.

"How George Floyd's Death Became a Catalyst for Change." National Museum of African American History and Culture. Accessed December 28, 2024. https://nmaahc.si.edu/explore/stories/how-george-floyds-death-became-catalyst-change.

Howland, Daphne. "No, Not All Companies Are Abandoning Diversity, Equity, and Inclusion. Here's Why." Retail Dive, September 23, 2024. Accessed December 22, 2024. https://www.retaildive.com/news/retail-dei-diversity-equity-inclusion-woke-policy-changes/723103.

HR News Canada. "Goodbye DEI, Hello I&D: SHRM Adopts New Acronym for Diversity." HR News Canada, July 9, 2024. https://hrnewscanada.com/goodbye-dei-hello-id-shrm-adopts-new-acronym-for-diversity.

HSBC. 2020. "HSBC Shares UK Employee Ethnic Representation Data." October 28, 2020. https://www.about.hsbc.co.uk/news-and-media/hsbc-shares-uk-employee-ethnic-representation-data.

Huet, Ellen. "Salesforce Begins Paving a Long Road to Equal Pay." Forbes, August 19, 2015. https://www.forbes.com/sites/ellenhuet/2015/08/19/salesforce-begins-paving-a-long-road-to-equal-pay-most-innovative-companies.

Humphries, Fred. "Our Annual Report: 'Racial Equity Initiative: Strengthening Our Communities.'" Microsoft (blog), June 9, 2021. https://blogs.microsoft.com/blog/2021/06/09/our-annual-report-racial-equity-initiative-strengthening-our-communities/.

Hunt, Vivian, Dennis Layton, and Sara Prince. "Diversity Matters." McKinsey & Company, February 2, 2015. https://www.mckinsey.com/~/media/mckinsey/business%20functions/people%20and%20organizational%20performance/our%20insights/why%20diversity%20matters/diversity%20matters.pdf.

IBM. "Our History." Accessed December 18, 2024. https://www.ibm.com/impact/be-equal/history.

Ighodaro, Omose. "How Google Is Sticking to—and Soaring Past—Its DEI Goals." BBC Worklife, February 15, 2024. https://www.bbc.com/worklife/article/20240213-bbc-interview-melonie-parker-google.

Impelli, Matthew. "Is Starbucks Banning Pride Decorations? What We Know." Newsweek, June 13, 2023. https://www.newsweek.com/republicans-celebrate-starbucks-banning-pride-decorations-stores-1806375.

Impelli, Matthew. "Trump Ramps Up His War on 'Woke.'" Newsweek, March 2, 2023. https://www.newsweek.com/trump-ramps-his-war-woke-1785208.

Irwin, Lauren. "Another Republican Labels Harris 'DEI Hire.'" The Hill, July 24, 2024. https://thehill.com/homenews/house/4790468-hageman-harris-dei-hire.

James, Ervin III. "Floyd, George Perry, Jr. (1973–2020)." Handbook of Texas Online. Texas State Historical Association, May 10, 2023. Accessed December 28, 2024. https://www.tshaonline.org/handbook/entries/floyd-george-perry-jr.

Jani, Namee. "Generative AI and the Future of Recruitment: Insights from Microsoft's Push for AI-Powered Diversity Hiring." Datafloq, October 25, 2024. https://datafloq.com/read/generative-ai-future-recruitment.

Jeffery-Morrison, Michaela. "Attracting and Retaining Gen-Z Through Diversity and Inclusion." Forbes, June 9, 2023. https://www.forbes.com/councils/forbesbusinesscouncil/2023/06/09/attracting-and-retaining-gen-z-through-diversity-and-inclusion.

Johnson, Bryce. "When Designing for the Disabled, Fit Is the Finish." Microsoft Design, March 6, 2024. https://microsoft.design/articles/when-designing-for-the-disabled-fit-is-the-finish.

Johnson, Marty. "Transcript of George Floyd Death Shows He Said He Was Dying, Officers Said He Was Fine Because He Could Speak." The Hill, July 8, 2020. Accessed December 28, 2024. https://thehill.com/homenews/state-watch/506491-transcript-of-george-floyd-death-shows-he-said-he-was-dying-officers/.

JPMorgan Chase. "JPMorgan Chase Announces Initiatives to Support Minority-Owned and Diverse-Led Financial Institutions." Press Releases, February 23, 2021. https://www.jpmorganchase.com/newsroom/press-releases/2021/jpmc-announces-initiatives-to-support-minority-owned-and-diverse-led-financial-institutions.

JPMorgan Chase. "JPMorgan Chase Launches Diverse Supplier Grant Initiative to Address Barriers to Opportunity for Underrepresented Businesses." March 24, 2022. https://www.jpmorganchase.com/newsroom/press-releases/2022/jpmc-chase-launches-diverse-supplier-grant-initiative.

JPMorgan Chase. "Racial Equity Commitment Audit Report." November 21, 2022. https://www.jpmorganchase.com/content/dam/jpmc/jpmorgan-chase-and-co/documents/2022-Racial-Equity-Commitment-Audit-Report.pdf.

K, Judita. "After All These Years, George Floyd's 2nd-Grade Teacher Kept His Essay on How He Wanted to Become a Supreme Court Justice." Bored Panda, June 8, 2020. Accessed December 28, 2024. https://www.boredpanda.com/george-floyd-teacher-essay-supreme-court-justice.

Kamar, Lucile. "Debunking 5 Misconceptions Around Diversity and Inclusion." All Things Insights, February 29, 2024. https://allthingsinsights.com/content/debunking-5-misconceptions-around-diversity-and-inclusion.

KARE 11 Staff. "Read George Floyd's Full Autopsy Report." WTSP, June 3, 2020. Last updated January 4, 2022. Accessed December 28, 2024. https://www.wtsp.com/article/news/local/george-floyd/hennepin-county-medical-examiner-releases-george-floyds-full-autopsy-results/89-2f8e7de2-2cfa-4b37-9235-c4c045f497d6.

Keenan, Sara. "Companies Are Ditching the E in DEI to Avoid Legal Risks." People of Color in Tech, October 29, 2024. https://peopleofcolorintech.com/articles/companies-are-ditching-the-e-in-dei-to-avoid-legal-risks.

Keenan, Sara. "Major Media Companies Lose 4 Black Diversity Leaders—A Step Backwards?" People of Color in Tech, July 3, 2023. https://people ofcolorintech.com/articles/major-media-companies-loose-4-black-diversity-leaders-a-step-backward.

Keizer, Gregg. "Microsoft Writes off Nearly $1B to Account for Surface RT Bomb." ComputerWorld, July 19, 2013. https://www.computerworld .com/article/1409993/microsoft-writes-off-nearly-1b-to-account-for-surface-rt-bomb.html.

Kerber, Ross, and Simon Jessop. "American Companies Facing Pressure to Reveal Data on Diversity of Employees." Insurance Journal, July 6, 2020. https://www.insurancejournal.com/news/national/2020/07/06/5743 80.htm.

Kessler, Will. "Big Business Took a Beating From Conservatives Over Woke Marketing in 2023, But Did It Change Anything?" Daily Caller, January 1, 2024. https://dailycaller.com/2024/01/01/big-business-beating-conservatives-woke-marketing.

Kessler, Will. "Businesses Ditch 'Diversity' Initiatives in Droves Amid Economic Uncertainty." The Daily Caller, November 27, 2023. https://dailycaller .com/2023/11/27/businesses-diversity-equity-inclusion-economic-uncertainty.

King, Esther. "Europe Seeks Own Response to Black Lives Matter." Politico, June 10, 2020. https://www.politico.eu/article/us-style-civil-rights-protests-come-to-europe-george-floyd-black-lives-matter.

Kirby, Jen. 2020. "'Black Lives Matter' Has Become a Global Rallying Cry Against Racism and Police Brutality." Vox, June 12, 2020. https://www.vox.com/2020/6/12/21285244/black-lives-matter-global-protests-george-floyd-uk-belgium.

Klawans, Justin. 2024. "Companies That Have Rolled Back DEI Initiatives." The Week, December 3, 2024. https://theweek.com/business/companies-dei-rollback.

Klein, Katherine, Nancy Rothbard, and Sigal Barsade. "Is Cultural Fit a Qualification for Hiring or a Disguise for Bias?" Knowledge at Wharton, July 16, 2015. https://knowledge.wharton.upenn.edu/article/cultural-fit-a-qualification-for-hiring-or-a-disguise-for-bias/.

Knight, Rebecca. 2024. "As Some Companies Scale Back on DEI, Others Double Down on Their Efforts." Business Insider. October 23, 2024. https://www.businessinsider.com/companies-data-driven-strategies-tools-refine-dei-belonging-efforts-decisions-2024-10.

Kobie, Nicole. "'Reverse Mentorship': How Young Workers Are Teaching Bosses." BBC Worklife, November 14, 2022. https://www.bbc.com/worklife/article/20221110-reverse-mentorship-how-young-workers-are-teaching-bosses.

Kyte, Robert. "Protests Erupt Across the World in Response to Police Killing of George Floyd." Free Speech Project, Georgetown University, June 28, 2020, updated March 10, 2022. Accessed December 28, 2024. https://freespeechproject.georgetown.edu/tracker-entries/protests-erupt-across-the-world-in-response-to-police-killing-of-george-floyd/.

Lang, Cady. "What the Artists Behind George Floyd Murals Around the World Want Us to Remember." Time, May 25, 2022. https://time.com/6180773/george-floyd-murals.

Lattice. "All Hands: IBM's Obed Louissaint on the Importance of Skills-Based Hiring." Lattice, July 7, 2022. https://lattice.com/articles/all-hands-ibms-obed-louissaint-on-the-importance-of-skills-based-hiring.

Laws, Elaine P., Elizabeth Loia, and Michael Merritt. "The AT&T Labs Fellowship Program—35 Years of Mentoring Women and Underrepresented Minorities—An Update." In Proceedings of the WEPAN 2007 Conference. Copyright 2007, WEPAN-Women in Engineering Programs and Advocates Network.

Lay-Flurrie, Jenny. "Disability Data: Improving Representation to Drive AI Innovation." Microsoft On the Issues (blog), October 17, 2024. https://blogs.microsoft.com/on-the-issues/2024/10/17/disability-data-improving-representation-to-drive-ai-innovation.

Leonard, Jonathan S. "Antidiscrimination or Reverse Discrimination: The Impact of Changing Demographics, Title VII, and Affirmative Action on Productivity." The Journal of Human Resources 19, no. 2 (Spring 1984): 145–174. Published by the University of Wisconsin Press. https://www.jstor.org/stable/145562.

Lorenzo, Rocio, and Martin Reeves. "How and Where Diversity Drives Financial Performance." Harvard Business Review, January 30, 2018. https://wilbankspartners.com/wp-content/uploads/2020/12/Harvard-Business-Review-Diversity-Drives-Financial-Performance-January-2018.pdf.

Louis Casiano, "Target Reopening Looted, Ransacked Minneapolis Store—But with New Focus on Catering to Black Shoppers," Fox Business, November 12, 2020, https://www.foxbusiness.com/retail/target-ransacked-minneapolis-black-shoppers.

Luminate. "Entertainment Diversity Progress Report." https://luminatedata.com/wp-content/uploads/2024/06/Luminate-Diversity-Report-2024.pdf.

M&T Bank. "M&T Bank Expands Financial Access, Removes Language Barriers with 100 New Multicultural Banking Centers." PR Newswire. January 13, 2022. https://www.prnewswire.com/news-releases/mt-bank-expands-financial-access-removes-language-barriers-with-100-new-multicultural-banking-centers-301459851.html.

Maersk. "LGBTQIA+ Inclusion at Maersk." Accessed December 21, 2024. https://www.maersk.com/careers/diversity-equity-and-inclusion/lgbtqi-plus.

Mamchii, Oleksandra. "Barack Obama's Presidency: Policies, Impact and Legacy." Best Diplomats, February 22, 2024. https://bestdiplomats.org/barack-obama-presidency.

Mao, Frances. "George Floyd Death: Australians Defy Virus in Mass Anti-Racism Rallies." BBC News, June 6, 2020. https://www.bbc.com/news/world-australia-52947115.

Markovitz, Gayle. "The Legacy of George Floyd: Here's How Business Can Address Inequality and Promote Justice." World Economic Forum, June 5, 2020. https://www.weforum.org/stories/2020/06/the-legacy-of-george-floyd-here-s-how-business-can-address-inequality-and-promote-justice/.

Martin Luther King, Jr. Research and Education Institute. "Watts Rebellion (Los Angeles)." Stanford University. https://kinginstitute.stanford.edu/watts-rebellion-los-angeles.

Massie, Graeme. "Elon Musk Slammed for Saying DEI Is 'Another Word for Racism.'" The Independent, January 4, 2024. https://www.independent.co.uk/news/world/americas/elon-musk-mark-cuban-dei-b2473473.html.

Masterson, Victoria. 2023. "These Countries Are the Best at Attracting, Developing and Retaining Talent." World Economic Forum, November 16, 2023. https://www.weforum.org/stories/2023/11/most-talent-competitive-countries-2023.

Mathur, Priyamvada. "VC Firms Strive to Improve Diversity with New Industry Certification." PitchBook, March 16, 2021. https://pitchbook.com/news/articles/vc-firms-diversity-certification.

Mazziotta, Julie. 2020. "CrossFit CEO's Racist Tweet Prompts Many Gyms—and Reebok—to Cut Ties with the Brand." People, June 8, 2020. https://people.com/health/crossfit-gyms-reebok-end-affiliation-after-ceos-racist-comments/.

McCall, Scott, and Megan Crozier. "Accelerating Our Commitment to Diverse and Minority Suppliers." Walmart Corporate Newsroom, April 28, 2021. https://corporate.walmart.com/news/2021/04/28/accelerating-our-commitment-to-diverse-and-minority-suppliers.

McCarthy, Bill. "What the First Police Statement About George Floyd Got Wrong." PolitiFact, April 22, 2021. https://www.politifact.com/article/2021/apr/22/what-first-police-statement-about-george-floyd-got.

McGlauflin, Paige, and Paolo Confino. "How Mastercard Is Using A.I. to Streamline Its Recruiting Process." Yahoo Finance, June 28, 2023. https://finance.yahoo.com/news/mastercard-using-streamline-recruiting-process-113349249.html.

McIntyre, Lindsay-Rae. "Microsoft's 2024 Global Diversity and Inclusion Report: Our Most Global, Transparent Report Yet." Microsoft Blog. October 23, 2024. https://blogs.microsoft.com/blog/2024/10/23/microsofts-2024-global-diversity-inclusion-report-our-most-global-transparent-report-yet.

McIntyre, Lindsay-Rae. 2022. "2022 Diversity and Inclusion Report: Driving Progress Through Greater Accountability and Transparency." Microsoft Blog, October 27, 2022. https://blogs.microsoft.com/blog/2022/10/27/2022-diversity-inclusion-report-driving-progress-through-greater-accountability-and-transparency.

McKinney, Jeffrey. "How 12 Black DEI Trailblazers Are Driving Transformation at US Corporations After the George Floyd Murder." Black Enterprise, October 29, 2021. https://www.blackenterprise.com/how-12-black-dei-trailblazers-are-driving-transformation-at-us-corporations-after-the-george-floyd-murder.

McKinney, Jeffrey. "JPMorgan Chase Makes $30 Billion Commitment to Help Close the Racial Wealth Gap." Black Enterprise, October 9, 2020. https://www.blackenterprise.com/jpmorgan-chase-makes-30-billion-commitment-to-help-close-the-racial-wealth-gap.

McKinsey & Company. Diversity Wins: How Inclusion Matters. McKinsey & Company, 2020. https://www.mckinsey.com/featured-insights/diversity-and-inclusion/diversity-wins-how-inclusion-matters.

McLaughlin, Justin. "Netflix Marketing Strategy: Streaming Success." Brand Credential, December 8, 2023. https://www.brandcredential.com/post/netflix-marketing-strategy-streaming-success.

McMinn, Tl. "Looking Back, Planning Forward: The History of DEI and Priorities Moving into 2022." Lunaria Solutions. Accessed December 21, 2024. https://lunariasolutions.com/blog-post/deipriority2022.

McNary, Dave. "WarnerMedia CEO John Stankey on Diversity: 'We've Got More Work to Do.'" Yahoo Entertainment, September 26, 2019. https://www.yahoo.com/entertainment/warnermedia-ceo-john-stankey-diversity-233038651.html.

Mensik, Hailey. "How Booz Allen and Bank of America Are Training Managers to Be More Neuro-Inclusive." WorkLife News, October 15, 2024. Accessed December 22, 2024. https://www.worklife.news/talent/how-booz-allen-and-bank-of-america-are-training-managers-to-be-more-neuro-inclusive.

Meyersohn, Nathaniel. "Costco Is Pushing Back—Hard—against the Anti-DEI Movement." CNN, December 27, 2024. https://edition.cnn.com/2024/12/27/business/costco-dei/index.html.

Mgbolu, Charles. "Cannes 2024: African Films Make Bold Statements." TRT Afrika, May 16, 2024. https://www.trtafrika.com/lifestyle/cannes-2024-african-films-make-bold-statements-18163220.

Microsoft. "About Microsoft." Accessed December 19, 2024. https://www.microsoft.com/en-us/about.

Microsoft. "Racial Equity Initiative: Four-Year Fact Sheet." June 13, 2024. https://query.prod.cms.rt.microsoft.com/cms/api/am/binary/RW1lWJA.

Microsoft. "Six Principles to Guide Microsoft's Facial Recognition Work." Microsoft On the Issues (blog), December 17, 2018. https://blogs.microsoft.com/on-the-issues/2018/12/17/six-principles-to-guide-microsofts-facial-recognition-work/.

Milano, Ashley. "JPMorgan Chase Settles Mortgage Discrimination Lawsuit for $55M." Top Class Actions, January 24, 2017. https://topclassactions.com/lawsuit-settlements/consumer-products/jpmorgan-chase-settles-mortgage-discrimination-lawsuit-55m

Miller, Conrad, and Ian M. Schmutte. "The Dynamics of Referral Hiring and Racial Inequality: Evidence from Brazil." NBER Working Paper Series, no. 29246 (September 2021). National Bureau of Economic Research. http://www.nber.org/papers/w29246.

Milne, Stefan. "AI Tools Show Biases in Ranking Job Applicants' Names According to Perceived Race and Gender." University of Washington News, October 31, 2024. https://www.washington.edu/news/2024/10/31/ai-bias-resume-screening-race-gender.

Minkin, Rachel. "Diversity, Equity and Inclusion in the Workplace." Pew Research Center, May 17, 2023. https://www.pewresearch.org/social-trends/2023/05/17/diversity-equity-and-inclusion-in-the-workplace.

Mishra, Subodh. "Racial and Ethnic Diversity on U.S. Corporate Boards—Progress Since 2020." Harvard Law School Forum on Corporate Governance, July 21, 2022. https://corpgov.law.harvard.edu/2022/07/21/racial-and-ethnic-diversity-on-u-s-corporate-boards-progress-since-2020.

MIT Sloan Management Review. "Should Companies Refrain from Making Political Statements?" MIT SMR Strategy Forum, May 31, 2023. https://sloanreview.mit.edu/strategy-forum/should-companies-refrain-from-making-political-statements.

Mitchell, Aaron, and Shannon Alwyn. 2020. "Building Economic Opportunity for Black Communities." Netflix, June 30, 2020. https://about.netflix.com/en/news/building-economic-opportunity-for-black-communities.

Moats, Castañón, Leah Malone Maria, and Christopher Hamilton. "The Evolving Role of ESG Metrics in Executive Compensation Plans." Harvard Law School Forum on Corporate Governance, March 19, 2022. https://

corpgov.law.harvard.edu/2022/03/19/the-evolving-role-of-esg-metrics-in-executive-compensation-plans.

Mohan, Pavithra. "SHRM, a Leading HR Organization, Is No Longer Focusing on 'Equity' in Its DEI Approach." Fast Company, July 12, 2024. https://www.fastcompany.com/91154675/shrm-hr-organization-dropped-equity-from-dei.

Moore, Stephanie Y., and Curshanda Cusseaux Woods. "Influencing Our Ecosystem to Promote Racial Justice." February 23, 2022. https://blogs.cisco.com/csr/influencing-our-ecosystem-to-promote-racial-justice.

Moran, Catherine Douglas, "5 Ways Target Is Pushing Customer-Driven Innovations in Omnichannel, Grocery," Grocery Dive, January 19, 2023. https://www.grocerydive.com/news/5-ways-target-is-pushing-customer-driven-innovations-in-omnichannel-grocer/640577.

Morrison, Ann M., Carol T. Schreiber, and Karl F. Price. A Glass Ceiling Survey: Benchmarking Barriers and Practices (Greensboro, NC: Center for Creative Leadership, 1995). https://cclinnovation.org/wp-content/uploads/2021/02/glassceilingsurvey.pdf.

Morrison, Carol. 2020. "ERGs Continue to Evolve as Powerful Allies During Pandemic." i4cp, August 10, 2020. https://www.i4cp.com/coronavirus/employee-resource-groups-continue-to-evolve-as-powerful-allies-during-the-pandemic.

Murray, Rachel. "A History of DEI and the Future of Work." Inclusion Geeks, October 4, 2024. https://www.inclusiongeeks.com/articles/a-history-of-dei-and-the-future-of-work.

Murray, Sarah. "Rescuing Diversity from the DEI Backlash." Financial Times, June 20, 2024. https://www.ft.com/content/18a8e9c4-d515-4d9b-aac1-d88c02b46028.

Nakintu, Stacy. "Diversity, Equity and Inclusion: Key Terms and Definitions." National Association of Counties, November 29, 2021. https://www.naco.org/resources/featured/key-terms-definitions-diversity-equity-inclusion.

Natalie Sherman. "George Floyd: Why Are Companies Speaking Up This Time?" BBC News, June 6, 2020. https://www.bbc.com/news/business-52896265.

National Center for Education Statistics. "Degrees Conferred by Race/Ethnicity and Sex." Accessed December 23, 2024. https://nces.ed.gov/FastFacts/display.asp?id=72.

Naughton, Eileen. "Our Focus on Pay Equity." Google Blog, April 11, 2017. https://blog.google/outreach-initiatives/diversity/our-focus-pay-equity.

NCRC. 2021. "PNC Bank, NCRC Announce $88 Billion Community Investment Commitment." National Community Reinvestment Coalition, April 27, 2021. https://ncrc.org/pnc-bank-ncrc-announce-88-billion-community-investment-commitment.

Neeson, Johanna. "26 Powerful George Floyd Murals Seen Around the World." Reader's Digest, December 9, 2022. https://www.rd.com/list/george-floyd-murals/.

Neira, Juliana. "For Once, Don't Do It—Nike's New Powerful Anti-Racism Campaign." Designboom, June 1, 2020. https://www.designboom.com/design/for-once-dont-do-it-nike-anti-racism-ad-01-06-2020.

Nesvig, Kara K., and Sara Delgado. "Munroe Bergdorf Joins L'Oréal Paris as Consultant After Calling Out the Brand." Teen Vogue, June 9, 2020. https://www.teenvogue.com/story/munroe-bergdorf-loreal-paris-black-lives-matter.

Newsweek Staff. "Texaco's Troubles." Newsweek, November 24, 1996. Updated March 13, 2010. https://www.newsweek.com/texacos-troubles-176224.

Nguyen, Kevin. "Enormous Crowds March in Sydney Black Lives Matter Protest After Last-Ditch Win in Court of Appeal." ABC News, June 6, 2020. https://www.abc.net.au/news/2020-06-06/arrests-at-sydney-black-lives-matter-protests/12329066.

Norfleet, Nicole. "Target CEO Says Company Taking Steps to Be 'True Leader' in Diversity, Inclusion." Star Tribune, May 22, 2021. https://www.startribune.com/target-ceo-says-company-taking-steps-to-be-true-leader-in-diversity-inclusion/600059849.

Nielsen. "COVID-19: Tracking the Impact on Media Consumption." Nielsen, March 2020.

Norwood, Candice. "Racial Bias Trainings Surged After George Floyd's Death. A Year Later, Experts Are Still Waiting for 'Bold' Change." PBS NewsHour, May 25, 2021. https://www.pbs.org/newshour/nation/racial-bias-trainings-surged-after-george-floyds-death-a-year-later-experts-are-still-waiting-for-bold-change.

NSDC NAACP. "ACT-SO." Accessed December 15, 2024. https://www.nsdcnaacp.org/act-so.

Nudd, Tim. "Heinz Apologizes and Pulls Ad with Imagery Reminiscent of Blackface." Ad Age, October 7, 2024. https://adage.com/article/marketing-news-strategy/heinz-apologizes-and-pulls-ad-imagery-reminiscent-blackface/2585706.

Ogbogu, Stephanie. 2020. "PepsiCo CEO Pledges Over $400 Million to Empower Black Employees & Their Communities." AfroTech, June 16, 2020. https://afrotech.com/pepsico-400-million-empower-black-employees-communities.

Ojha, Shankar. "HR Software Evolution: A Comprehensive Journey from Manual Processes to Fully Automated Systems in Modern Human Resources." QHRM Blog, August 2, 2024. https://qhrm.io/qhrm-blog/details/The-Evolution-of-HR-Software.

Olson, Alexandra, Haleluya Hadero, and Anne D'Innocenzio. "As Diversity, Equity, and Inclusion Comes Under Legal Attack, Companies Quietly Alter Their Programs." AP News, January 14, 2024. https://apnews.com/article/dei-diversity-corporations-affirmative-action-309864f08e6ec63a45d18ca5f25d7540.

Olson, Rochelle, Stephen Montemayor, and Matt McKinney. "Descended from Cops, Thomas Lane Saw His Minneapolis Police Career Last 4 Days." Star Tribune, August 29, 2020. Accessed December 28, 2024. https://www.startribune.com/descended-from-cops-thomas-lane-saw-his-minneapolis-police-career-last-4-days/572263492.

Origins of Diversity Training: A Historical Overview. Accessed December 18, 2024. https://hyperspace.mv/origins-of-diversity-training-a-historical-overview.

Otten, Tori. "Starbucks Denies Union Allegations of a Ban on Pride Decorations." The New Republic, June 13, 2023. https://newrepublic.com/post/173589/starbucks-take-down-pride-decorations-disgusting-cave-far-right.

Ousterout, Jamie. The Latest DEI Trends & Predictions for 2024: Insights from The Diversity Movement's Work with Clients in 2023. The Diversity Movement, 2024. https://thediversitymovement.com/wp-content/uploads/2024/02/Trends-and-Predictions-for-2024.pdf.

Out Leadership. 2016. "Out Leadership-Sponsored Study Released by the Center for Talent Innovation in Davos." January 22, 2016. https://outleadership.com/news/out-leadership-sponsored-study-released-by-the-center-for-talent-innovation-in-davos.

Parisi, Kristen. "The Next DE&I Component to Rebrand: Employee Resource Groups." HR Brew, August 27, 2024. https://www.hr-brew.com/stories/2024/08/27/the-next-de-and-i-component-to-rebrand-employee-resource-groups.

Park, Andrea. "WarnerMedia and Michael B. Jordan Launch Company-Wide Inclusion Rider." CBS News, September 5, 2018. https://www.cbsnews.com/news/warnermedia-and-michael-b-jordan-launch-company-wide-inclusion-rider.

Parker, Melonie. "Focused on Progress: Our 2022 Diversity Annual Report." Google Blog, May 19, 2022. https://blog.google/outreach-initiatives/diversity/diversity-annual-report-2022.

Participedia. "Black Lives Matter (BLM) and Repercussions in Brazil." Participedia. Accessed December 21, 2024. https://participedia.net/case/vidas-negras-importam-blm-e-repercusses-no-brasil.

Pasquini, Maria. "Sharon Osbourne Speaks Out After Exiting 'The Talk' Following Controversy: 'I'm Angry, I'm Hurt.'" People, April 16, 2021. https://people.com/tv/sharon-osbourne-speaks-out-after-the-talk-exit.

Paul, Stan. "Disadvantages Persist in Neighborhoods Impacted by 1992 L.A. Riots." UCLA Luskin School of Public Affairs, April 27, 2017. https://luskin.ucla.edu/disadvantages-persist-neighborhoods-impacted-1992-l-riots.

Perez Alfaro, Clara, John McAllister, Ashley Jones, Amarachi Ekekwe, and Marina Cavalcanti. "A Path for Greater Diversity in Film Festivals." Arts Management & Technology Laboratory, November 19, 2021. https://amt-lab.org/blog/2021/11/a-path-for-greater-diversity-in-film-festivals.

Perez-Chao, F. A., and E. Pipic. These Companies Are Successfully Scaling Up Diversity, Equity and Inclusion (DEI) Initiatives Across the Globe. World Economic Forum, January 8, 2024. https://www.weforum.org/stories/2024/01/organizations-impactful-corporate-dei-initiatives

Pew Research Center. "Progressive Left." Pew Research Center, November 9, 2021. https://www.pewresearch.org/politics/2021/11/09/progressive-left.

Pfeifer, Sylvia. "Rolls-Royce Hardwires Inclusion into Its Systems." Financial Times, November 19, 2024. https://www.ft.com/content/4bb7911a-d238-4e10-adae-7e8f701a7997.

Pichai, Sundar. "Our Commitments to Racial Equity." Google Blog, June 17, 2020. https://blog.google/inside-google/company-announcements/commitments-racial-equity.

Piers Morgan Leaves ITV's Good Morning Britain After Row Over Meghan Remarks. BBC News, March 10, 2021. https://www.bbc.com/news/entertainment-arts-56334082.

Planting, Sasha. "Clicks Stores Trashed Over Racist Ad." Daily Maverick, September 8, 2020. https://www.dailymaverick.co.za/article/2020-09-08-clicks-stores-trashed-over-racist-ad/.

Pop Culture Dictionary. "Cancel Culture." July 31, 2020. https://www.dictionary.com/e/pop-culture/cancel-culture.

Portocarrero, Sandra, and James T. Carter. "Diversity Initiatives in the US Workplace: A Brief History, Their Intended and Unintended Consequences." Sociology Compass 16, no. 7 (2022): e13001. https://doi.org/10.1111/soc4.13001.

Press, Joy. "Hollywood's DEI Programs Have Begun to D-I-E. How Hard Did the Industry Really Try?" Vanity Fair, December 18, 2024. https://www.vanityfair.com/hollywood/story/hollywoods-dei-programs-have-begun-to-die.

Price, Caleb. "Consumer Boycotts Impacting Major Brands: A Historical Look." Investors Hangout, updated September 4, 2024. https://investorshangout.com/consumer-boycotts-impacting-major-brands-a-historical-look-6634-/.

Provost, Taran. "Texaco Will Pay Historic Settlement." TIME, November 15, 1996. https://time.com/archive/6929429/texaco-will-pay-historic-settlement.

Quillian, Lincoln, Devah Pager, Ole Hexel, and Arnfinn H. Midtbøen. "Meta-analysis of Field Experiments Shows No Change in Racial Discrimination in Hiring over Time." Proceedings of the National Academy of Sciences of the United States of America 114, no. 41 (September 12, 2017): 10870–10875. https://doi.org/10.1073/pnas.1706255114.

Rajesh, Ananya Mariam, David Shepardson, and Nora Eckert. "Automaker Ford to Modify Diversity Policy, Internal Memo Says." Reuters, August 28, 2024, 3:48 PM. Accessed December 22, 2024. https://www.reuters.com/business/autos-transportation/automaker-ford-modify-diversity-policy-internal-memo-says-2024-08-28.

Ray, Susanna. "New Ideas and Energized Employees Fuel Microsoft's Ongoing Efforts toward Racial Equity." Microsoft Source (blog), March 10, 2021. https://news.microsoft.com/source/features/diversity-inclusion/new-ideas-and-energized-employees-fuel-microsofts-ongoing-efforts-toward-racial-equity.

Reinstein, Julia, and Stephanie K. Baer. "Two Black Men Were Arrested in Starbucks. Witnesses Say They 'Didn't Do Anything.'" BuzzFeed News, April 14, 2018. https://www.buzzfeednews.com/article/juliareinstein/starbucks-arrest-viral-black-men-waiting-philadelphia.

Reinstein, Julia. "Cate Blanchett, Ava DuVernay, Kristen Stewart, And Salma Hayek Just Protested in Cannes." BuzzFeed News, May 12, 2018. https://www.buzzfeednews.com/article/juliareinstein/cate-blanchett-cannes-film-festival-times-up-me-too.

Research Finds DEI Initiatives During Certain Presidencies Can Affect Bottom Line. University of New Hampshire, September 28, 2023. https://www.unh.edu/unhtoday/news/release/2023/09/28/research-finds-dei-initiatives-during-certain-presidencies-can-affect-bottom.

Ricci v. DeStefano. Casebriefs. Accessed December 29, 2024. https://www.casebriefs.com/blog/law/constitutional-law/constitutional-law-keyed-to-brest/race-and-the-equal-protection-clause/ricci-v-destefano/.

Rinderle, Susana. "The Enemies of Inclusion: Cancelling, Consensus, and Perfection." TLNT, March 18, 2021. https://www.tlnt.com/articles/the-enemies-of-inclusion-cancelling-consensus-and-perfection.

Rivero, Nicolás. "The Influential Project That Sparked the End of IBM's Facial Recognition Program." Quartz, June 10, 2020. https://qz.com/1866848/why-ibm-abandoned-its-facial-recognition-program.

Robertson, Nick. "Moore Denounces DEI Blame for Bridge Collapse: 'I Have No Time for Foolishness.'" The Hill, March 31, 2024. https://thehill.com/homenews/state-watch/4566162-moore-denounces-dei-blame-for-bridge-collapse-i-have-no-time-for-foolishness.

Robinson, Joseph. "How Are Companies Adapting Their Leadership Development Programs to Foster Greater Diversity and Inclusion?" Flevy Insights. Accessed December 24, 2024. https://flevy.com/topic/diversity/question/enhancing-diversity-inclusion-modern-leadership-development-programs.

Roma Rights Activists Take Police Killing of Stanislav Tomáš to European Court. European Roma Rights Centre, August 10, 2023. https://www.errc.org/press-releases/roma-rights-activists-take-police-killing-of-stanislav-tomas-to-european-court.

Romano, Aja. "Google Has Fired the Engineer Whose Anti-Diversity Memo Reflects a Divided Tech Culture: James Damore's Sexist Screed Indicted All of Silicon Valley." Vox, August 8, 2017. https://www.vox.com/identities/2017/8/8/16106728/google-fired-engineer-anti-diversity-memo.

Rose, Lily. "Twitter Reacts to Starbucks Racial Bias Training Closures." The Daily Meal, 29 May 2018. https://www.thedailymeal.com/drink/starbucks-closures-twitter.

Ruble, Kayla. "South African Plaintiffs Are Using an 18th Century Law to Take IBM to Task for Allegedly Facilitating Apartheid." Vice, February 25, 2015. https://www.vice.com/en/article/south-african-plaintiffs-are-using-an-18th-century-law-to-take-ibm-to-task-for-allegedly-facilitating-apartheid.

Ryan, Tom. "Will Giant Food's Shelf Labels with Diversity Call-Outs Drive Sales?" RetailWire, January 4, 2021. https://retailwire.com/discussion/will-giant-foods-shelf-labels-with-diversity-call-outs-drive-sales.

Saez de Tejada Cuenca, Anna. "U.S. and Europe Lead Global Efforts to Diversify Suppliers." IESE Insight, October 30, 2024. https://www.iese.edu/insight/articles/diversity-supply-chains-suppliers-sustainability.

Saha, Rubel, Md Nurul Kabir, Syed Asif Hossain, and Sheikh Mohammad Rabby. "Impact of Diversity and Inclusion on Firm Performance: Moderating Role of Institutional Ownership." Journal of Risk and Financial Management 17, no. 8 (2024): 344. https://www.mdpi.com/1911-8074/17/8/344.

Salvation Army Northern Division. "Remembering Mr. George Floyd." The Salvation Army, May 29, 2020. Accessed December 28, 2024. https://centralusa.salvationarmy.org/northern/harborlightcenter/news/remembering-mr-george-floyd/.

Sault, Samantha. "Davos Agenda: What You Need to Know About the Future of Work." World Economic Forum, January 24, 2021. https://

www.weforum.org/stories/2021/01/davos-agenda-2021-society-and-the-future-of-work-skills-gap-jobs-of-tomorrow-diversity-inclusion-worker-well-being/.

Scarcella, Mike, "Target Must Face Shareholder Lawsuit Over Pride Backlash, US Judge Rules," Yahoo Finance, updated December 4, 2024, https://finance.yahoo.com/news/target-must-face-shareholder-lawsuit-202851198.html.

Schifrin, Nick, and Layla Quran. "Outrage Over George Floyd Catalyzes Movements for Racial Justice Abroad." PBS NewsHour, June 11, 2020. https://www.pbs.org/newshour/show/outrage-over-george-floyd-catalyzes-movements-for-racial-justice-abroad.

Schmidt, Ann. "JPMorgan's Jamie Dimon Reacts to Floyd Protests: 'We Are Committed to Fighting Racism.'" Fox Business, May 30, 2020. https://www.foxbusiness.com/money/jpmorgan-jamie-dimon-reacts-george-floyd-protests.

Schott, Bryan. "Baltimore Bridge Collapse Caused by DEI Efforts, Utah Rep. Phil Lyman Says." The Salt Lake Tribune, March 26, 2024. https://www.sltrib.com/news/politics/2024/03/26/baltimore-bridge-collapse-caused.

Schwarz, Robert. 2021. "Corporate Racial Equality Investments—One Year Later." Harvard Law School Forum on Corporate Governance, August 30, 2021. https://corpgov.law.harvard.edu/2021/08/30/corporate-racial-equality-investments-one-year-later/.

Schwerin, Dan. "CEOs Can't Hide from This Election." Fast Company, April 9, 2024. https://www.fastcompany.com/91088907/ceos-cant-hide-from-this-election.

Sethi, Vaamanaa. "Apple Is Hiring Engineers and Interns for Their Tech Team in India." Business Insider India, October 22, 2021. https://www.businessinsider.in/careers/news/apple-is-hiring-engineers-and-interns-for-their-tech-team-in-india/articleshow/87205763.cms.

Shahani, Aarti. "Is the Memo Controversy a Pivot Point on Diversity for Google?" All Things Considered, NPR, August 9, 2017. https://www.npr.org/sections/alltechconsidered/2017/08/09/542412661/is-the-memo-controversy-a-pivot-point-on-diversity-for-google.

Shepherd, Tiah. "GOP Rep. Burchett Calls Harris a 'DEI Hire.'" The Hill, July 22, 2024. https://thehill.com/homenews/4787275-gop-rep-burchett-kamala-harris-dei-hire.

Sherman, Louise. "Celebrating Black History Month at HSBC." February 16, 2021. https://www.business.us.hsbc.com/en/campaigns/commercial-banking-blog/blackhistorymonth.

Sheth, Sudev, Geoffrey Jones, and Morgan Spencer. "Bollywood, Skin Color and Sexism: The Role of the Film Industry in Emboldening and Contesting Stereotypes in India after Independence." Working Paper 21-077. The Lauder Institute, Wharton, and Harvard Business School, 2021. https://www.hbs.edu/ris/Publication%20Files/21-077_6547bcf4-d0eb-4d54-ad62-c99e604e797f.pdf.

Simonite, Tom. "Photo Algorithms ID White Men Fine—Black Women, Not So Much." Wired, February 6, 2018. https://www.wired.com/story/photo-algorithms-id-white-men-fineblack-women-not-so-much.

Smith, Carl. "How Much Could Younger Voters Affect Future Election Outcomes?" Governing, April 10, 2023. https://www.governing.com/now/how-much-could-younger-voters-affect-future-election-outcomes.

Smith, Jake. "Big Business Scales Back 'Diversity' Initiatives as Legal Pressure Mounts." BizPac Review, December 24, 2023. https://www.bizpacreview.com/2023/12/24/big-business-scales-back-diversity-initiatives-as-legal-pressure-mounts-1422472.

Sony Music. "Sony Music Group Appoints Tiffany R. Warren Executive Vice President, Chief Diversity and Inclusion Officer." Sony Music, October 4, 2020. https://www.sonymusic.com/sonymusic/sony-music-group-appoints-tiffany-r-warren-executive-vice-president-chief-diversity-and-inclusion-officer.

Speed, Madeleine. "Diageo Campaigns Capture the Spirit of the Times." Financial Times, November 19, 2024. https://www.ft.com/content/9ad7b5e8-0071-40e3-bfdc-55f007aea38e.

Statista Research Department. "Number of People Shot to Death by the Police in the United States from 2017 to 2024, by Race." Statista, December 9, 2024. https://www.statista.com/statistics/585152/people-shot-to-death-by-us-police-by-race.

Steven, Khris. "30+ Important Employee Resource Groups Statistics." KhrisDigital, September 19, 2024. https://khrisdigital.com/employee-resource-groups-statistics.

Stewart, Emily. "George Floyd and the Cascade of Crises in Black America." Vox, June 1, 2020. Accessed December 28, 2024. https://www.vox.com/covid-19-coronavirus-economy-recession-stock-market/2020/6/1/21276909/george-floyd-police-coronavirus-crisis-minnesota-unemployment-protests.

Street Law, Inc. "Case Summary: Regents of the University of California v. Bakke (1978)." Landmark Cases. https://s3.amazonaws.com/landmarkcases.org/Bakke/Student/Case_Summary_MS_Bakke_Student.pdf

Supplier.io. 2023 Supplier Diversity Benchmarking Report. Supplier.io, 2023. https://supplier.io/wp-content/uploads/2023/03/2023-Supplier.io-Supplier-Diversity-Benchmarking-Report.pdf.

Sydell, Laura. "Google CEO Cuts Vacation Short to Deal with Crisis over Diversity Memo." NPR, August 8, 2017. https://www.wunc.org/2017-08-08/google-ceo-cuts-vacation-short-to-deal-with-crisis-over-diversity-memo.

Syeda, Sahlah. "Study Predicts 3 Ways Gen Z Will Continue to Change the Workplace in 2025—Including Bringing Back the 'Cheesy Office Christmas Party.'" YourTango, December 13, 2024. https://www.yourtango.com/self/study-predicts-ways-gen-z-continue-change-workplace.

Szabo, Liz. "Rubber Bullets Are Supposed to Be 'Less Than Lethal,' But They Can Still Kill or Maim." PBS NewsHour, June 3, 2020. https://www.pbs.org/newshour/health/at-close-range-police-fire-rubber-bullets-that-can-maim-or-kill-protesters.

Target Commits $100 Million Through 2025 for Black Communities. Philanthropy News Digest, October 13, 2021. https://philanthropynewsdigest.org/news/target-commits-100-million-through-2025-for-black-communities.

Target Corporation. "Our Locations." Target Corporation, accessed December 19, 2024, https://corporate.target.com/about/locations.

Target Debuts New Larger-Format Store Featuring Modern Design and Expanded Space to Fuel Popular Same-Day Fulfillment Services. Target Corporation, November 10, 2022. https://corporate.target.com/press/release/2022/11/target-debuts-new-larger-format-store-featuring-mo.

Target Provides Update on Commitment to Spend $2 Billion with Black-Owned Businesses and Announces New Media Fund Initiative. Target Corporation, May 10, 2022. https://corporate.target.com/press/release/2022/05/target-provides-update-on-commitment-to-spend-2-bi.

Taveras, Juan. "Historical Context of DEI in the Workplace." DEI Pro Finder, October 12, 2023. Accessed December 18, 2024. https://www.deiprofinder.com/blog/historical-context-of-dei-in-the-workplace.

Telford, Taylor, and Julian Mark. "DEI Is Getting a New Name. Can It Dump the Political Baggage?" The Washington Post, May 5, 2024. Accessed December 22, 2024. https://css.washingtonpost.com/business/2024/05/05/dei-affirmative-action-rebrand-evolution.

The Conference Board. "US Corporate Board Diversity: Boards Are More Diverse than Ever, But the Pace of Growth Is Slowing." The Conference Board, November 9, 2023. https://www.conference-board.org/press/press-release-board-diversity-2023.

The Editorial Board. "Cast in Colour: Pervasive Brutality in India." The Telegraph India, June 13, 2020. https://www.telegraphindia.com/opinion/caste-discrimination-and-violence-in-india/cid/1780756.

The Talk: Sharon Osbourne Leaves US Show After Racism Row. BBC News, March 27, 2021. https://www.bbc.com/news/world-us-canada-56547718.

Thier, Jane. "College Degrees Could Become Obsolete—and It Could Be the First Step in Giving Your Job to Someone Else." Yahoo Finance, updated January 9, 2023. https://finance.yahoo.com/news/college-degrees-could-become-obsolete-133000993.html.

Thomas, David A. "IBM Finds Profit in Diversity." Harvard Business School Working Knowledge, September 27, 2004. https://www.library.hbs.edu/working-knowledge/ibm-finds-profit-in-diversity.

Thomas, Rhys. "JPMorgan Chase: The Gold Standard in Diverse Spend." Procurement Magazine, January 5, 2022. https://procurementmag.com/company-reports/jpmorgan-chase-gold-standard-diverse-spend.

Thorbecke, Catherine. "Starbucks to Tie Executive Compensation to Meeting Its Diversity Goals." ABC News, October 15, 2020. https://abcnews.go.com/Business/starbucks-tie-executive-compensation-meeting-diversity-goals/story?id=73629368.

Tilo, Dexter. "Did the Aftermath of George Floyd's Murder Lead to Positive Change in the Workplace?" Human Capital America. June 20, 2023. https://www.hcamag.com/us/specialization/diversity-inclusion/did-the-aftermath-of-george-floyds-murder-lead-to-positive-change-in-the-workplace/449927.

Toraif, Noor, Neha Gondal, Pujan Paudel, and Alison Frisellaa. "From Colorblind to Systemic Racism: Emergence of a Rhetorical Shift in Higher Education Discourse in Response to the Murder of George Floyd." PLOS ONE. August 3, 2023. https://doi.org/10.1371/journal.pone.0289545.

Truu, Maani. "George Floyd: How a Nine Minute Video Reignited a Decades-Old Civil Rights Movement in Australia." SBS News, April 21, 2021. https://www.sbs.com.au/news/article/george-floyd-how-a-nine-minute-video-reignited-a-decades-old-civil-rights-movement-in-australia/bbgzy0mug.

U.S. Bureau of Labor Statistics. "Healthcare Occupations." Accessed December 24, 2024. https://www.bls.gov/ooh/healthcare.

U.S. Bureau of Labor Statistics. "Payroll Employment Down 20.5 Million in April 2020." The Economics Daily, May 8, 2020.

U.S. Bureau of Labor Statistics. "The Employment Situation—April 2020." News Release, May 8, 2020.

U.S. Department of Labor. "About OFCCP: History." Accessed December 18, 2024. https://www.dol.gov/agencies/ofccp/about/history.

U.S. Department of Labor. "Executive Order 11246." Accessed December 18, 2024. https://www.dol.gov/agencies/ofccp/executive-order-11246.

U.S. Equal Employment Opportunity Commission. "What You Should Know: ABCs of the EEOC." Accessed December 18, 2024. https://www .eeoc.gov/laws/guidance/what-you-should-know-abcs-eeoc.

U.S. Senate. "Senator Vance & Rep. Cloud Introduce Legislation to Eliminate All DEI Programs from the Federal Government." Press release, June 12, 2024. https://www.vance.senate.gov/press-releases/senator-vance-rep-cloud-introduce-legislation-to-eliminate-all-dei-programs-from-the-federal-government.

UC Office of the President. "UC Statement on Protests, Violence Following George Floyd's Death." University of California, May 31, 2020. https:// www.universityofcalifornia.edu/press-room/uc-statement-protests-violence-following-george-floyds-death.

Unilever. "A Beacon of Diversity and Inclusion." Unilever, accessed December 17, 2024. https://www.unilever.com/sustainability/equity-diversity-and-inclusion/a-beacon-of-diversity-and-inclusion.

Unilever. 2021. "Unilever Commits to Help Build a More Inclusive Society." January 21, 2021. https://www.unilever.com/news/press-and-media/press-releases/2021/unilever-commits-to-help-build-a-more-inclusive-society.

United Minds. How Chief Diversity Officers Are Meeting the Challenges of Today and Tomorrow. October 2021. https://cms.webershandwick.com/wp-content/uploads/2023/01/United-Minds_CDO_Study.pdf.

United States Government Accountability Office. Financial Services Industry: Representation of Minorities and Women in Management and Practices to Promote Diversity, 2007–2015. Statement of Daniel Garcia-Diaz, Director, Financial Markets and Community Investment. Testimony Before the Subcommittee on Diversity and Inclusion, Committee on Financial Services, House of Representatives. February 27, 2019. https:// www.gao.gov/assets/gao-19-398t.pdf.

United States Supreme Court. Grutter v. Bollinger, 539 U.S. 306 (2003). Cornell Law School Legal Information Institute. https://www.law.cornell .edu/supct/html/02-241.ZS.html.

University of Michigan History Labs. "Government Investigations and Civil Rights/Black Power Pushback." Detroit Under Fire: Police Violence, Crime Politics, and the Struggle for Racial Justice in the Civil Rights Era. https://policing.umhistorylabs.lsa.umich.edu/s/detroitunderfire/page/investigations.

University of Michigan History Labs. "III. Uprising and Occupation, 1967." Detroit Under Fire: Police Violence, Crime Politics, and the Struggle for Racial Justice in the Civil Rights Era. https://policing.umhistorylabs.lsa .umich.edu/s/detroitunderfire/page/1967.

Unzipped Staff. 2020. "Elizabeth A. Morrison Named New Chief Diversity, Inclusion & Belonging Officer." Levi Strauss & Co. November 17, 2020. https://www.levistrauss.com/2020/11/17/elizabeth-morrison-diversity-inclusion-belonging-officer.

Unzipped Staff. 2024. "Quick Questions with Our New Chief DE&I and Talent Officer." Levi Strauss & Co. August 25, 2024. https://www.levistrauss.com/2024/08/25/quick-questions-dei-talent-officer.

Valentine, Rebekah. "Microsoft DEI Lead Blasts Company in Internal Email After Team Is Reportedly Laid Off." IGN, July 16, 2024. https://www.ign.com/articles/microsoft-dei-lead-blasts-company-in-internal-email-after-team-is-reportedly-laid-off.

Vedantam, Shankar. "Most Diversity Training Ineffective, Study Finds." The Washington Post, January 20, 2008. https://www.washingtonpost.com/archive/national/2008/01/20/most-diversity-training-ineffective-study-finds/f44ed0f5-bd4a-408b-aa34-1f326198f9b8/.

Velazquez, Diego. "The Americans with Disabilities Act and Its Strong Impact Upon Corporate Employment Practices." June 18, 2019. https://www.jvattorneys.com/2019/06/18/the-american-with-disabilities-act-and-its-strong-impact-upon-corporate-employment-practices.

Vera, Amir and Daniel Wolfe. "Seeking Justice: A Timeline Since the Death of George Floyd." CNN, March 2021. https://www.cnn.com/interactive/2021/03/us/george-floyd-case-timeline.

Vespa, Jonathan, David M. Armstrong, and Lauren Medina. Demographic Turning Points for the United States: Population Projections for 2020 to 2060 (Washington, DC: U.S. Census Bureau, February 2020). https://www.census.gov/content/dam/Census/library/publications/2020/demo/p25-1144.pdf.

Vinik, D. Frank. "Disparate Impact." Britannica. https://www.britannica.com/topic/disparate-impact.

Vogels, Emily A., Monica Anderson, Margaret Porteus, Chris Baronavski, Sara Atske, Colleen McClain, Brooke Auxier, Andrew Perrin, and Meera Ramshankar. "Americans and 'Cancel Culture': Where Some See Calls for Accountability, Others See Censorship, Punishment." Pew Research Center, May 19, 2021. https://www.pewresearch.org/internet/2021/05/19/americans-and-cancel-culture-where-some-see-calls-for-accountability-others-see-censorship-punishment.

Walker, Corey. "Don't Blame DEI for Baltimore Bridge Collapse." Washington Examiner, March 28, 2024. https://www.washingtonexaminer.com/opinion/2942380/dont-blame-dei-for-baltimore-bridge-collapse.

Wang, Alexandr. "Meritocracy at Scale." Scale AI, June 13, 2024. https://scale.com/blog/meritocracy-at-scale.

Ward, Marguerite, and Allana Akhtar. "JPMorgan's Multibillion-Dollar Push for Racial Equity Continues with New $100 Million Investment in Black and Hispanic Banks." Business Insider, Updated September 29, 2021. https://www.businessinsider.com/jpmorgan-racial-equity-economy-within-own-walls-2021-3.

WarnerMedia Celebrates 20 Years of Supplier Diversity. Business Wire, March 30, 2022. https://www.businesswire.com/news/home/20220330005775/en/WarnerMedia-Celebrates-20-Years-of-Supplier-Diversity.

Watson, Katy. "Brazil's Racial Reckoning: 'Black Lives Matter Here, Too.'" BBC News, July 24, 2020. https://www.bbc.com/news/world-latin-america-53484698.

Weber Shandwick. "Speak Up," Americans Demand of Corporate Leaders. August 11, 2023. https://webershandwick.com/news/speak-up-americans-demand-of-corporate-leaders.

White, Jonno. "Top 450 Leadership Quotes on Diversity and Inclusion." Consult Clarity, March 13, 2023. https://www.consultclarity.org/post/top-450-leadership-quotes-on-diversity-and-inclusion.

Wiggins, Christopher. "Anheuser-Busch Execs on Leave after Right-Wing Fuss Over Dylan Mulvaney Collaboration." Advocate. April 24, 2023. https://www.advocate.com/business/budweiser-execs-dylan-mulvaney-partnership.

Williams, Trey. "IBM's HR Team Saved 12,000 Hours in 18 Months after Using A.I. to Automate 280 Tasks: 'We're Spending Time on Things That Matter.'" Yahoo Finance, June 26, 2023.

Wilson, Valerie, and William M. Rodgers, III. "Black-White Wage Gaps Expand with Rising Wage Inequality." Economic Policy Institute, September 20, 2016. https://www.epi.org/publication/black-white-wage-gaps-expand-with-rising-wage-inequality/.

Winick, Erin. "Amazon Ditched AI Recruitment Software Because It Was Biased Against Women." MIT Technology Review, October 10, 2018. https://www.technologyreview.com/2018/10/10/139858/amazon-ditched-ai-recruitment-software-because-it-was-biased-against-women.

Winslow, George. "WarnerMedia Issues Diversity Report Showing Progress and Challenges." TV Technology, October 14, 2021. https://www.tvtechnology.com/news/warnermedias-issues-diversity-report-showing-progress-and-challenges.

Winsor, Morgan, and Kelly McCarthy. "Men Arrested at Starbucks Were There for Business Meeting Hoping to Change 'Our Lives.'" ABC News, April 19, 2018. https://abcnews.go.com/GMA/News/men-arrested-starbucks-business-meeting-hoping-change-lives/story?id=54578217.

Wise, Chelsea Higgs, "Black Beyond Measure—Lessons on Celebrating Black History Month and Building Inclusive Cultures—Target's Story," The Spark Mill, February 14, 2020, https://www.thesparkmill.com/blog-posts/2020/2/12/target-black-beyond-measurenbsp.

Wolf, Jessica. "2020 Hollywood Diversity Report: A Different Story Behind the Scenes." UCLA Newsroom, February 6, 2020. https://newsroom.ucla.edu/releases/2020-hollywood-diversity-report.

Woodward, Jennifer. "Borrowed Agency: The Institutional Capacity of the Early Equal Employment Opportunity Commission." Journal of Policy History, published online by Cambridge University Press, March 1, 2023. https://www.cambridge.org/core/journals/journal-of-policy-history/article/borrowed-agency-the-institutional-capacity-of-the-early-equal-employment-opportunity-commission/53C695DB106317949CA32F24 76473E69.

World Economic Forum. The Future of Jobs Report 2023, April 30, 2023. https://www.weforum.org/publications/the-future-of-jobs-report-2023.

Wright, B.C.T. "'Be less white': Coca-Cola addresses backlash for employees' training program 'Confronting Racism." NewsOne, February 22, 2021. https://newsone.com/4095905/coca-cola-white-training-controversy.

Xerox Corporation. "Diversity at Xerox." Xerox Corporation. Accessed December 17, 2024. https://www.xerox.com/downloads/usa/en/n/nr_Xerox_Diversity_Timeline_2008.pdf.

Yadidsion, Danny. "Understanding California's Pay Transparency Laws: What Employers Need to Know in 2024." Labor Law PC. Accessed December 24, 2024. https://www.laborlawpc.com/blog/understanding-californias-pay-transparency-laws-what-employers-need-to-know-in-2024.

Yost, Billy. "WarnerMedia Drives Changes for All to See." Hispanic Executive, March 7, 2022. https://hispanicexecutive.com/warner-media.

Zhang, Hannah. "The Pressure Is On for VC Firms to Take Diversity Seriously." Institutional Investor, April 18, 2023. https://www.institutionalinvestor.com/article/2bstsei2jl2xgthp7k1kw/culture/the-pressure-is-on-for-vc-firms-to-take-diversity-seriously.

Zheng, Hongwei, Weihua Li, and Dashun Wang. "Expertise Diversity of Teams Predicts Originality and Long-Term Impact in Science and Technology." arXiv preprint, October 10, 2022. https://arxiv.org/abs/2210.04422.

Acknowledgments

WHEN UNDERTAKING A project of this scope, one accumulates many debts of gratitude. First and foremost, I must thank the countless professionals who shared their experiences, insights, and stories with me over the decades. Your trust and candor have made this book possible.

Special thanks to my early mentors at ABC News, who gave me my first opportunity in journalism and taught me the power of storytelling. My time as an on-air reporter for *Long Island News Tonight* in the 1990s shaped my understanding of how to communicate complex issues to diverse audiences.

I am deeply grateful to the executives, managers, and employees at organizations like Moody's, Dentsu International, WPP Hill and Knowlton, and countless others who allowed me to witness their transformation journeys firsthand. Your commitment to creating genuine change, even in challenging times, continues to inspire me.

To my colleagues at DTI, Diversity Talent International, thank you for helping build a platform that has enabled us to impact organizations worldwide. Your dedication to excellence and inclusion has been instrumental in shaping the ideas presented in this book.

To the board members at Mogulai.com, AAF, Urban Word, ALPFA, and Education Africa—your perspectives have enriched my understanding of how inclusion drives innovation across sectors and cultures.

To my research partners at UPENN Wharton School, the Tapestry Network, and Coqual, thank you for helping develop the empirical foundation that underlies many of this book's insights.

Finally, my deepest gratitude goes to my family, whose unwavering support made this work possible. You've reminded me daily why building inclusive organizations matters—not just for business success, but for creating a world where everyone can thrive.

About the Author

DK BARTLEY IS a pioneering voice in corporate diversity, equity, and inclusion, whose career spans the intersections of media, technology, and organizational transformation. Currently serving as Global Chief Diversity, Equity, and Inclusion Officer at WPP's Hill and Knowlton, one of the world's leading public relations firms, Bartley brings over two decades of experience in helping organizations leverage diversity as a competitive advantage.

Beginning his career as a researcher at ABC News and on-air reporter for *Long Island News Tonight* in the 1990s, Bartley developed a keen understanding of how to communicate complex issues to diverse audiences. This foundation in journalism would later prove invaluable in helping organizations navigate sensitive conversations about inclusion and change.

As Chief Diversity Officer at Moody's, Bartley led the company's strategic acceleration of DEI as a business imperative, helping drive the organization's most profitable year and entrance into the Fortune 500. His work has been featured in *Fortune*, *Forbes*, *USA Today*, *Diversity Inc*, *Savoy*, and *Fintech Magazine*.

Previously, as Senior Vice President and Head of Diversity and Inclusion for Dentsu International, Bartley managed talent solutions for global clients including Microsoft, American Express, Proctor & Gamble, and Mastercard. His innovative approach to talent acquisition led to groundbreaking successes, including the strategic hiring of over 400 diverse advertising professionals for Microsoft, resulting in significant multicultural revenue growth.

Bartley currently serves as an Independent Corporate Board Director for Mogulai.com and holds board positions with several influential organizations including AAF (the American Advertising Federation), Urban Word, and ALPFA (the Association of Latino Professionals for America). His global perspective is enhanced through his work as a trustee of Education Africa and membership in the Executive Leadership Council.

A sought-after global speaker, Bartley frequently addresses audiences worldwide on topics including DEI and AI, DEI as a Business Imperative, Creating Effective DEI Strategies, Embedding DEI into Talent Acquisition, and the intersection of DEI with ESG initiatives. He has visited over 140 countries, bringing a truly global perspective to diversity and inclusion work.

Bartley holds a master's degree in communications from the New York Institute of Technology and a Bachelor of Arts in Political Science from Stony Brook University. He is certified in Diversity and Inclusion Management from Cornell University ILR. His pioneering research partnerships with UPENN Wharton School, the Tapestry Network, and Coqual have helped advance understanding of how diversity drives business performance.

Throughout his career, Bartley has maintained that excellence and inclusion strengthen each other. This book represents the culmination of his experiences helping organizations transform diversity from a compliance issue into a competitive advantage.

Index